When You're Entertaining

When You're Entertaining

by the editors of SPHERE Magazine
wine editor/Paul Kovi

Golden Press   New York
Western Publishing Company, Inc.
Racine, Wisconsin

Contents

Acknowledgments

Editing a cookbook is a formidable task, but a joyous one that we hope is reflected in the pages of *When You're Entertaining*. The test kitchen staff of SPHERE Magazine—Sue Spitler, Food Editor, and her assistants: Eileen Wheeler, Kathie Thuerk, Judy Vance—carefully selected the best recipes from SPHERE Magazine with an eye to creating a comprehensive and complete guide for entertaining. All recipes, menus and party plans were tested in the Betty Crocker Kitchens of General Mills, Inc.

Wine Suggestions accompany each menu, and for them we thank Paul Kovi, SPHERE Wine Editor. A partner in the famed Four Seasons Restaurant in New York (which boasts the largest wine cellar in the United States), he is an internationally respected expert on wine as well as food. We are proud of his association with the magazine and with this book.

Production of *When You're Entertaining* could never have been accomplished without many hours of work by SPHERE staff members, including Harriet Dalaskey, Patricia Joseph, Luci Nadjari, Elizabeth Rhein and Karen Sullivan. Chapter and menu introductions were written by Corinne Ross. And other helping hands were supplied by Michael Bell, Vickie Leonard and Sheldon Widmer.

We also wish to thank all of the fine photographers who contributed to *When You're Entertaining*. A list of their names and the pages on which their work appears is on page 255.

Joan Leonard
Editor, SPHERE Magazine

Chicago, Illinois
July 22, 1974

Introduction

This is a cookbook for people who entertain, and most of us do. But people entertain in many different ways; so *When You're Entertaining* is divided into nine chapters, and each chapter covers different kinds of parties—from The Casual Scene through Buffet Spectaculars and elegant sit-down Dinners to Remember. We've taken the guesswork out of party planning by providing a selection of complete menus within each chapter, all beautiful to serve and easy to prepare.

Each menu includes a Party Plan, a time schedule that tells in outline form exactly when to prepare each recipe so everything is ready just when you need it and nothing is forgotten. The recipes themselves have appeared in SPHERE Magazine and have all been subjected to rigorous testing standards. Recipes are printed in a format that makes them clear and easy to follow.

Photography is an integral part of *When You're Entertaining.* Nearly every recipe is pictured, so you can see how the food will look when it's presented to your guests. Where an unusual cooking technique is involved, Step-By-Step Recipes use photographs to illustrate each procedure in the recipe. None of the recipes in *When You're Entertaining* requires unusual cooking equipment; where ingredients might be seasonal or uncommon, substitutes are suggested. For your convenience, mail order sources for specialty foods are listed on page 255.

To round out each of the menus, SPHERE's Wine Editor, Paul Kovi, has personally selected one or more wines (or another beverage, if he deemed wine inappropriate for the menu). Mr. Kovi has selected wines from the best vineyards, both foreign and domestic. If a specific wine is not available in your area, Mr. Kovi recommends that you ask your local wine merchant to give you a similar variety.

We've attempted to make *When You're Entertaining* one of the most comprehensive cookbooks for entertaining ever published. Within each individual party menu we've tried to include everything the busy hostess needs to know. We want you to enjoy the party, too!

1 The Casual Scene

Parties are fun—to give or to go to, and some of the best are the casual ones. Reflecting the informal lifestyle most of us follow today, a simple get-together should be relaxed and comfortably undemanding. Food is a vital part of every entertaining occasion, and if your party is to have a light, friendly mood, you need meals that incorporate both ease of preparation and no-fuss serving.

Many of the recipes included in this chapter may be prepared well in advance of your guests' arrival. Some use convenience foods that can be purchased ahead, ready for quick assembly just before serving. The first three menus are planned for twelve people, the last two for six—but you can increase or decrease them easily to serve a different number of guests.

The hearty menu of chili, salad and rich Sunshine Sherry Cake is guaranteed to satisfy hungry guests when the weather is cold and blustery. Chili originated in Mexico and first became popular in America's Southwest. Its full name is *chile con carne,* or "peppers with meat."

Summer is an ideal time to serve the Chutney Chicken Menu. Served with ease buffet style, the two entrée salads can be prepared in advance. Top off this buffet with a Strawberry Meringue Cake, simply made from a packaged cake mix.

A group of twelve will enjoy an out-of-the-ordinary party meal based on three hot and savory soups. People tend to congregate in the kitchen anyway, so these soups are planned for easy serving straight from the stove. A choice of two desserts completes the informal meal.

In some circles, dunking might be considered impolite. But it depends on how you do your dunking. Thanks to the good people of Switzerland, the art of selective dunking has spread around the world in the form of fondue. Fondues—hot sauces in which other foods are dipped—often use beef or bread cubes as the main dunking ingredient. The fondue menu introduces a new twist—potato dunking.

Paella is a traditional Spanish dish made with cooked rice and a wide variety of other ingredients, often chicken and seafood. The Paella Menu is unusually simple to prepare. With the components on hand in cupboard or freezer, you will be able to put together an impromptu feast without turning a hair.

Sunshine Sherry Cake: it's easy to make and elegant to eat (see menu on page 12).

Midwinter Party

Make chili with beef cubes for a hearty party dish.

You can do almost everything in advance in this menu except add the dressing to the salad and the topping to the cake. Start with a lime, vodka and wine punch. It has a tart and refreshing citrus taste that's not too sweet for spicy foods. Then bring on the Chunky Chili, full of ample bites of tender beef, tomatoes and kidney beans. This recipe provides generously large servings, so if you have a smaller guest list, you might want to cut the recipe in half and prepare it in a single Dutch oven.

A cornmeal loaf, warm from the oven, is the perfect accompaniment to chili. This one is easily made from packaged hot roll mix. If you plan to make two or more loaves, make each one separately rather than increasing the recipe. The loaves can be baked ahead and reheated in foil. The crisp spinach and cucumber salad has a unique dressing made with avocado dip and prepared salad dressing.

Round out the meal with a Sunshine Sherry Cake. This rich cake is ultra-moist and ultra-easy, too, since it is made with lemon cake mix and lemon instant pudding. Spread sherry glaze between the layers and top the cake with a whipping cream-sherry topping to add a beautiful touch to the meal. Serves 12.

Wine Suggestion: If you want to serve wine with this menu, it should be in complete balance with the food it accompanies. To equalize the spiciness of chili, select a red wine with strength and body. My choice is an Italian Barbaresco—or a good California Barbera, maybe from Davis Bynum. Vintage? It should be young.

Lime Punch, a popcorn medley and cheeses set a party mood.

PARTY PLAN FOR CHUNKY CHILI MENU

2 Days Before:
Prepare Chunky Chili through step 2 in recipe; cover and refrigerate.

1 Day Before:
Prepare Sunshine Sherry Cake through step 2 in recipe; wrap layers in aluminum foil and refrigerate.
Make Corn Bread; cool and wrap in aluminum foil. Refrigerate.
Make Avocado Goddess Dressing; cover and refrigerate.
Make Hodge Podge Cocktail Snack; store in airtight container.

3 Hours Before Serving:
Make Tossed Salad; cover and refrigerate.
Prepare garnishes for menu; cover and refrigerate.
Complete Sunshine Sherry Cake.

10 Minutes Before Guests Arrive:
Make Lime Punch.

30 Minutes Before Serving:
Complete Chunky Chili.
Heat Corn Bread in foil in oven (350°) until hot, 10 to 15 minutes.

HODGE PODGE COCKTAIL SNACK

Makes 12 cups

⅓ cup butter or margarine, melted
1 teaspoon lemon pepper
½ teaspoon dried oregano leaves
¼ teaspoon garlic powder
¼ teaspoon dry mustard
*8 cups popped corn
1 can (4 ounces) shoestring potatoes
1 package (4 ounces) toasted sunflower nuts (about ¾ cup)

Heat oven to 350°

Mix butter, lemon pepper, oregano, garlic and mustard; toss with remaining ingredients. Spread popped corn mixture in jelly roll pan, 15½ x 10½ x 1 inch. Bake, stirring once, 8 to 10 minutes.

*TIP: *⅓ cup unpopped corn makes about 2½ quarts popped corn.*

LIME PUNCH

Makes about 3 quarts

2 cans (6 ounces each) frozen limeade concentrate
1½ cups vodka, chilled
1½ cups sauterne, chilled
⅓ cup orange liqueur
2 bottles (32 ounces each) carbonated water, chilled
½ tray ice cubes
  Mint sprigs
  Lemon slices

Place limeade, vodka, sauterne and orange liqueur in blender container; cover. Blend until mixed. Pour into chilled punch bowl. Stir in carbonated water and ice cubes. Garnish with mint sprigs and lemon slices.

CHUNKY CHILI

8 pounds beef for stew, cut into 1-inch cubes
⅓ cup vegetable oil
6 medium onions, sliced (about 3 cups)
4 cloves garlic, crushed
⅓ cup butter or margarine
4 cans (28 ounces each) tomatoes
6 cans (16 ounces each) red kidney beans, undrained
2 cans (6 ounces each) tomato paste
6 to 7 tablespoons chili powder
2 tablespoons salt
2 teaspoons beef stock base
1 teaspoon red pepper sauce
¾ cup water
½ cup cornstarch
4 green peppers, cut into rings

1. Brown meat, ⅓ at a time, in oil in 8-quart Dutch oven or kettle; remove. Cook and stir onions and garlic in butter and meat drippings in Dutch oven until onions are tender.

2. Drain tomatoes, reserving liquid; cut tomatoes into quarters. Stir tomatoes, reserved liquid, kidney beans, tomato paste, chili powder, salt, beef stock base and red pepper sauce into onion mixture. Measure 3 quarts chili into 5-quart Dutch oven; stir in 6 cups of the meat. Stir remaining meat into chili in 8-quart Dutch oven. Heat to boiling; reduce heat and cover. Simmer, stirring occasionally, 2 to 2½ hours, until meat is tender.* Skim fat from chili.

3. Mix ½ cup of the water and 5 tablespoons of the cornstarch. Stir cornstarch mixture and two-thirds of the green peppers into chili in 8-quart Dutch oven. Mix remaining water and cornstarch. Stir cornstarch mixture and remaining green peppers into chili in 5-quart Dutch oven. Simmer, stirring occasionally, 5 minutes.

*TIP: *Chili can be made to this point in advance. Cool slightly and cover. Refrigerate no longer than 48 hours. To serve, skim fat from chili. Heat chili to boiling; reduce heat and cover. Simmer until meat is hot, about 20 minutes. Proceed with step 3.*

*CORN BREAD

Makes 1 loaf

¾ cup warm water (105° to 115°)
1 egg, beaten
1 package (13¾ ounces) hot roll mix

1. Dissolve yeast (from hot roll mix package) in ¾ cup warm water in large bowl. Stir in egg and hot roll mix; cover. Let rise in warm place until double, about 45 minutes. (Dough is ready if impression remains.)

2	tablespoons butter or margarine, melted
⅓	cup cornmeal
½	teaspoon salt
¼	cup water
½	teaspoon cornstarch
1	tablespoon cornmeal

2. Turn dough onto lightly floured board. Roll dough into rectangle, 14 x 10 inches; brush with butter. Mix ⅓ cup cornmeal and the salt; sprinkle on buttered dough. Roll up, beginning at long end. Place on greased jelly roll pan, 15½ x 10½ x 1 inch; cover. Let rise 30 minutes.

3. Heat oven to 375°. Mix water and cornstarch in saucepan. Heat to boiling, stirring constantly; cool slightly. Brush loaf with cornstarch mixture; sprinkle with 1 tablespoon cornmeal. Bake until golden brown, about 30 minutes. Cool on wire rack. Serve warm or cold.

*TIP: *For this menu, you may want to make additional bread. Make each loaf separately rather than increasing recipe.*

TOSSED SALAD WITH AVOCADO GODDESS DRESSING

1	can (7¾ ounces) frozen avocado dip, thawed
1	cup green goddess salad dressing
1	head lettuce
1	pound spinach
1	cup sliced celery
1	cup thinly sliced cucumber
1	cup thinly sliced Bermuda onion
½	cup sliced pitted ripe olives
2	hard-cooked eggs, sliced

1. Mix avocado dip and green goddess dressing; cover and refrigerate.

2. Tear lettuce and spinach into bite-size pieces. Toss with remaining ingredients except egg slices. Garnish with egg slices. Serve with Avocado Goddess Dressing.

SUNSHINE SHERRY CAKE

1	package (18.5 ounces) lemon cake mix
1	package (3¾ ounces) lemon instant pudding
½	cup vegetable oil
1	cup sherry
4	eggs
1	tablespoon freshly grated orange peel
	Orange-Sherry Glaze (recipe follows)
	Sherry Topping (recipe follows)
1	can (11 ounces) mandarin orange segments, drained, chilled

Heat oven to 350°

| 1 | jar (16 ounces) orange marmalade |
| 3 | tablespoons sherry |

1	cup chilled whipping cream
2	tablespoons sugar
1	tablespoon sherry

1. Beat cake mix (dry), pudding (dry), vegetable oil, sherry, eggs and orange peel in large mixer bowl on low speed 1 minute, scraping bowl occasionally. Beat on medium speed 4 minutes. Pour batter into well-greased 10-inch tube pan. (Position oven rack so that top of tube pan is in center of oven.)

2. Bake until top of cake springs back when touched lightly with finger, about 45 minutes. Cool right side up on wire rack 15 minutes. Remove from pan; cool completely.

3. Make Orange-Sherry Glaze. Cut cooled cake in half horizontally to make 2 layers. Place top half of cake cut side up on serving plate. Pour half the cooled Orange-Sherry Glaze over cut side of cake; spread to edge. Place remaining layer cut side down on top of glaze. Spread remaining glaze over top of cake, allowing some to drip down side.

4. Make Sherry Topping. Spoon large dollops of Sherry Topping on top of cake; garnish with mandarin orange segments.*

*TIP: *Refrigerate cake if not serving immediately for no longer than 4 hours.*

ORANGE-SHERRY GLAZE
Mix marmalade and sherry in saucepan. Heat to boiling, stirring occasionally. Reduce heat; simmer 5 minutes. Cool to room temperature.

SHERRY TOPPING
Beat cream, sugar and sherry in chilled small mixer bowl until stiff peaks form.

A Springtime Buffet

Two entrée salads star in this buffet menu.

Chutney, that pungent relish from India, can be found bottled on most grocery shelves, but it's really not hard to make it yourself. This chutney uses fresh cantaloupe or honeydew melon, brown sugar, raisins and onion, blended with vinegar and spices. It's incorporated here into Chutney Chicken, but you might want to make an extra amount: homemade chutney is an excellent condiment served separately with meats.

Let your buffet guests sample two salads this spring. As a complement to Chutney Chicken, choose Molded Ham Aspic. A clear gelatin mold flavored with chicken broth, this aspic has a layer of sliced avocado and hard-cooked egg; then ham rolls are arranged in rows to allow easy slicing. Plan to make the aspic ahead of time since you must wait for the gelatin to set between layers. If you need extra help, the Step-By-Step Recipe shows the procedure.

Then make a springtime version of Baked Alaska for dessert. Angel food cake, strawberry ice cream and meringue are enhanced with fresh berries and strawberry sauce. This recipe uses a packaged mix, but a purchased cake or your favorite angel food recipe will work just as well. The amount of ice cream needed will vary according to the size of the cake. Other fruits and other flavors of ice cream or sherbet could also be used in this recipe. Serves 12.

Wine Suggestion: May I suggest with this menu a wine which is light, pleasantly fruity and, of course, white: Liebfraumilch Blue Nun or a California Johannisberg Riesling by Simi.

This Strawberry Meringue Cake is filled with ice cream and served with fresh berries.

PARTY PLAN FOR CHUTNEY CHICKEN MENU

2 Days Before:	Prepare Molded Ham Aspic through step 4 in recipe. Prepare Strawberry Meringue Cake through step 4 in recipe. Freeze cake; refrigerate sauce.
1 Day Before:	Make Toasted Nut Nibbles, Cheese Breadsticks and Party Herb Melba; cool completely and store in airtight containers. Prepare Chutney Chicken through step 1 in recipe; refrigerate.
2 Hours Before Serving:	Complete Chutney Chicken; cover and refrigerate. Complete Molded Ham Aspic; refrigerate. Prepare relishes, cheeses and garnishes for menu; cover and refrigerate.
30 Minutes Before Guests Arrive:	Make Artichoke Puffs. Make Orange-Wine Punch.
20 Minutes Before Dessert:	Complete Strawberry Meringue Cake.

ORANGE-WINE PUNCH
Makes about 9 cups

2   cups orange juice
1   can (6 ounces) frozen
     lemonade concentrate, thawed
½   cup orange liqueur
1   bottle (⅘ quart) sauterne, chilled
2   bottles (10 ounces each)
     carbonated water, chilled
½   tray ice cubes

Mix orange juice, lemonade concentrate, orange liqueur and sauterne in chilled punch bowl. Stir in carbonated water and ice cubes, Garnish with fruit slices if desired.

17

TOASTED NUT NIBBLES

Makes about 11 cups

3½ cups toasted oat cereal
3½ cups bite-size toasted corn
 cereal
⅓ cup butter or margarine, melted
1 tablespoon lemon juice
1 teaspoon onion powder
1 teaspoon garlic salt
¼ teaspoon seasoned pepper
4 cups nuts

Heat oven to 250°

Mix oat and corn cereals in jelly roll pan, 15½ x 10½ x 1 inch. Mix remaining ingredients except nuts; pour over cereal mixture. Stir gently until evenly coated. Stir in nuts. Bake 15 minutes. Stir gently. Bake 15 minutes longer.

ARTICHOKE PUFFS

Makes about 3 dozen

36 slices small party rye bread
2 cans (14 ounces each) artichoke
 hearts, drained
2 egg whites
¼ cup mayonnaise or salad
 dressing
¼ cup grated Parmesan cheese
2 tablespoons shredded Cheddar
 cheese
 Dash cayenne pepper
 Paprika

Heat oven to 400°

1. Place bread slices on baking sheet. Cut artichoke hearts in half; place one half cut side down on each bread slice.

2. Beat egg whites until stiff. Fold in remaining ingredients except paprika. Top each artichoke half with about 1½ teaspoons egg white mixture. Sprinkle with paprika.

3. Bake until golden brown, 10 to 15 minutes.

CHUTNEY CHICKEN

3 cups chopped cantaloupe
 or honeydew melon
1 cup plus 2 tablespoons packed
 brown sugar
½ cup raisins
⅓ cup chopped onion
3 tablespoons cider vinegar
½ teaspoon ground cinnamon
½ teaspoon ground ginger
½ teaspoon ground allspice
¼ teaspoon salt

2¼ cups dairy sour cream
9 cups cubed cooked chicken
3¾ cups chopped celery
1 tablespoon salt
½ teaspoon pepper
 Salad greens
⅓ cup chopped salted peanuts

1. Heat cantaloupe, brown sugar, raisins, onion, vinegar, spices and ¼ teaspoon salt to boiling; reduce heat. Simmer uncovered, stirring occasionally, about 25 minutes. Drain; cool mixture slightly.

2. Stir sour cream into fruit mixture. Fold in chicken, celery, 1 tablespoon salt and the pepper; cover. Refrigerate at least one hour, no longer than 2 hours. Arrange in greens-lined bowl. Sprinkle with peanuts.

MOLDED HAM ASPIC   *See STEP-BY-STEP RECIPE on page 21.*

CHEESE BREADSTICKS   *Makes 8 dozen*

1½ cups all-purpose flour
½   cup grated Parmesan cheese
¼   teaspoon garlic powder
¼   teaspoon salt
¼   cup butter or margarine
1   cup shredded Cheddar cheese
    (about 4 ounces)
¼   cup finely chopped green
    onions
2   tablespoons finely chopped
    jalapeño pepper
½   cup milk

    Cornmeal

    Heat oven to 400°

1. Measure flour, Parmesan cheese, garlic powder and salt into bowl; cut in butter. Stir in Cheddar cheese, onions and pepper to coat. Add milk; stir just until dough forms. Refrigerate 1 hour.

2. Sprinkle cornmeal on wooden board. Divide dough in half. Roll each half on board into rectangle, 12 x 8 inches. Cut each rectangle horizontally in half; cut each half into sticks ½ inch wide. Twist sticks; place on buttered baking sheet.

3. Bake until light brown, about 10 minutes. Cool on wire rack.

PARTY HERB MELBA   *Makes about 3 dozen*

⅓   cup butter or margarine,
    softened
1   teaspoon parsley flakes
1   teaspoon dried basil leaves
¾   teaspoon dried oregano
    leaves
¾   teaspoon dried tarragon
    leaves
¼   teaspoon dried marjoram
    leaves
1   loaf (8 ounces) party rye
    bread slices

    Heat oven to 350°

1. Mix butter, parsley flakes, basil, oregano, tarragon and marjoram. Spread mixture on bread slices; place on baking sheet.

2. Bake until crisp and light brown, 15 to 20 minutes.

STRAWBERRY MERINGUE CAKE

1   package (15 or 16 ounces)
       white angel food cake mix

½   gallon strawberry ice cream,
       softened

1   pint strawberries, sliced
¼   cup strawberry jelly, melted
¼   cup strawberry or orange
       liqueur

3   egg whites
¼   teaspoon cream of tartar
6   tablespoons sugar
½   teaspoon vanilla
       Strawberry halves
       Mint sprigs

1. Bake cake mix according to package directions; cool and remove cake from pan.

2. Place cake upside down; cut down into cake with serrated knife 1 inch from outer edge and 1 inch from edge of hole, leaving substantial "wall" on each side. Remove cake within cuts, being careful to leave base of cake 1 inch thick.

3. Spoon ice cream into hollowed-out portion of cake. Wrap and freeze.

4. Mix 1 pint strawberries, the jelly and liqueur to make strawberry sauce; cover and refrigerate.

5. Heat oven to 450°. Beat egg whites and cream of tartar until foamy. Beat in sugar, 1 tablespoon at a time; beat until stiff and glossy. Beat in vanilla. Place frozen cake on heatproof plate or wooden cutting board.* Spread meringue on cake, covering top of cake and ice cream completely. Bake until meringue is golden, about 3 minutes. Garnish with strawberry halves and mint.

6. To serve, slice cake into wedges. Spoon strawberry sauce over wedges.

*TIP: *Cake can also be placed on a baking sheet. Transfer to serving platter after baking.*

1.

2.

3.

4.

5.

6.

7.

8.

3	packages (4¼ ounces each) thinly sliced cooked ham (12 slices)
2	jars (5 ounces each) sharp cheese spread
3	cans (10¾ ounces each) condensed chicken broth
¾	cup water
1	small onion, sliced
2	stalks celery, quartered
3	envelopes unflavored gelatin
¾	cup water
1	avocado
	Lemon juice
1	hard-cooked egg, sliced
	Salad greens

1. Spread each ham slice with generous tablespoon cheese spread. Roll up tightly (photo 1) and cover. Refrigerate.

2. Heat chicken broth, ¾ cup water, the onion and celery to boiling; reduce heat. Simmer 15 minutes; strain (photo 2). Add water, if necessary, to measure 4 cups. Sprinkle gelatin over ¾ cup water to soften; stir into broth mixture (photo 3). Heat, stirring constantly, until gelatin is dissolved; cool. Pour 1 cup gelatin mixture into baking dish, 8 x 8 x 2 inches. Refrigerate until mixture mounds slightly when dropped from a spoon (photo 4).

3. Peel avocado; cut lengthwise in half and remove pit. Slice avocado crosswise; dip slices in lemon juice to prevent discoloration. Arrange half of the avocado slices and the egg slices in gelatin in dish (photo 5). Refrigerate until set.

4. Arrange ham rolls in 2 rows over gelatin in dish; pour 2 cups gelatin mixture over ham rolls (photo 6). Refrigerate until firm, 45 to 50 minutes. Dip remaining avocado slices in gelatin mixture and arrange along sides of dish (photo 7). Pour remaining 1 cup gelatin on top. Refrigerate until set, about 40 minutes.

5. Unmold onto greens and, if desired, garnish with pimiento cutouts and parsley (photo 8).

Informal Party for Twelve

Three soups—all hearty and hot—make party fare for informal entertaining.

SAVORY SOUP MENU

- •CHICKEN SOUP A LA MARIA
- •FRENCH-STYLE VEGETABLE SOUP
- •CHEESY CLAM CHOWDER
  ASSORTED CONDIMENTS

  CHILLED RELISH TRAY
  HARD ROLLS AND BREADS

- •CHEESECAKE-MINCE PIE
- •PUMPKIN CHIFFON PIE
  COFFEE

•Recipes included

Here's a hearty soup and dessert menu, excellent during the crisp days of autumn. Three distinctive soups are kept simmering hot on the stove, filling the air with tempting aromas.

Invite everyone into the kitchen and let them ladle out mugs of chicken soup boasting homemade tortellini, pasta rings filled with chicken. Similar to ravioli, tortellini are round instead of square. They take a while to prepare—both pasta and filling are made from scratch—and are well worth the effort. Make them ahead and freeze them.

Don't let your guests forget zesty French-style Vegetable Soup, chunky with tomatoes, potatoes and cauliflower, or a New England-style clam chowder enlivened with Cheddar cheese. The chicken and vegetable soups may be made the day before, but the Cheesy Clam Chowder should be made fresh. It's difficult to reheat and still maintain a good consistency. You can assemble all of the ingredients in advance, however.

For dessert, bring out the traditional fall flavors of mince and pumpkin, this time in two new guises—Cheesecake-Mince Pie and Pumpkin Chiffon Pie. Both may be made a day ahead. Add garnish just before serving. Serves 12.

Wine Suggestion: If it is a white wine, it should be a pleasant, uncomplicated one such as the Italian Lugana or the Emerald Dry of Paul Masson.

PARTY PLAN FOR SAVORY SOUP MENU

1 Day Before:

Make Cheesecake-Mince Pie and Pumpkin Chiffon Pie, except do not garnish. Cover and refrigerate.
Prepare Chicken Soup à la Maria through step 4 in recipe; cover and refrigerate.
Prepare French-Style Vegetable Soup through step 2 in recipe; cover and refrigerate.

3 Hours Before Serving:

Prepare ingredients for Cheesy Clam Chowder; cover separately and refrigerate.
Prepare relishes and garnishes for menu; cover and refrigerate.

50 Minutes Before Serving:

Complete French-Style Vegetable Soup.
Complete Chicken Soup à la Maria.
Make Cheesy Clam Chowder.

10 Minutes Before Dessert:

Garnish Cheesecake-Mince Pie and Pumpkin Chiffon Pie.

CHICKEN SOUP A LA MARIA WITH HOMEMADE TORTELLINI

Makes 3 quarts

*2   **broiler-fryer chickens (about 2½ pounds each), cut up**
6   **cups water**
1   **stalk celery with leaves, cut into 1-inch pieces**
1   **carrot, pared, cut into 1-inch pieces**
1   **onion, quartered**
2   **sprigs parsley**
1   **bay leaf**
2½   **teaspoons salt**
1   **teaspoon peppercorns**

1½   **cups all-purpose flour**
1   **egg**
1   **egg white**
1   **tablespoon olive oil**
1   **teaspoon salt**

2   **tablespoons grated Parmesan cheese**
1   **egg yolk, slightly beaten**
⅛   **teaspoon grated lemon peel**
⅛   **teaspoon salt**
  Dash ground nutmeg or mace
  Dash pepper

2   **cups water**
2   **tablespoons snipped parsley**
¼   **cup grated Parmesan cheese**

1. Place chicken, 6 cups water, celery, carrot, onion, parsley sprigs, bay leaf, 2½ teaspoons salt and the peppercorns in large Dutch oven or kettle. Heat to boiling; reduce heat and cover. Simmer until thickest pieces are tender, about 45 minutes. Refrigerate until cool. Strain broth; remove meat from bones, separating dark meat. Chop enough dark meat to measure ¾ cup; cover and refrigerate. Place remaining chicken meat in broth; cover and refrigerate no longer than 24 hours.

2. To make tortellini dough, measure flour into bowl. Make a well in center; add egg, egg white, oil and salt. Mix until dough gathers into a ball; sprinkle with few drops of water if dry. Knead dough on lightly floured board until smooth and elastic, about 10 minutes. Cover and let rest 10 minutes.

3. Mix ¾ cup chopped dark chicken meat, 2 tablespoons Parmesan cheese, the egg yolk, lemon peel, ⅛ teaspoon salt, the nutmeg and pepper.

4. Divide dough in half. Roll one half on lightly floured board into 10-inch square. Cut into twenty-five 2-inch circles. Place ¼ teaspoon chicken mixture in center of each circle. Moisten edges of each circle with water. Fold circle in half; seal edges. Shape into rings by stretching the tips of each half circle slightly and wrapping the ring around index finger. Gently press tips together. Repeat with remaining half of dough; cover. Freeze until firm.**

5. To serve, remove fat from broth. Heat broth with meat and 2 cups water to boiling. Add frozen tortellini and snipped parsley. Heat to boiling; reduce heat and cover. Simmer until tortellini are tender, about 30 minutes. Sprinkle servings with ¼ cup Parmesan cheese.

*TIPS: *If available, one 4- to 5-pound stewing chicken, cut up, can be substituted for the broiler-fryer chickens. Simmer until tender, 2½ to 3½ hours.*

**Tortellini can be stored in freezer 24 hours.

FRENCH-STYLE VEGETABLE SOUP

Makes about 3 quarts

*1½ **pounds veal for stew, cubed**
2 **tablespoons vegetable oil**
½ **cup chopped onion**
¼ **cup sliced carrot**
¼ **cup chopped celery**

*1 **veal knuckle (about 1¾ pounds)**
8 **cups water**
1 **tablespoon salt**
2 **bay leaves**
6 **peppercorns**
3 **cloves**
¼ **teaspoon pepper**

½ **cup chopped onion**
½ **cup sliced celery**
1 **can (16 ounces) tomatoes**
1½ **cups cubed pared potatoes**
½ **small head cauliflower, separated into cauliflowerets**

1 **package (10 ounces) frozen mixed vegetables, if desired**

1. Brown cubed veal in oil in Dutch oven. Remove veal; add ½ cup chopped onion, the carrot and ¼ cup celery. Cook and stir over medium heat until onion is transparent.

2. Return veal to Dutch oven. Add veal knuckle, water, salt and spices. Heat to boiling; reduce heat and cover. Simmer 4 hours. Refrigerate at least 12 hours.

3. Skim fat from broth. Remove bone, gristle, fat, bay leaves, peppercorns and cloves. Return meat to Dutch oven. Stir in ½ cup chopped onion, ½ cup sliced celery, the tomatoes, potatoes and cauliflower. Heat to boiling; reduce heat and cover. Simmer 30 minutes.

4. Add frozen mixed vegetables. Heat to boiling; reduce heat and cover. Simmer until vegetables are tender, about 10 minutes longer.

*TIP: *Beef can be substituted for the veal in this recipe.*

CHEESY CLAM CHOWDER

Makes about 3 quarts

6 **slices bacon**
½ **cup diced carrot**
½ **cup chopped celery**
½ **cup finely chopped onion**
¼ **cup all-purpose flour**
1 **tablespoon cornstarch**
½ **teaspoon salt**
¼ **teaspoon pepper**

3 **cans (8 ounces each) minced clams, drained (reserve liquor)**
2 **cans (8 ounces each) clam juice**
1 **quart milk**

1 **cup cubed cooked potatoes**
*1 **pound white Cheddar cheese, diced**
Parsley

1. Cook bacon in Dutch oven until crisp; remove bacon, drain and crumble. Reserve. Cook and stir carrot, celery and onion in bacon fat until onion is transparent. Stir in flour, cornstarch, salt and pepper. Cook and stir until mixture is bubbly.

2. Add reserved clam liquor to clam juice to measure 3½ cups. Stir juice and milk into vegetable mixture. Heat just to boiling, stirring occasionally, until mixture thickens.

3. Add clams, potatoes and cheese; stir until cheese is melted. Sprinkle with reserved bacon. Garnish with sprig of parsley.

*TIP: *White and yellow Cheddar cheese are the same in flavor; only the color differs.*

CHEESECAKE-MINCE PIE

4 **packages (3 ounces each) cream cheese, softened**
2 **eggs**
½ **cup sugar**
2 **teaspoons grated orange peel**
1 **tablespoon orange juice**

1. Beat cream cheese, eggs, ½ cup sugar, the orange peel and juice until smooth.

2. Mix 2 cups mincemeat and the nuts. Spoon mincemeat mixture into pie shell. Pour cream cheese mixture evenly over mincemeat.

Offer a choice of Cheesecake-Mince and Pumpkin Chiffon Pies for dessert.

2 cups mincemeat
½ cup chopped walnuts
10-inch baked pie shell

1 cup dairy sour cream
½ teaspoon vanilla
2 tablespoons sugar

Heat oven to 375°

3. Bake 20 minutes. Mix sour cream, vanilla and 2 tablespoons sugar; spread evenly on top of baked pie. Bake 10 minutes. Chill at least 6 hours.

4. Garnish with orange segments and mincemeat, if desired.

PUMPKIN CHIFFON PIE

½ cup packed brown sugar
1 envelope unflavored gelatin
¼ teaspoon salt
¼ teaspoon ground cinnamon
¼ teaspoon ground nutmeg
1 teaspoon finely chopped
    crystallized ginger
¾ cup canned pumpkin
2 egg yolks
⅓ cup milk

2 egg whites
¼ teaspoon cream of tartar
⅓ cup granulated sugar

8-inch baked pie shell
Sweetened whipped cream
Caramelized Almonds
    (recipe follows)

2 tablespoons sugar
½ cup sliced almonds

1. Mix brown sugar, gelatin, salt, cinnamon, nutmeg and ginger in small saucepan. Mix pumpkin, egg yolks and milk; stir into brown sugar mixture.

2. Cook over medium heat, stirring constantly, just until mixture boils. Place pan in bowl of ice and water or in refrigerator; stir occasionally until mixture mounds slightly when dropped from spoon.

3. Beat egg whites and cream of tartar until foamy. Beat in granulated sugar, 1 tablespoon at a time; beat until stiff and glossy. (Do not underbeat.)

4. Fold pumpkin mixture into egg whites. Spoon into baked pie shell. Refrigerate until set, at least 3 hours. Garnish with whipped cream and Caramelized Almonds just before serving.

CARAMELIZED ALMONDS
Cook and stir sugar in skillet over low heat until sugar is melted and light brown. Stir in almonds. Pour into greased shallow pan; cool. Crumble and separate into pieces.

Fondue Supper for Six

Cinnamon-Sour Cream Sauce adds a perfect touch to Blueberry-Pear Compote.

SWISS DUNKING SUPPER MENU

•SWISS DUNKING POTATOES

ASSORTED COLD MEATS AND

   CHEESES

HOT BRATWURST

TOSSED GREEN SALAD

VEGETABLE RELISHES

•BLUEBERRY-PEAR COMPOTE

COOKIES

COFFEE

•Recipes included

Nearly everyone owns a fondue pot and fork set, and those who don't can find fondue sets in almost any gourmet cookware shop or department store. Many fondue pots are electric, while others receive heat from a small burner using denatured alcohol or canned cooking fuel.

Fondue is a favorite, and this innovative fondue supper uses precooked new potatoes dipped into a pungent hot oil and vinegar sauce. Guests determine at dunking time whether or not to peel the potatoes. Larger potatoes may be used if they are cut into small pieces before cooking. Hot bratwurst or any favorite sausage and a lavish assortment of cold meats and cheeses are served with the potatoes. Select slices of rare roast beef, thin-sliced Danish ham, headcheese and liverwurst, and for cheese, Muenster, Cheddar, Swiss, mozzarella and brick. For texture and color contrast, serve a crisp tossed salad and relishes.

Cookies can be served as an accompaniment to a delicious compote made with poached pears and lightly stewed blueberries, topped with cinnamon-flavored sour cream. The cooking has been timed so that pears and blueberries come out piping hot. Baked apples could be a tasty substitute for the pears, if you like. Serves 6.

Wine Suggestion: And why not? A compromising rosé wine, pleasantly chilled, could be just the thing. But don't look for any sophisticated finds. Almadén Grenache Rosé will be just fine.

PARTY PLAN FOR SWISS DUNKING SUPPER MENU

1 Day Before:	Make Cinnamon-Sour Cream Sauce; cover and refrigerate.
2 Hours Before Serving:	Make salad, relishes and garnishes for menu; cover and refrigerate.
40 Minutes Before Serving:	Make Swiss Dunking Potatoes. Prepare Blueberry-Pear Compote through step 2 in recipe. Arrange cold meats and cheeses on platter; cover and refrigerate.
10 Minutes Before Serving:	Cook bratwurst.
20 Minutes Before Dessert:	Complete Blueberry-Pear Compote.

SWISS DUNKING POTATOES (Stupfete)

2	pounds small new potatoes, washed
¾	cup cider vinegar
1	cup finely chopped onion
½	cup vegetable oil
¼	cup butter or margarine
2	teaspoons caraway seed
2	teaspoons salt
½	teaspoon black pepper

1. Heat 1 inch salted water (1 teaspoon salt to 1 cup water) to boiling in 3-quart saucepan. Add potatoes; cover. Cook until fork tender, about 25 minutes. Drain. Return to saucepan. Shake over low heat until dry. Place in napkin-lined serving dish or basket.

2. Mix remaining ingredients in small saucepan. Heat to boiling; reduce heat. Simmer 5 minutes. Pour sauce into fondue pot. Place pot on stand and ignite denatured alcohol burner or canned cooking fuel.

3. Potatoes can be eaten unpared or can be pared as you go, then cut into halves or quarters. Using a fondue fork, dip each potato or potato section into hot sauce. For added flavor, allow potatoes to remain in sauce 30 seconds or more. Transfer to regular dinner fork before eating.

BLUEBERRY-PEAR COMPOTE

6	pears
1	cup packed brown sugar
⅔	cup water
½	teaspoon grated lemon peel
2	tablespoons lemon juice
2	tablespoons butter or margarine
1	package (10 ounces) frozen blueberries, partially thawed Cinnamon-Sour Cream Sauce (recipe follows)

Heat oven to 350°

½	cup dairy sour cream
1	tablespoon sugar
¼	teaspoon ground cinnamon

1. Core pears from the blossom end up leaving the stems on. Arrange pears in oblong baking dish (size will be determined by size of pears). Mix brown sugar, water, lemon peel, lemon juice and butter in small saucepan. Heat to boiling. Pour over pears; cover.

2. Bake until pears are tender, 60 to 65 minutes, basting occasionally. Uncover for the last 15 minutes.

3. Remove pears to serving dish. Pour syrup into saucepan. Heat syrup to boiling. Boil syrup down to half the amount (about ⅔ cup), stirring occasionally, about 15 minutes. Add blueberries and heat to boiling. Spoon warm blueberry sauce around pears. Top with Cinnamon-Sour Cream Sauce.

CINNAMON-SOUR CREAM SAUCE
Mix all ingredients; cover and refrigerate.

Take-It-Easy Dinner

Toasted coconut tops it off.

Paella is a traditional Spanish dish of rice with meats and seafood.

PAELLA MENU

- SANGRIA

- STUFFED CELERY

- GOOD 'N' EASY PAELLA

- MARINATED SALAD
  ROLLS AND BUTTER
  CORN CHIPS

- PEACH-CINNAMON CREAM
  DESSERT
  COFFEE

- Recipes included

If you love paella but think it is complicated and time-consuming to make, rest easy. This menu utilizes work-saving canned and convenience foods to create an elegant dinner suitable for year-around serving.

This Spanish-inspired paella includes chicken, sausages, shrimp and clams, mingled with saffron-garlic rice. Frozen fried chicken and canned clams help make it a fast and easy dish to prepare. A salad of green beans and carrots marinated in a piquant dressing is rapidly chilled by placing it in your freezer for thirty minutes. For a tangy difference, try dilled cauliflower as a substitute for the green beans.

Add a basket of corn chips, a dish of olives, and your favorite hot rolls with butter to round out the feast. Fruity Sangría, a traditional Spanish beverage, looks especially attractive served in tall iced glasses, garnished with orange slices. Peach-Cinnamon Cream Dessert is quickly made with peach halves, pound cake and cinnamon-flavored vanilla pudding, sprinkled with toasted coconut. Any canned fruit would work just as well as peaches. Serves 6.

Wine Suggestion: It is a lot of fun to serve Sangría just before the dinner; but when it is time for the magnificent paella, we'd better go for a finer wine, and it should be Spanish if possible. How about Federico Paternina's *Reserva* Especial?

28

PARTY PLAN FOR PAELLA MENU

1 Hour 10 Minutes Before Serving: Make Good 'n' Easy Paella.
Prepare Stuffed Celery through Step 1
in recipe; refrigerate.

35 Minutes Before Serving: Make Marinated Salad.
Refrigerate canned peaches.

20 Minutes Before Serving: Prepare Sangría through step 1 in recipe.
Complete Stuffed Celery.

As Guests Arrive: Complete Sangría.

20 Minutes Before Dessert: Complete Peach-Cinnamon Cream Dessert.

SANGRIA
Makes about 9 cups

1 can (6 ounces) frozen
    lemonade concentrate
6 to 8 ice cubes
1 bottle (4/5 quart) red wine
1 package (10 ounces) frozen
    mixed fruit
¼ cup grenadine syrup

1 bottle (32 ounces) club soda
    Half orange slices, if desired

1. Mix frozen lemonade concentrate, ice cubes, wine, fruit and grenadine syrup in pitcher or punch bowl; mix and let stand at room temperature 20 minutes.

2. Just before serving, stir in club soda. Place orange slices on tall glasses and pour beverage.

STUFFED CELERY
Makes about 24

2 hard-cooked eggs, quartered
1 can (4½ ounces) deviled
    ham
2 teaspoons honey
2 teaspoons lemon juice
1 teaspoon Worcestershire
    sauce
    Dash red pepper sauce

    Small bunch celery
    Green olive slices

1. Place all ingredients except celery and olive slices in blender container; cover. Blend until smooth. Store covered in refrigerator.

2. Cut celery into 1-inch lengths. Fill each with 1 teaspoon egg mixture. Garnish with olive slices.

GOOD 'N' EASY PAELLA

*1   package (16 ounces) frozen fried chicken pieces
2   tablespoons olive oil
½   cup finely chopped onion
1   package (8 ounces) frozen brown and serve sausages

1   package (12 ounces) frozen peeled uncooked shrimp
1   teaspoon instant chicken bouillon
¾   cup hot water
1   can (16 ounces) tomato wedges, undrained
1   package (10 ounces) frozen peas
1   can (24 ounces) clams in the shell, drained
1   can (14 ounces) artichoke hearts, drained
2   cups uncooked quick-cooking rice
1   jar (4 ounces) whole pimiento, drained, cut into ¼-inch strips
2½   teaspoons salt
¼   teaspoon garlic powder
½   teaspoon ground saffron

1. Remove chicken from freezer; separate pieces and place on ungreased baking sheet. Heat chicken in oven according to package directions except bake only 20 minutes. Remove from oven. During last 10 minutes of baking, heat oil in Dutch oven. Cook and stir onion and sausages in oil until onion is tender, about 7 minutes, turning sausages frequently.

2. Rinse shrimp under cold running water just to remove ice crystals. Dissolve bouillon in water. Add chicken, shrimp, bouillon and remaining ingredients to Dutch oven. Heat to boiling, stirring frequently; reduce heat and cover. Simmer 10 minutes, stirring frequently; remove from heat. Cover; let stand 10 minutes. Arrange in paella pan or large platter to serve.

*TIP: *1 package (17¼ ounces) fried chicken halves, cut into pieces, can be substituted for chicken pieces.*

MARINATED SALAD

*1   can (16 ounces) cut green
      beans, drained
1   can (16 ounces) sliced
      carrots, drained
¼   cup Italian salad dressing
      Salad greens

Toss beans and carrots in freezer container. Pour dressing over vegetables; toss lightly and cover. Chill in freezer 30 minutes. Stir; serve on greens.

TIP: *1 jar (15½ ounces) dilled cauliflower (with liquid) can be substituted for the green beans. Omit Italian dressing.

PEACH-CINNAMON CREAM DESSERT

1   can (16 ounces) peach halves
1   package (11¼ ounces) frozen
      pound cake
2   cans (5 ounces each) vanilla
      pudding
¼   teaspoon ground cinnamon
1   cup frozen whipped topping,
      thawed

½   cup toasted coconut

1. Chill peaches in refrigerator 45 minutes. Remove cake from freezer; cut six ½-inch slices from cake. Place each slice on plate; thaw about 20 minutes. Mix vanilla pudding, cinnamon and whipped topping.

2. Place 1 peach half cut side up on each cake slice. Fill cavity with about ¼ cup pudding-topping mixture. Sprinkle with coconut.

2   Late Suppers

Entertaining with a late supper gives a delightful fillip to an evening. Food at evening's end should be fairly light and uncomplicated—a multi-course dinner would be too heavy. All the ideal late supper needs is one sensational main dish, a salad and a dessert.

These four late-supper menus range from peasant simple to gourmet elegant. Many of the recipes may be made ahead of time with only a little last-minute preparation. Late suppers can be pleasantly economical, too, since they don't require as much food as a full-fledged dinner. These menus are designed for two or three couples but may easily be increased to accommodate a larger group of people.

If you have a fireplace, light a crackling fire as a cheerful background for a menu of skewered scallops and Caesar Salad. People tend to unwind when they are near a home fire—perhaps it's a carry-over reaction from prehistoric days, when a fire was the main symbol of security. In any case, good feelings and good food together make a memorable occasion.

Buffet meals are always popular with hostesses—the food can be dished up all at once, ready for guests to help themselves. The Beef Ragout Menu is beautifully suitable for buffet serving, but it's easily adaptable for a sit-down supper, too. Ragout is fairly filling, so a light dessert of sherbet and fresh fruit is all you need to round out the meal.

For a late and luxurious supper for four, serve the Sherried Sweetbreads Menu. Sweetbreads have a tender, delicate taste and texture. They're very much worth getting to know. A make-ahead chocolate meringue dessert provides you with more time to spend with guests.

For anytime, try a late-evening menu with a flavor of Italy. This nicely balanced meal includes a chilled antipasto salad and ice cream and a slightly different hot pasta main dish.

Serve crisp, flavorful Caesar Salad as an entrée for late evening entertaining.

Fireside Feasting

Peachy Pecan Pie is delicious.

A skewered scallop appetizer complements Caesar Salad.

CAESAR SALAD MENU

- **LEMON-BASTED SCALLOPS**
- **CAESAR SALAD**
  CRUSTY ROLLS AND BUTTER

- **RED DEVIL'S FOOD LAYER**
  CAKE OR
- **PEACHY PECAN PIE**
  COFFEE OR TEA

- Recipes included

Pictured on page 33.

Lemon-Basted Scallops are attractive as hors d'oeuvres or may be served along with the Caesar Salad entrée. The scallops are skewered with chunks of pimiento and brushed with a tangy lemon and herb mixture during broiling. If you like, shrimp may be used in place of scallops.

The Caesar Salad begins with a base of romaine lettuce and raw spinach. It's tossed with an olive oil dressing, croutons, anchovies and grated Parmesan, and garnished with tomato wedges. Pass crusty rolls and butter to round out the meal. Although it is suggested as an entrée in this menu, the Caesar Salad would also be excellent with a larger meal—the recipe will make twelve individual accompaniment servings.

The scallops and salad are just filling enough to leave everyone with room for an out-of-the ordinary dessert. This menu offers a choice: Red Devil's Food Layer Cake or Peachy Pecan Pie. The cake is the old-fashioned variety—made from scratch to be ultra-moist. Peaches make the pie a delicious variation on traditional pecan pie which can be made the day before and refrigerated. Serves 6.

Wine Suggestion: Nothing could be better than a dry white wine of the Chablis type for this. Maybe a Petite Chablis of Sichel or a California Chablis.

PARTY PLAN FOR CAESAR SALAD MENU

1 Day Before:	Make Peachy Pecan Pie; cover and refrigerate.
	Prepare Caesar Salad through step 2 in recipe. Cover and refrigerate dressing; store croutons in airtight container.
That Afternoon:	Make Red Devil's Food Layer Cake.
20 Minutes Before Serving:	Make Lemon-Basted Scallops.
	Complete Caesar Salad.

LEMON-BASTED SCALLOPS

¼ cup butter or margarine, melted
2 tablespoons lemon juice
1 small clove garlic, crushed
½ teaspoon Worcestershire sauce
½ teaspoon salt
¼ teaspoon dried tarragon
   leaves
¼ teaspoon dried basil leaves

1 package (16 ounces) frozen
   scallops, thawed
1 jar (4 ounces) whole
   pimiento, drained, cut into
   ½-inch pieces

Watercress, if desired
Lemon wedges

Heat oven to broil and/or
   550°

1. Mix butter, lemon juice, garlic, Worcestershire sauce, salt, tarragon and basil; reserve.

2. Thread scallops and pimiento on twelve 6-inch skewers. Place on broiler pan; brush with butter mixture.

3. Broil kabobs 3 inches from heat, turning once and brushing with butter, 5 to 8 minutes. Garnish with watercress and lemon wedges.

CAESAR SALAD

¼ cup olive oil
1 tablespoon fresh lemon juice
¼ teaspoon salt
¼ teaspoon cracked pepper
¼ teaspoon Worcestershire sauce
⅛ teaspoon dry mustard

*3 slices bread
   *Soft butter or margarine
   *Garlic powder

1 clove garlic, cut in half
1 large bunch romaine
1 package (12 ounces) spinach

1 egg

¼ cup grated Parmesan cheese
6 anchovy fillets, cut in half
1 medium tomato, cut into 6
   wedges

Heat oven to 400°

1. Mix olive oil, lemon juice, salt, pepper, Worcestershire sauce and dry mustard; reserve.

2. Trim crusts from bread. Butter both sides of bread generously; sprinkle one side with garlic powder. Cut bread into ½-inch cubes; place on baking sheet. Bake, turning occasionally, until brown and crisp, about 12 minutes.

3. Rub large salad bowl with cut clove of garlic; discard. Tear romaine and spinach into bite-size pieces into salad bowl; set aside.

4. To coddle egg, place egg in the shell in bowl of warm water. In saucepan, heat enough water to cover egg completely to boiling. Immerse egg in boiling water with slotted spoon. Remove pan from heat; cover and let stand 30 seconds. Place egg in cold water immediately.

5. Pour olive oil mixture over salad greens; toss until leaves are coated. Break egg onto greens; toss until leaves are coated. Sprinkle with croutons, cheese and anchovies; toss. Garnish with tomato wedges.

*TIP: *1½ cups packaged seasoned croutons can be substituted.*

RED DEVIL'S FOOD LAYER CAKE

1¾ cups all-purpose flour
1   cup granulated sugar
½   cup packed brown sugar
1½ teaspoons baking soda
¾   teaspoon salt
1¼ cups buttermilk
½   cup shortening
2   eggs
2   squares (1 ounce each)
     unsweetened chocolate,
     melted, cooled
1   teaspoon vanilla
½   teaspoon red food color

     Chocolate Frosting (recipe
     follows)

     Heat oven to 350°

1   package (3 ounces) cream
     cheese, softened
3   tablespoons milk
     Dash salt
3   cups powdered sugar
2   squares (1 ounce each)
     unsweetened chocolate,
     melted, cooled

1. Measure all ingredients except Chocolate Frosting into large mixer bowl. Beat on low speed, scraping bowl constantly, ½ minute. Beat on high speed, scraping bowl occasionally, 3 minutes. Pour into 2 greased and floured round layer pans, 8 or 9 x 1½ inches.

2. Bake until wooden pick inserted in center comes out clean, 30 to 35 minutes. Cool.

3. Prepare Chocolate Frosting; frost cooled cake.

CHOCOLATE FROSTING
Beat cream cheese, milk and salt in small mixer bowl on low speed until smooth. Beat in powdered sugar gradually, scraping bowl occasionally. Add chocolate; beat until smooth.

PEACHY PECAN PIE

Pastry for 9-inch one-crust
    pie
3   eggs
⅔   cup sugar
⅔   cup corn syrup
⅓   cup butter or margarine,
    melted
1   teaspoon vanilla
½   teaspoon salt
1   package (10 ounces) frozen
    sliced peaches, thawed,
    well-drained, cut up
    (⅔ cup)
1   cup pecan halves

Heat oven to 375°

1. Prepare pastry. Beat eggs, sugar, corn syrup, butter, vanilla and salt with rotary beater. Stir in peaches and pecans. Pour mixture into pastry-lined pie plate.

2. Bake until filling is set, 35 to 40 minutes. Cool completely before cutting. Serve with whipped cream if desired.

Buffet for Six

A buffet features Beef Ragout as a make-in-advance entrée.

Hearty ragout and an unusual Marinated Pepper Salad are the basics for this simple buffet. The Beef Ragout, seasoned with Burgundy wine and spices, may be prepared almost to completion two days ahead.

The word *ragout* comes from the French, meaning "to renew the taste," and this recipe does just that. Besides chunks of beef, the ragout includes mushrooms, carrots and a taste of bacon, all precooked and ready to reheat and dish over hot noodles. Serve in a chafing dish if you wish, or spoon servings into individual ramekins. Tomato juice may be substituted for the wine, if preferred.

Choose peppers—green or red—for the salad course. Marinate them in a garlicky Italian dressing and serve the salad on fresh greens. The dessert is light; tart lime sherbet is pleasurably cool to the tongue after the spicy ragout. Offer your favorite cookies and a seasonal selection of fresh fruit—apples, bananas and pears, for example. Piled high in a bowl, they provide a festive centerpiece for your buffet and a refreshing taste and texture combination as well. Serves 6.

Wine Suggestion: Ragouts and Beaujolais wines make a wonderful marriage. One of the best is Brouilly, but equally fine is a wine made from the same grape variety, California's Gamay Beaujolais of Sebastiani.

PARTY PLAN FOR BEEF RAGOUT MENU

2 Days Before:	Prepare Beef Ragout through step 2 in recipe; cover and refrigerate. Prepare Marinated Pepper Salad through step 3 in recipe; cover and refrigerate.
20 Minutes Before Serving:	Complete Beef Ragout. Complete Marinated Pepper Salad.

BEEF RAGOUT

3 slices bacon, diced
2 pounds beef for stew, cut into 1½-inch cubes
1 medium onion, sliced
2 cloves garlic, crushed

1 cup beef bouillon
1 cup red Burgundy wine
4 medium carrots, thinly sliced (about 2 cups)
½ cup snipped parsley
1 small bay leaf
1½ teaspoons salt
½ teaspoon dried thyme leaves
½ teaspoon dried savory leaves
¼ teaspoon pepper

½ pound mushrooms (small to medium), quartered
¼ cup water
3 tablespoons flour
8 ounces noodles, cooked

1. Cook bacon in Dutch oven until crisp; remove bacon and reserve. Cook and stir meat, onion and garlic in bacon fat until meat is brown and onion is tender.

2. Stir in reserved bacon, the bouillon, wine, carrots, parsley, bay leaf, salt, thyme, savory and pepper. Heat to boiling; reduce heat and cover. Simmer until meat is tender, 1½ to 2 hours.*

3. Stir in mushrooms. Shake water and flour in tightly covered jar; stir gradually into meat mixture. Heat to boiling, stirring constantly. Boil and stir 1 minute. Serve on cooked noodles.

*TIP: *Beef Ragout can be made to this point in advance. Cool slightly and cover. Refrigerate no longer than 48 hours. To serve, heat Beef Ragout to boiling; reduce heat and cover. Simmer until meat is hot, about 15 minutes. Proceed with step 3.*

MARINATED PEPPER SALAD

2 cups vegetable oil
3 large red or green peppers

1 bottle (8 ounces) Italian salad dressing
2 tablespoons chopped pimiento
4 large cloves garlic, finely chopped

Salad greens

1. Heat oil in 2-quart saucepan to 250°; add peppers. Cook, turning occasionally, until light brown and tender, about 15 minutes.

2. Remove peppers from oil with slotted spoon; plunge into cold water. Remove outer skin of peppers; place peppers in 1½-quart bowl.

3. Mix dressing, pimiento and garlic; pour over peppers and cover. Refrigerate at least 3 hours, no longer than 48 hours.

4. Cut peppers into eighths; remove seeds and stems. Arrange peppers on greens; spoon small amount of dressing on peppers.

A Special Supper for Four

An elegant Chocolate Meringue.

Sherried Sweetbreads have a distinct and delicate flavor.

SHERRIED SWEETBREADS MENU

• SHERRIED SWEETBREADS
CRISP GREEN SALAD
BREADSTICKS

• CHOCOLATE MERINGUES
COFFEE OR TEA

• Recipes included

Veal sweetbreads in a sauce of chicken broth, sherry and cream, served over crisp toast points, will delight even those who've never tried this treat before. (If you can't find sweetbreads at your meat counter, ask your butcher or order them in advance.) For a variation, serve the sweetbreads in fluted pastry shells, which you can make yourself or buy at your local bakery.

A simple salad of bibb lettuce and artichoke hearts with a light vinegar and oil dressing offers a pleasant contrast to the creamy-rich sweetbreads. Serve breadsticks as an additional taste complement.

Chocolate Meringues, made in individual servings, will be a handsome dessert. Layered meringue shells with a chocolate fudge/whipped cream/chopped pecan filling are made even more irresistible with a sprinkling of chocolate curls. Another time, consider substituting a different kind of ice cream topping for the chocolate fudge topping used in the meringue. Special boon to the hostess: meringues can be prepared and frozen weeks in advance. In fact, this dessert is at its mellowest if frozen for at least one week. Serves 4.

Wine Suggestion: Sherried Sweetbreads is an elegant dish and deserves a wine of equal nobility. Find a nice Bordeaux for it like Chateau Monbousquet 1969 or even 1970, or a fine Cabernet from California—one of the best is Christian Brothers.

PARTY PLAN FOR SHERRIED SWEETBREADS MENU

1 Week Before:	Make Chocolate Meringues; freeze.
3 Hours Before Serving:	Prepare Sherried Sweetbreads through step 1 in recipe; cover and refrigerate. Make salad; cover and refrigerate.
30 Minutes Before Serving:	Complete Sherried Sweetbreads.

SHERRIED SWEETBREADS

2 quarts water
2 tablespoons lemon juice
2 teaspoons salt
1 pound veal sweetbreads

¼ cup butter or margarine
2 tablespoons finely chopped
   onion
3 tablespoons flour
¼ teaspoon salt
1 cup chicken broth
½ cup light cream or
   half-and-half
1 egg yolk, beaten
2 tablespoons dry sherry
1 teaspoon lemon juice
  *Toast points
  Vegetable relishes, if
   desired

1. Heat water, 2 tablespoons lemon juice and 2 teaspoons salt to boiling; add sweetbreads. Heat to boiling; reduce heat and cover. Simmer 20 minutes; drain. Plunge sweetbreads into cold water. Remove membrane and veins and cut sweetbreads into ⅜-inch slices.

2. Melt butter in large skillet. Cook and stir sweetbreads in butter until light brown. Remove sweetbreads from skillet. Cook and stir onion in butter until tender. Stir in flour and ¼ teaspoon salt; remove from heat. Stir in chicken broth and cream. Heat to boiling, stirring constantly. Boil and stir 1 minute. Add small amount hot broth mixture to egg yolk; stir egg yolk mixture into remaining broth mixture. Heat to boiling; boil 1 minute. Stir in sherry, 1 teaspoon lemon juice and the sweetbreads. Heat *just* until hot. Serve on toast points. Garnish with vegetable relishes.

*TIP: *Trim crusts from 4 slices white toast; cut slices diagonally into 4 pieces.*

CHOCOLATE MERINGUES

3 egg whites
¼ teaspoon cream of tartar
¾ cup sugar

1 cup chilled whipping cream
½ cup milk chocolate fudge
   topping
½ teaspoon vanilla
½ cup chopped pecans
  Chocolate curls

Heat oven to 275°

1. Beat egg whites and cream of tartar until foamy. Beat in sugar, 1 tablespoon at a time, beating until stiff and glossy. Do not underbeat.

2. Drop meringue by ⅓ cupfuls onto baking sheet covered with brown paper. Shape mounds into eight 3½-inch circles, building up sides.

3. Bake 1 hour. Turn off oven; leave meringues in oven with door closed 1½ hours. Remove from oven and finish cooling meringues away from draft.

4. Beat cream in chilled bowl until soft peaks form. Beat in fudge topping and vanilla on low speed. Fold in pecans. Spread about ¼ cup filling on each meringue shell. Place 4 of the shells on top of the others. Decorate with chocolate curls.

5. Freeze uncovered until filling is firm, about 3 hours.

TIP: This dessert mellows if frozen 1 week or longer. Freeze covered no longer than 1 month.

A Pasta Repast

"Hearty, not heavy" is the rule for summer eating with this menu.

PROSCIUTTO PASTA MENU

- •ANTIPASTO SALAD
- •PROSCIUTTO PASTA
  HARD ROLLS

  NEAPOLITAN ICE CREAM
  COFFEE OR TEA

- •Recipes included

Popular antipasto appears in a new guise in this menu—it's a colorful salad. Iceberg and romaine lettuce form a base for slices of zucchini, cubes of provolone cheese, ripe olives and green onions, garnished with anchovies and hard-cooked eggs. Make your own dressing with the recipe included here, or use any bottled Italian dressing. *Antipasto* literally means "before the food," but you may certainly serve it along with the pasta entrée, if you wish.

Tender rotini, little corkscrews of pasta, are a different twist for the entrée. Regular spaghetti may also be used. The classic ground beef and tomato sauce has a difference, too. Red wine and paper-thin strips of spicy prosciutto make the subtle distinction. The sauce can be made a day ahead and refrigerated.

Stay in the Italian vein with this summery mealtime conclusion: tricolored Neapolitan ice cream—strawberry, chocolate and vanilla. Or try that other Italian favorite, spumoni—an ice cream dessert containing nuts and candied fruit. Still another traditional Italian dessert idea is a simple array of fresh fruits and cheeses. Serves 6.

Wine Suggestion: This simple but very pleasant Italian menu calls for those charming light red wines which come from the Lake Garda region of Italy, such as Valpolicella; or if you prefer, choose a Hearty Burgundy by Gallo.

PARTY PLAN FOR PROSCIUTTO PASTA MENU

1 Day Before:

Prepare Prosciutto Pasta through step 2 in recipe; cover and refrigerate.
Prepare Italian Dressing; cover and refrigerate.

30 Minutes Before Serving:

Complete Prosciutto Pasta.
Complete Antipasto Salad.

ANTIPASTO SALAD

½   head iceberg lettuce
1   small bunch romaine
1   medium zucchini, thinly sliced
½   cup cubed provolone or
     fontina cheese
½   cup sliced celery
½   cup sliced ripe olives
⅓   cup sliced green onions
2   hard-cooked eggs, chopped
     Anchovy fillets, if desired

     Italian Dressing
     (recipe follows)

1. Tear salad greens into bite-size pieces. Arrange remaining ingredients except dressing on top.

2. Just before serving, toss with dressing.

ITALIAN DRESSING   *Makes 1½ cups*
Shake all ingredients in tightly covered jar; refrigerate.

⅓   cup olive oil
1   tablespoon red wine vinegar
1   tablespoon lemon juice
1   tablespoon snipped parsley
2   teaspoons grated onion
½   teaspoon salt
¼   teaspoon Worcestershire sauce
⅛   teaspoon pepper
1   small clove garlic, finely
     chopped

PROSCIUTTO PASTA

2   tablespoons olive oil
1   pound ground beef
2   medium onions, sliced
2   cloves garlic, finely chopped

1   tablespoon sugar
2   teaspoons salt
1   teaspoon ground nutmeg
½   teaspoon dried rosemary
      leaves, crushed
½   teaspoon pepper
*¼   pound prosciutto, cut into thin
      strips
2   cups dry red wine
2   cans (28 ounces each)
      tomatoes, undrained

1   pound rotini or mostaccioli
      Grated Parmesan cheese

1. Heat oil in Dutch oven. Cook and stir ground beef, onion and garlic in oil until meat is light brown and onion is tender.

2. Stir in remaining ingredients except pasta and cheese; cover. Heat to boiling; reduce heat. Simmer 15 minutes, stirring occasionally. Uncover and simmer, stirring occasionally, until sauce has thickened, about 1½ hours.**

3. Cook pasta according to package directions; drain. Serve sauce on hot cooked pasta. Sprinkle with Parmesan cheese.

TIPS: *Thinly sliced smoked ham can be substituted for the prosciutto.

**Sauce can be made ahead and stored covered in refrigerator no longer than 24 hours. To serve, heat until hot.

3 Dinners for Two

Cooking for two can be a welcome opportunity to try out new recipes. Since you don't need large quantities of food, you can go ahead and splurge on a roast, seafood or steak.

Hibachis are great fun to use and they're popular now, so consider making a purchase. They're small portable braziers with a grill and they burn charcoal. Use one at the table, placed in a fireplace or transported to the porch or patio. The Lemon-Peppered Steak Menu employs this fun technique in a tasty grilled shrimp appetizer.

Cook an extra-special dinner for two with an extra-special touch—flaming Cognac. The technique is called *flambé,* and it can be used with just about any food—a simple dousing with preheated liquor plus a lighted match will do the trick. Be sure to burn off all the alcohol before serving. Our Chicken Cognac Menu gives you a chance to try your hand at it with a flaming entrée of chicken breasts.

Get away from the standard, dull choice of sandwiches or, worse still, an unimaginative box of commercial fried chicken, next time you create a *picnique à deux.* This outdoor menu will please any fresh-air appetites with its surprisingly different recipes. It even includes a soup, and most of it is easily prepared a day ahead.

Use your best china and crystal for the elegant dinner of stuffed Oriental Pork Roast. Several of the less common spices take their place in this menu—ginger in the pork stuffing, nutmeg in the Twice-Baked Squash and a touch of cardamom in the Crème Cake dessert. They're all added with a light hand, so don't worry about the meal being over-spiced. The cake can be made the day before.

Lemon-Peppered Steak offers elegance with ease in a menu for two (see menu on page 46).

A Very Special Dinner

Hibachi Shrimp.

The pears come out on top of this special upside-down cake.

LEMON-PEPPERED STEAK MENU

•HIBACHI SHRIMP

•LEMON-PEPPERED STEAK
FRESH GREEN BEANS
PARSLIED POTATOES
CRISP TOSSED SALAD
CROISSANTS AND BUTTER

•UPSIDE-DOWN PEAR CAKE
ICED TEA OR COFFEE

•Recipes included

Pictured on page 45.

Bring out the hibachi for this menu. Then stuff jumbo shrimp with anchovies, roll them in bacon and grill them over hot coals. Use your kitchen broiler if you prefer. Hibachi Shrimp make excellent appetizers for a large crowd, and this recipe is easily increased to serve more.

Beef rib steaks are sprinkled with tart lemon pepper; be sure you press the pepper well into the meat so it can absorb the flavor. Quickly pan-fried in butter, the steaks are served with a hot onion, cream and brandy sauce. Green beans are a good choice for a vegetable. Use fresh if they are available.

In Upside-Down Pear Cake, milk-chocolate batter is poured over an arrangement of pears and maraschino cherries. After baking, the cake is inverted so that the syrupy layer of pears is on top. Then it's decorated with sweetened whipped cream.

Any combination of fruit may be substituted for the pears. Make the dessert the day you'll serve it so it will be at its freshest. This type of cake can become overly moist if it sits too long. Serves 2.

Wine Suggestion: A big rib steak goes well with a big, husky, mellow Burgundy wine. Nuits St. Georges, Clos de la Maréchale, by Faiveley will salute this great dinner.

46

PARTY PLAN FOR LEMON-PEPPERED STEAK MENU

That Afternoon: Prepare Upside-Down Pear Cake through step 3 in recipe; cool.
Prepare salad greens and slice tomatoes; cover and refrigerate.

50 Minutes Before Serving: Make Lemon-Peppered Steak.
Make Hibachi Shrimp.
Cook potatoes.

20 Minutes Before Serving: Cook green beans.

15 Minutes Before Serving: Complete Upside-Down Pear Cake.

HIBACHI SHRIMP

6	to 8 fresh or thawed frozen jumbo shrimp
6	to 8 anchovy fillets, if desired
3	or 4 slices bacon, cut in half

1. Shell shrimp; split down back, removing sand vein. Place an anchovy in each slit. Roll shrimp in bacon; secure with wooden picks.

2. Grill bacon-wrapped shrimp 3 inches from hot coals until bacon is crisp, about 7 minutes on each side. (Do not overcook.)

LEMON-PEPPERED STEAK

2	beef rib steaks (about 12 ounces each)
2	teaspoons lemon pepper
1	tablespoon butter or margarine
1	tablespoon vegetable oil
	Salt
2	tablespoons chopped green onions and tops
1	tablespoon butter or margarine
2	teaspoons flour
¼	teaspoon salt
½	cup whipping cream
1	tablespoon brandy

1. Pat steaks dry with paper toweling. Sprinkle both sides of steaks with lemon pepper, pressing it into the meat; cover. Let stand 30 minutes.

2. Heat 1 tablespoon butter and the oil in large skillet. Brown steaks 3 to 4 minutes on each side. Remove to hot platter; sprinkle with salt and keep warm.

3. Pour fat from skillet. Cook and stir green onions in 1 tablespoon butter 1 minute; mix in flour and ¼ teaspoon salt. Stir in cream and brandy gradually. Cook and stir until bubbly. Pour over steaks.

UPSIDE-DOWN PEAR CAKE

¼	cup butter or margarine
⅓	cup granulated sugar
1	can (16 ounces) sliced pears, drained
11	maraschino cherries, drained
½	package (18.5-ounce size) milk chocolate cake mix (about 2 cups)
⅔	cup water
1	egg
1	teaspoon instant coffee
½	cup chilled whipping cream
1	tablespoon powdered sugar
	Heat oven to 350°

1. Melt butter in round layer pan, 9 x 1½ inches; stir in granulated sugar. Arrange pears and cherries in pan.

2. Measure cake mix, water, egg and instant coffee into small mixer bowl. Blend ½ minute on low speed, scraping bowl constantly. Beat 4 minutes medium speed, scraping bowl frequently. Pour batter slowly over fruit.

3. Bake until top springs back when touched lightly, about 30 minutes. Invert immediately onto heatproof serving plate; let pan remain over cake 1 minute to allow syrup to run down over cake. Remove pan and cool.

4. Beat whipping cream and powdered sugar in chilled bowl until stiff. Pipe whipped cream around edge of cake with decorator's tube or spoon on dollops.

An Intimate Dinner

Chicken Cognac is flamed before serving.

Flaming dishes are an impressive sight whenever they are served. But they don't have to be complicated. In this menu, chicken breasts are dipped into a coating lightly spiced with paprika, then baked until tender.

Just before serving, heated Cognac is ignited and poured over the chicken. As soon as the flames die down, a creamy sauce is ladled on. Made with heavy cream, sliced green onions, butter and beaten egg yolk, this sauce is also delicious over veal.

Baked potato halves sprinkled with Parmesan cheese are served along with Vegetables California. The familiar flavor of glazed carrots is enhanced by a tang of lemon and the addition of celery cooked just to the crisp-tender stage. To accent the meal, offer croissants and a chilled salad of raw spinach and cherry tomatoes.

Keep the conclusion simple. Place ripe Camembert or Gouda cheese on a wooden serving board. Bring the cheese to room temperature before serving; it tastes better when the chill is off. Alongside, arrange bunches of green grapes and a variety of crisp crackers. Serves 2.

Wine Suggestion: This rich chicken recipe calls for a full-bodied, big mellow wine, like the big white Burgundies: Chassagne Montrachet, Abbaye de Morgeot, or the pride of California, a Pinot Chardonnay of Robert Mondavi.

PARTY PLAN FOR CHICKEN COGNAC MENU

3 Hours Before Serving:	Make salad; cover and refrigerate.
	Prepare vegetables for Vegetables California; cover and refrigerate.
1 Hour 15 Minutes Before Serving:	Make Chicken Cognac.
	Make Buttery Potato Halves.
10 Minutes Before Serving:	Complete Vegetables California.

CHICKEN COGNAC

2 chicken breasts, split
2 tablespoons milk
¼ cup biscuit baking mix
½ teaspoon salt
½ teaspoon paprika

¼ cup sliced green onions
1 tablespoon butter or margarine
1 egg yolk
½ cup whipping cream

¼ cup Cognac

Heat oven to 425°

1. Dip chicken pieces in milk; drain. Mix baking mix, salt and paprika; coat chicken. Place chicken, skin side down, in greased baking pan, 9 x 9 x 2 inches.

2. Bake 30 minutes; turn chicken. Bake until chicken is tender, 20 to 30 minutes. Keep warm.

3. Cook and stir onions in butter in saucepan until onions are tender. Beat egg yolk and cream; stir gradually into onions. Cook and stir over low heat until thickened.

4. Heat Cognac in small saucepan just until hot. Pour Cognac over chicken; ignite. When flame dies out, pour sauce over chicken.

BUTTERY POTATO HALVES

1 large baking potato
   Vegetable oil
2 teaspoons butter or margarine
   Salt
   Dash pepper

1 tablespoon grated Parmesan
   cheese

Heat oven to 425°

1. Scrub potato and rub with oil. Cut in half lengthwise; score cut surfaces. Dot with butter and season with salt and pepper. Wrap each half in aluminum foil.

2. Bake until tender, 50 to 60 minutes. Unwrap. Sprinkle with cheese.

VEGETABLES CALIFORNIA

1 cup carrots, thinly sliced
   (3 medium)
1 cup celery, thinly sliced
   diagonally (2 stalks)
2 tablespoons butter or margarine
1 tablespoon packed brown sugar
2 tablespoons lemon juice

Cook and stir carrots and celery in butter in skillet until carrots are crisp-tender, about 4 minutes. Stir in sugar and lemon juice.

A Gourmet Picnic

New foods for your next picnic: Shrimp Marinade and Watercress Soup.

SHRIMP MARINADE MENU

- **CHEESE SPREAD**
- **WATERCRESS SOUP**
- **SHRIMP MARINADE**
  HARD-COOKED EGGS

- **FRUIT BITES**
- **SPICY TRIANGLE COOKIES**
  ICED TEA OR LEMONADE

- Recipes included

Light and easily packed in Thermos containers, this is an ideal picnic lunch to take along anywhere you please. Everything can be made in advance, so it's ready to go whenever you are.

Watercress, usually seen in salads or tea sandwiches, appears as pungent bits in an interestingly textured soup. This rich soup is equally good hot or cold. However, since the rest of the meal is chilled, you might prefer to serve it hot.

Shrimp are another unique picnic dish. Our shrimp are marinated in tarragon wine vinegar, herbs and vegetables and served with a cold Rice Salad. The rice is also marinated in a flavorful dressing along with chopped walnuts, celery, bits of green pepper and olives.

Hard-cooked eggs, cherry tomatoes and crisp carrot and celery sticks are ideal accompaniments. Fruit Bites—dried apricots and prunes stuffed with marshmallow halves, dipped in orange syrup and rolled in coconut—are served with Spicy Triangle Cookies. Serves 2.

Wine Suggestion: Serve this fine summer menu with a Bordeaux white such as Blanc de Blancs, Sauvignon, from Sichel or a Semillon St. Michelle from the new vineyards in Washington state or a quality California Semillon.

PARTY PLAN FOR SHRIMP MARINADE MENU

2 Days Before:	Make Cheese Spread; cover and refrigerate.
	Make Spicy Triangle Cookies; store in airtight container.
1 Day Before:	Make Watercress Soup; cover and refrigerate. (If serving hot, heat until hot just before serving.)
	Make Shrimp Marinade and Rice Salad; cover separately and refrigerate.
That Afternoon:	Make Fruit Bites.
	Make hard-cooked eggs.

CHEESE SPREAD   *Makes about 2 cups*

1   jar (5 ounces) Cheddar
     cheese spread
1   jar (5 ounces) Roquefort
     cheese spread
1   package (4 ounces)
     Camembert cheese, rind
     removed
1   package (3 ounces)
     cream cheese
¼   cup butter or margarine,
     softened
2   tablespoons Cognac
2   teaspoons prepared mustard
1   teaspoon soy sauce
     Party-size breads or crackers

Bring cheeses to room temperature. Blend with remaining ingredients except bread. Serve spread with breads or crackers.

TIP: Cheese Spread can be stored covered in refrigerator no longer than 3 days.

WATERCRESS SOUP   *Makes about 2 cups*

1   tablespoon butter or margarine
⅓   cup sliced green onions and
     tops
¼   cup sliced celery
1   can (13¾ ounces) chicken
     broth
½   cup snipped watercress
     (about 1 small bunch)
⅓   cup instant mashed potato
     puffs (dry)
¼   teaspoon pepper
½   cup light cream

1. Melt butter in saucepan; cook and stir onions and celery in butter until onions are tender. Stir in chicken broth. Heat to boiling; reduce heat. Simmer until celery is tender, about 5 minutes. Stir in watercress and potato puffs. Heat just until watercress is wilted, about 2 minutes. Remove from heat; cool slightly.

2. Pour watercress mixture into blender container; cover. Blend until smooth, about 20 seconds. Pour into saucepan. Stir in pepper and cream. Heat just to boiling. Serve hot or cold.

SHRIMP MARINADE

1   package (12 ounces) frozen
      cooked cleaned shrimp,
      thawed
½   cup sliced fresh carrot,
      turnip or cauliflowerets
5   slices lemon
2   slices onion, separated into
      rings
⅓   cup tarragon wine vinegar
¼   cup olive oil
1   teaspoon sugar
½   teaspoon salt
⅛   teaspoon dried basil leaves,
      crushed
1   bay leaf, crumbled
      Rice Salad (recipe follows)
      Salad greens, if desired

1   cup cooled cooked rice
¼   cup chopped walnuts
2   tablespoons sliced celery
2   tablespoons chopped green
      pepper
2   tablespoons sliced green
      onions
2   tablespoons chopped pimiento-
      stuffed olives
2   teaspoons snipped parsley
1   tablespoon French salad
      dressing
1   teaspoon vinegar
¼   teaspoon salt
      Dash pepper

Arrange shrimp, carrot, lemon and onion in baking dish, 11¾ x 7½ x 1¾ inches. Mix remaining ingredients except Rice Salad and salad greens; pour over shrimp and cover. Refrigerate at least 8 hours, stirring occasionally. Drain; transport shrimp and vegetables in insulated or vacuum container. Serve with Rice Salad. Garnish with salad greens.

RICE SALAD
Mix all ingredients; cover and refrigerate at least 8 hours.

FRUIT BITES
Makes 9 pieces

½   cup frozen orange juice
      concentrate, thawed
¼   cup water
2   tablespoons light corn syrup
6   pitted large prunes
3   large marshmallows, snipped
      in half
12   dried apricot halves

      Shredded coconut

1. Mix orange juice concentrate, water and corn syrup in small saucepan. Heat to boiling; reduce heat. Simmer 3 minutes. Remove from heat; cool slightly.

2. Wrap 3 prunes around 3 marshmallow halves; fasten with wooden picks. Place each remaining marshmallow half between 2 apricot halves; fasten with wooden picks. Wrap each of remaining prunes around 2 apricot halves; fasten with wooden picks.

3. Dip into orange juice mixture; roll in coconut. Dry on wire rack; remove wooden picks.

SPICY TRIANGLE COOKIES

Makes 4 dozen

1 cup butter or margarine, softened
1 cup packed brown sugar
1 egg yolk
1 teaspoon vanilla
2 cups all-purpose flour
¼ teaspoon salt
1 teaspoon ground cardamom
1 egg white
1 can (5 ounces) diced roasted almonds

Heat oven to 275°

1. Mix butter, sugar, egg yolk and vanilla. Stir in flour, salt and cardamom. Spread evenly in ungreased jelly roll pan, 15½ x 10½ x 1 inch. Brush dough with egg white. Sprinkle almonds on top; press into dough. Bake 1 hour.

2. While warm, cut into 2½-inch squares, then cut each square diagonally in half. Cool.

TIP: Spicy Triangle Cookies can be stored covered in freezer no longer than 4 months. Remove 20 minutes before serving and unwrap. Thaw uncovered at room temperature.

53

Good and Easy Dinner

This entrée features a uniquely stuffed pork roast.

ORIENTAL PORK ROAST MENU

- •ORIENTAL PORK ROAST
- •TWICE-BAKED SQUASH
  GREEN BEANS
  HOT ROLLS AND BUTTER
- •CREME CAKE
  COFFEE

•Recipes included

Spices are everywhere in this menu, and the result is truly spectacular. Four deep pockets are easily cut in a pork roast and then stuffed with bread crumbs, peanut butter, soy sauce and ginger. These traditional Oriental flavors blend well with the delicate taste of the pork.

Quickly cooked green beans add a note of color, as does our recipe for acorn squash. The squash halves are baked, then the squash is removed from the shells and mixed with mandarin orange syrup and spices. Add cranberry sauce cubes and orange segments, then spoon the mixture into the shells.

The made-from-scratch Crème Cake is split into two layers and drizzled with rum syrup. Then the layers are put together with vanilla pudding laced with rum-soaked raisins and coconut, and decorated with sliced almonds. Serves 2.

Wine Suggestion: A typical hearty menu, which calls for a gutsy, heady wine. Try to find a good Grignolino from Italy or California.

54

PARTY PLAN FOR ORIENTAL PORK ROAST MENU

1 Day Before:	Make Crème Cake; cover and refrigerate.
2 Hours Before Serving:	Make Oriental Pork Roast. Make Twice-Baked Squash.
15 Minutes Before Serving:	Make green beans.

ORIENTAL PORK ROAST

3   **pound pork loin center rib roast, backbone loosened**
2   **tablespoons peanut butter**
1   **tablespoon hot water**
1   **tablespoon soy sauce**
1   **clove garlic, finely chopped**
¼   **teaspoon ground ginger**
½   **cup soft bread crumbs**

Heat oven to 325°

1. Cut four deep pockets almost through meaty side of roast between ribs; spread apart. Mix peanut butter, water, soy sauce, garlic, ginger and bread crumbs. Spoon mixture into pockets of roast.

2. Place roast fat side up in open shallow roasting pan. Insert meat thermometer so tip is in center of thickest part of meat and does not touch bone or rest in fat or stuffing. Do not add water. Roast uncovered until meat thermometer registers 170°, about 1½ hours. Let meat stand 20 minutes before carving.

TWICE-BAKED SQUASH

1   **medium acorn squash**
1   **tablespoon mandarin orange syrup**
1   **tablespoon butter or margarine**
¼   **teaspoon salt**
⅛   **teaspoon pepper**
     Dash ground nutmeg
¾   **cup jellied cranberry sauce, cubed**
¼   **cup mandarin orange segments**

Heat oven to 325°

1. Cut squash in half; remove seeds and fibers. Place cut sides down in baking pan; fill with water to depth of ¼ inch. Bake until tender, about 1 hour.

2. Remove squash from shells, reserving shells. Spoon squash into small mixer bowl. Add orange syrup, butter, salt, pepper and nutmeg. Beat until smooth.*

3. Mix squash mixture, cranberry sauce and mandarin orange segments. Spoon into squash shells. Bake 25 to 35 minutes.

*TIP: *Mixture can be prepared to this point and refrigerated covered no longer than 24 hours.*

1¼ cups all-purpose flour
1   cup granulated sugar
1½ teaspoons baking powder
¾   teaspoon ground cardamom
½   teaspoon salt
¾   cup milk
⅓   cup shortening
1   egg
1   teaspoon vanilla

¼   cup water
2   tablespoons granulated
       sugar
⅓   cup dark rum or
       1 tablespoon rum flavoring
½   cup finely chopped raisins

1   package (3¼ ounces) vanilla
       regular pudding and pie
       filling
⅓   cup flaked coconut

     Sliced almonds

     Heat oven to 350°

1. Measure flour, 1 cup granulated sugar, the baking powder, cardamom, salt, milk, shortening, egg and vanilla into large mixer bowl. Blend ½ minute on low speed, scraping bowl constantly. Beat 3 minutes high speed, scraping bowl occasionally. Pour into greased and floured square pan, 8 x 8 x 2 or 9 x 9 x 2 inches. Bake until wooden pick inserted in center comes out clean, 45 to 55 minutes. Cool.

2. Heat water and 2 tablespoons granulated sugar until sugar is dissolved. Stir in rum and raisins. Remove from heat. Let stand at least 30 minutes.

3. Prepare pudding according to package directions for pudding except use only 1½ cups milk. Stir in coconut; cool.

4. Split cake horizontally to make 2 layers. Remove raisins from rum mixture (reserve mixture); stir raisins into cooled pudding mixture. Prick each layer on cut side with long-tined fork. Drizzle rum mixture over pricked cake. Spread half of the raisin-coconut pudding over 1 layer. Replace top layer. Spread remaining raisin-coconut pudding on top of cake. Press in sliced almonds. Refrigerate at least 8 hours, no longer than 24 hours.

Crème cake is filled and topped with raisin-coconut pudding.

4   Brunch or Lunch

The late morning, noon or early afternoon meal has a unique personality all its own. These hours of the day are pleasant for entertaining—there is time to relax, to linger over coffee. Drinks are best kept on the light side, but there's a wide range of beverages from which to choose. For example, what could be nicer than wine, especially served in group-size or individual glass carafes?

An airy soufflé is an excellent luncheon idea any time of the year. The name is from the French *souffler,* "to puff up," and a soufflé is a fluffy dish made with egg yolks and stiffly beaten egg whites. Usually baked in a round, straight-sided casserole, it puffs up while cooking. Soufflés can be used as main dish or dessert. This soufflé menu is of the main-dish variety with crabmeat as its major addition.

Main-dish salads are always luncheon favorites, and should be fairly filling. The Choose-Your-Own Chef's Salad allows guests to be creative; they may also choose from three different dressings. This menu is a summertime joy—the food is refreshingly cool and everything can be prepared ahead.

An attractive dish at any hour, the ultra-thin pancakes called crêpes are especially nice for brunch or lunch and they're not too hard to make. The Crêpe Menu makes a particularly pretty spring brunch, yet is appealing year-around. Because crêpes are remarkably versatile, they've become increasingly popular; an infinite variety of fillings can turn them into inviting entrées, vegetable courses or desserts.

Traditional American cooking has always included a robust breakfast. Farmers needed a sturdy beginning to their long days. Loggers in the North Woods, too, enjoyed Paul Bunyanesque breakfasts. Nowadays, most of us are content with lighter fare for everyday, but there are times when a hearty yet leisurely breakfast brunch is the perfect repast. The Down-on-the-Farm Brunch is a comforting reminder of days past.

The last lunch-brunch menu offers an interesting variation on eggs and bacon. These two staple breakfast foods meet in an unusual cheese pie, accompanied by a salad, bread and fruit. It's a luncheon that knows no seasons—a pleasing choice whenever it is served. Light and totally uncomplicated, you'll be pleased with its simple elegance.

Airy soufflés are made with crabmeat for a luncheon entrée (see menu on page 60).

An Elegant Luncheon

Crisp salad and breadsticks are perfect accompaniments for a soufflé menu.

CRABMEAT SOUFFLE MENU

- **GREEN SALAD WITH LEMONY FRENCH DRESSING**
- **PARMESAN BREADSTICKS**
- **CRABMEAT SOUFFLE**
  Pictured on page 59.
- **BRAISED PEAS AND CELERY**

- **CITRUS DELIGHT**
  COFFEE OR TEA

- Recipes included

The fascinating puffiness of soufflés makes them look difficult and for that reason they frighten many cooks. But the technique is not that difficult. Directions for making Crabmeat Soufflé are given in the Step-By-Step Recipe. You can even prepare it hours in advance, all ready for baking. A soufflé's puffiness comes from air bubbles beaten into the egg whites. French chefs claim the best volume results when egg whites are beaten in an unlined copper bowl with a wire whisk.

Because of the addition of crabmeat, this soufflé is very moist and will rise only to a moderate height. To serve it correctly use two forks to separate the soufflé gently and lift it out to preserve the delicate texture.

Braised Peas and Celery and a simple green salad go well with the soufflé. The salad is tossed with a refreshing, Lemony French Dressing. Homemade Parmesan Breadsticks—crisp on the outside, moist and breadlike inside—add a nice contrast to the meal.

Fruit desserts are ideal for lunch and our Citrus Delight is a splendid way to serve grapefruit. The sectioned fruit is flavored with sugared fruit brandy or liqueur. Tops are replaced, with green grapes draped over and around for a graceful touch. In place of grapefruit, large oranges could also be used effectively. Serves 8.

Wine Suggestion: Soufflés are elegant by preparation and nature. So is a Moselblümchen from Sichel, or go to New York State for Dr. Konstantin Frank's Johannisberg Riesling.

PARTY PLAN FOR CRABMEAT SOUFFLE MENU

1 Day Before:	Make Lemony French Dressing; refrigerate. Prepare Citrus Delight through step 2 in recipe; cover and refrigerate.
4 Hours Before Serving:	Prepare Crabmeat Soufflé through step 3 in recipe; cover and refrigerate. Make Parmesan Breadsticks; cover. Prepare salad greens; cover and refrigerate. Prepare vegetables for Braised Peas and Celery; cover and refrigerate.
45 Minutes Before Serving:	Heat oven to 375°; complete Crabmeat Soufflé.
10 Minutes Before Serving:	Make Braised Peas and Celery. Complete salad.
5 Minutes Before Dessert:	Garnish Citrus Delight.

GREEN SALAD WITH LEMONY FRENCH DRESSING

½   cup olive oil
2   tablespoons white wine vinegar
2   tablespoons lemon juice
1¼ teaspoons salt
½   teaspoon pepper
2   cloves garlic, finely chopped

8   cups bite-size pieces salad
     greens (bibb lettuce, romaine,
     spinach), chilled

1. Measure all ingredients except salad greens into jar; cover. Shake well. Refrigerate.

2. Shake dressing; pour over salad greens. Toss dressing with the greens.

PARMESAN BREADSTICKS

Makes 32 breadsticks

1   package active dry yeast
⅔   cup warm water (105° to 115°)
2½ cups biscuit baking mix

¼   cup butter or margarine, melted
2   tablespoons grated Parmesan
     cheese

1. Dissolve yeast in warm water. Stir in baking mix; beat vigorously. Turn dough onto floured surface. Knead until smooth, about 20 times.

2. Roll dough into a rectangle, about 13 x 9 inches. Brush part of the butter in baking pan, 13 x 9 x 2 inches. Place dough in pan, pressing to fit bottom of pan. Cut dough crosswise into 16 strips, then cut lengthwise in half. Brush with remaining butter. Sprinkle with cheese; cover. Let rise in warm place until light, about 1 hour.

3. Heat oven to 425°. Bake until golden brown, about 15 minutes. Turn oven off. Allow breadsticks to remain in oven 15 minutes longer to crisp. Break apart to serve.

CRABMEAT SOUFFLE

See STEP-BY-STEP RECIPE on page 63.

Citrus Delight is a refreshing dessert.

BRAISED PEAS AND CELERY

2   packages (10 ounces each)
        frozen green peas
2   cups diagonally sliced celery
1   cup sliced green onions
1   cup water
1   teaspoon instant chicken
        bouillon

4   teaspoons cornstarch
2   tablespoons water
2   tablespoons butter or margarine
½   teaspoon salt
¼   teaspoon pepper

1. Mix peas, celery, onions, water and bouillon in saucepan. Heat to boiling; reduce heat and cover. Simmer 5 minutes.

2. Mix cornstarch and water. Stir into vegetables. Heat, stirring constantly, to boiling. Boil and stir 2 minutes. Stir in butter, salt and pepper.

CITRUS DELIGHT

8   small grapefruit

8   teaspoons powdered sugar
¼   cup fruit-flavored brandy or
        orange liqueur

     Mint sprigs
     Green grapes

1. Slice off top one-third of each grapefruit or orange; peel and reserve fruit for cap. Section fruit in bottom of grapefruit with grapefruit knife.

2. Mix sugar and brandy (if using oranges, omit sugar). Gently squeeze out 2 to 3 tablespoons juice from each grapefruit. Spoon sugar mixture over fruit. Place reserved caps over grapefruit; cover. Refrigerate at least 2 hours.

3. Serve in shallow stemmed glasses or dessert dishes. Garnish with mint and green grapes.

TIP: Fruits can be peeled completely, sectioned and mixed with brandy or the liqueur. Refrigerate until chilled. Spoon into shallow stemmed glasses or dessert dishes.

1.

2.

3.

4.

5.

1	cup finely chopped shallots or green onions
⅔	cup butter or margarine
½	cup all-purpose flour
2	teaspoons salt
1	teaspoon pepper
1¼	cups light cream
⅓	cup tomato paste
¼	teaspoon red pepper sauce
8	egg yolks, slightly beaten
2	packages (6 ounces each) frozen crabmeat, thawed, drained, flaked
½	teaspoon dried tarragon leaves
8	egg whites

1. Butter two 1½-quart soufflé dishes or casseroles or eight 1½-cup individual soufflé dishes or baking cups. Cook and stir shallots in butter in 3-quart saucepan until transparent. Stir in flour, salt and pepper (photo 1). Cook over low heat, stirring constantly, until mixture is smooth and bubbly. Remove from heat.

2. Stir in cream, tomato paste and pepper sauce. Heat to boiling, stirring constantly. Boil and stir 1 minute; reduce heat. Beat in egg yolks gradually (photo 2); remove from heat. Stir in crabmeat and tarragon leaves. Set saucepan in ice and water. Stirring occasionally, cool *just* to room temperature, 15 to 20 minutes.

3. Heat oven to 375°. Beat egg whites until stiff but not dry (photo 3). Stir about ¼ of the egg whites into crabmeat mixture. Gently fold mixture into remaining egg whites (photo 4). Divide the mixture (about 8½ cups) evenly into soufflé dishes.*

4. Bake until knife inserted halfway between edge and center comes out clean (center will be soft)—1½-quart soufflés 30 to 35 minutes, individual soufflés 25 to 30 minutes.

5. Serve immediately. To serve, divide soufflé into sections with 2 forks. Garnish with lemon wedges and parsley if desired.

*TIP: *Mixture can be covered and refrigerated no longer than 4 hours at this point.*

Summer Salad Lunch

Assemble ingredients ahead and join guests in putting together a hearty salad.

CHEF'S SALAD MENU

- CHOOSE-YOUR-OWN CHEF'S
  SALAD WITH ASSORTED
  DRESSINGS
- CRUSTY ROLLS AND BUTTER
- CHOCOLATE ECLAIRS
  ICED TEA

• Recipes included

This cool luncheon menu is light enough to win the favor of heat-wilted guests and hearty enough to please healthier appetites. And with little extra effort the recipes may easily be expanded to serve any number of people.

The recipe for Choose-Your-Own Chef's Salad offers a tempting variety of luncheon meats, cheeses, salmon and all kinds of vegetables. Feel free to add anything you like, or include fewer items. Then let your guests make any salad combination they desire. Add three distinctively different homemade dressings for your enterprising salad makers to enjoy. Crusty hard rolls, easily made from frozen bread dough, can be baked ahead and reheated or served cold.

A tray of chocolate-frosted eclairs brings a cool finish to this quickly prepared meal. The eclairs are filled with vanilla pudding flavored with banana liqueur—you can use any favorite flavoring. Serves 8.

Wine Suggestion: Anything else but a rosé wine would be pretentious: Tavel les Vignerons; Vin Rosé Sec from Paul Masson.

PARTY PLAN FOR CHEF'S SALAD MENU

1 Day Before:

Make salad dressings; cover separately and refrigerate.
Make Crusty Rolls; wrap in aluminum foil and refrigerate.

3 Hours Before Serving:

Prepare Choose-Your-Own Chef's Salad through step 2 in recipe; cover and refrigerate.
Make Chocolate Eclairs; refrigerate.
Make iced tea; refrigerate.

20 Minutes Before Serving:

Heat oven to 350°. Heat Crusty Rolls in foil in oven until hot, 10 to 15 minutes.

CHOOSE-YOUR-OWN CHEF'S SALAD WITH ASSORTED DRESSINGS

8   cups bite-size pieces salad
      greens (iceberg, spinach,
      butterhead lettuce, romaine)
1   large avocado, peeled,
      pitted, sliced
1   tablespoon lemon juice
12 ounces assorted sliced luncheon
      meats (salami, ham)
12 ounces assorted sliced cheeses
      (Swiss, Cheddar)
1   package (10 ounces) frozen
      asparagus spears, cooked
1   package (9 ounces) frozen
      green beans, cooked
1   cup cherry tomato halves
1   medium-size red onion, sliced
1   can (16 ounces) garbanzo beans,
      drained
1   can (7½ ounces) salmon,
      drained, flaked
½   cup croutons, if desired

Assorted dressings
(recipes follow)

1. Place salad greens in salad bowl; cover and refrigerate. (Place four 8-inch salad plates in refrigerator to chill at the same time.)

2. Sprinkle avocado with lemon juice. Cut meats and cheeses into 1-inch strips; arrange with avocado, vegetables and salmon on serving platter; cover. Refrigerate. Croutons can be placed in a bowl and covered until serving time.

3. Prepare salad dressings.

½   cup chili sauce
½   cup mayonnaise or salad
      dressing
1   hard-cooked egg, chopped
1   tablespoon pickle relish,
      drained
½   teaspoon instant minced onion

THOUSAND ISLAND DRESSING   *Makes 1⅓ cups*

Mix all ingredients and cover. Refrigerate until cold.

½   cup dairy sour cream
½   cup mayonnaise or salad
      dressing
1   clove garlic, crushed
¼   teaspoon white pepper
1   tablespoon milk
1   tablespoon snipped chives

CREAMY GARLIC DRESSING   *Makes 1 cup*

Mix all ingredients and cover. Refrigerate at least 24 hours.

2/3 cup olive oil
1/3 cup red wine vinegar
2 ounces blue cheese, crumbled

CHUNKY BLUE CHEESE DRESSING

Makes 1¼ cups

Mix all ingredients and cover. Refrigerate until cold.

CRUSTY ROLLS

Makes 12 rolls

2 loaves (16 ounces each) frozen bread dough
2 tablespoons butter or margarine, melted

½ cup water
1 teaspoon cornstarch
Caraway seeds, sesame seeds or instant minced onion

1. Let frozen dough stand at room temperature 1 hour and 15 minutes. Cut each loaf crosswise into 6 slices; shape into 4-inch circles. Place rolls on greased baking sheet; brush with melted butter. Let stand at room temperature 1 hour.

2. Heat oven to 350°. Mix water and cornstarch in small saucepan. Heat to boiling, stirring constantly; remove from heat. Cool slightly; brush rolls with cornstarch mixture. Sprinkle with caraway seeds.

3. Bake rolls until golden brown, 20 to 25 minutes.

CHOCOLATE ECLAIRS

Makes 16

2 packages (3 ounces each) vanilla regular pudding and pie filling
6 tablespoons banana liqueur, if desired

1 cup water
½ cup butter or margarine
1 cup all-purpose flour
4 eggs

1 cup chilled whipping cream

1/3 cup semisweet chocolate pieces
¼ cup evaporated milk
1 cup powdered sugar
1 teaspoon light corn syrup
½ teaspoon vanilla

1. Prepare pudding and pie filling according to package directions for pudding except use 3 cups milk. Remove from heat. Stir in banana liqueur and cover. Refrigerate.

2. Heat water and butter in 3-quart saucepan to boiling; reduce heat. Stir in flour. Stir vigorously over low heat until mixture leaves sides of pan and forms a ball. Remove from heat. Beat in eggs, all at once. Beat until smooth.

3. Heat oven to 400°. Shape dough by scant 3 tablespoonfuls 3 inches apart on ungreased baking sheet into finger-like shapes, 3¼ inches long and 1½ inches wide. Bake 35 to 40 minutes. Cool away from draft.

4. Beat whipping cream in chilled bowl until stiff. Fold vanilla pudding mixture into whipped cream. Cut tops off eclairs. Remove soft dough. Fill eclairs with filling; replace tops.

5. Heat chocolate pieces and evaporated milk over low heat until chocolate is melted. Remove from heat. Stir in sugar, corn syrup and vanilla until smooth. Frost eclairs and cover. Refrigerate until serving time, no longer than 2 hours.

Chocolate Eclairs are a perfect dessert for a luncheon menu.

The Ultimate Brunch

Fruit Sparkle is the perfect beginning for an elegant brunch.

CREPE MENU

- **FRUIT SPARKLE**

- **EGG AND HAM CREPES WITH MUSHROOM SAUCE**
- **BIBB LETTUCE SALAD WITH CLASSIC FRENCH DRESSING**

- **SHERBET COOLERS**
  ICED TEA

- Recipes included

Bubbling champagne poured over fruit in stemmed crystal glasses sets the effervescent note for this beautiful brunch. Ripe strawberries and Cognac-marinated apricots arranged in the glasses just before adding the champagne gives the festive appetizer its name—Fruit Sparkle. Any fresh or canned fruit combination would be excellent served this way.

Crêpes, rolled and stuffed with scrambled eggs and ham, are delicious with sour cream sauce spooned over them. Mushrooms, onion, mustard and a pinch of nutmeg add a zippy note to the sauce. You don't need a special crêpe pan—a small six- or seven-inch skillet with rounded bottom will do the job. If you've never made crêpes before, make the first crêpe or two a sample; you'll quickly acquire the knack. The crêpes may be made a day ahead and refrigerated. Then at serving time, reheat the crêpes, place the filling on the center of each crêpe and roll up.

The rich Egg and Ham Crêpes call for a light, crisp contrast, perfectly provided by a salad of bibb lettuce. Homemade French dressing takes the salad out of the realm of average. Miniature scoops of pastel-colored sherbets in a variety of subtle flavors make a simple but lovely dessert. Garnish the sherbet with sprigs of mint. We've chosen orange, lemon, lime and pineapple sherbets, but any varicolored assortment would be fine. Serves 4.

Wine Suggestion: Sip one of those beautiful country wines, which re-evoke hundreds of memories, with this menu: Moulin-à-Vent, Paul Bocuse; or Pinot Noir, Christian Brothers.

Egg and ham-filled crêpes are served with creamy Mushroom Sauce.

PARTY PLAN FOR CREPE MENU

1 Day Before:	Prepare Fruit Sparkle through step 1 in recipe; cover and refrigerate. Prepare Bibb Lettuce Salad with Classic French Dressing through step 2 in recipe; cover and refrigerate. Make Crêpes. Cool; wrap with aluminum foil to prevent drying out. Refrigerate. Chop ham for Egg and Ham Crêpes; cover and refrigerate.
30 Minutes Before Serving:	Heat oven to 325°. Make Mushroom Sauce; keep warm. Heat Crêpes in foil in oven until warm, 5 to 10 minutes. Reduce oven temperature to 200°. Prepare Egg and Ham Crêpes, except do not spoon Mushroom Sauce over top; cover. Keep warm in oven.
10 Minutes Before Serving:	Complete Fruit Sparkle. Complete Bibb Salad with Classic French Dressing. Spoon Mushroom Sauce over Egg and Ham Crêpes.
10 Minutes Before Dessert:	Make Sherbet Coolers.

FRUIT SPARKLE

1 cup fresh apricot halves or
   1 can (8¾ ounces) apricot
   halves, drained
¼ cup Cognac
2 tablespoons powdered sugar

1 cup fresh strawberries, cut
   in half
Chilled champagne

1. Measure apricots into small bowl. Mix Cognac and sugar; pour over fruit, stirring well. Cover. Refrigerate at least 12 hours.

2. Arrange strawberries and apricot-Cognac mixture in 4 chilled champagne glasses or sherbet dishes. Pour champagne over fruit just before serving.

EGG AND HAM CREPES WITH MUSHROOM SAUCE

Crêpes (recipe follows)

¼ pound fully cooked ham,
   finely chopped (about
   1¼ cups)
2 tablespoons butter or margarine

8 eggs
½ cup milk
¼ cup water
½ teaspoon pepper

Mushroom Sauce
   (recipe follows)

1 cup biscuit baking mix
1 egg
1 cup milk

1. Prepare Crêpes; cover and keep warm.

2. Cook and stir ham in butter over medium heat until light brown, about 5 minutes.

3. Mix eggs, milk, water and pepper with fork; pour over ham in skillet. As mixture begins to set at bottom and side, gently lift cooked portions with spatula so thin, uncooked portions can flow to bottom. Avoid constant stirring. Cook until eggs are thickened throughout but still moist, 3 to 5 minutes.

4. Spoon ¼ cup egg-ham mixture on center of each crêpe; roll up. Place seam side down on plate. Spoon Mushroom Sauce over top.

CREPES   *Makes 12*
1. Beat all ingredients with rotary beater until smooth. Spoon 2 tablespoons batter into hot lightly greased 6- or 7-inch skillet. Immediately rotate skillet until batter covers bottom.

2. Cook until light brown; turn and brown on other side. When removing from skillet, place crêpe so first cooked side is down on baking sheet or tray.

MUSHROOM SAUCE   *Makes about 1⅔ cups*
1. Cook and stir mushrooms and onion in butter until onion is tender and mushrooms are light brown, 3 to 5 minutes.

½ pound fresh mushrooms, sliced
2 tablespoons chopped onion
3 tablespoons butter or margarine

1 tablespoon flour
½ teaspoon salt
⅛ teaspoon ground nutmeg
⅛ teaspoon pepper

1 cup dairy sour cream
⅓ cup milk
1 teaspoon prepared mustard
2 tablespoons snipped parsley

2. Stir in flour, salt, nutmeg and pepper. Cook and stir over low heat until mixture is bubbly. Remove from heat.

3. Mix sour cream, milk, mustard and parsley; stir into mushroom mixture. Heat, stirring constantly, just to boiling.

Small scoops of pastel sherbet are a perfect ending for any brunch.

BIBB LETTUCE SALAD WITH CLASSIC FRENCH DRESSING

2	heads bibb lettuce or 4 cups other salad greens
¼	cup olive oil or vegetable oil
2	tablespoons tarragon or wine vinegar
¾	teaspoon salt
1	small clove garlic, crushed
¼	teaspoon monosodium glutamate
	Generous dash freshly ground pepper
2	to 3 tablespoons sliced pimiento-stuffed olives

1. Wash lettuce; cut each head in half lengthwise. Pat dry. Refrigerate.

2. Shake remaining ingredients except olives in tightly covered jar. Refrigerate. Shake again just before serving.

3. Arrange lettuce halves on salad plates; garnish with olive slices. Drizzle with salad dressing.

SHERBET COOLERS

½	pint orange sherbet
½	pint lemon sherbet
½	pint lime sherbet
½	pint pineapple sherbet
4	mint sprigs

Arrange small scoops of assorted sherbets in bowls. Garnish with sprigs of mint.

Down-on-the-Farm Brunch

Hash-brown potatoes are scrambled with eggs and served with fried pork slices.

SCRAMBLED EGGS AND PORK MENU

FRUIT JUICE

•HASH-BROWN SCRAMBLED EGGS

•FRESH SIDE PORK FRY

•FRIED APPLES

•KNEADED BREAKFAST BISCUITS

PRESERVES AND HONEY

COFFEE OR MILK

•Recipes included

Breakfast basics take on a new look and taste when scrambled eggs are combined with hearty hash-brown potatoes in one satisfying dish. Frozen hash browns make Hash-Brown Scrambled Eggs fast and easy to prepare.

Old-fashioned Fresh Side Pork Fry is a tasty change from ham or sausages. Side pork is uncured bacon, and here it is fried crisp in a cornmeal coating. Fresh side pork may have to be ordered specially. If you can't get it, a good substitute could be fried pork chops, since side pork has a similar taste when fried.

Pork and apples traditionally go well together, so apple rings cooked in butter and sugar and sprinkled with cinnamon are an excellent side dish. Round out the meal with light and flaky hot kneaded biscuits, made from scratch and served with honey or preserves. To avoid too much last-minute preparation, make the biscuits the day before and reheat in foil.

Start brunch with guests' choice of several fruit juices—use common favorites such as orange, grapefruit, apple or tangerine, or select some favorites of your own. Finish with plenty of steaming hot coffee and second helpings of biscuits. Serves 6.

Wine Suggestion: A fresh young wine could be a fine match for this menu: Mirassou's Zinfandel; Prince Noir from Barton & Guestier.

Fried Apples and petite biscuits complete this hearty brunch.

PARTY PLAN FOR SCRAMBLED EGGS AND PORK MENU

1 Day Before: Make Kneaded Breakfast Biscuits; cool and wrap in aluminum foil. Refrigerate.

45 Minutes Before Serving: Make Fresh Side Pork Fry; keep warm in oven.
Heat oven to 350°. Heat Kneaded Breakfast Biscuits in foil in oven until hot, about 10 minutes.
Make Fried Apples.
Make Hash-Brown Scrambled Eggs.

HASH-BROWN SCRAMBLED EGGS

⅓   cup vegetable oil
2   cups frozen hash browns
     (about 8 ounces)

8   eggs
⅓   cup cream
1   teaspoon salt
¼   to ½ teaspoon coarsely
     ground black pepper

1. Heat vegetable oil over high heat in 12-inch skillet. Carefully add frozen potatoes; cover. Cook over high heat, turning several times, until brown and crispy, about 5 minutes.

2. Beat eggs and cream. When potatoes are brown, stir egg mixture, salt and pepper into potatoes. Cook and stir uncovered over medium-high heat until eggs are firm. Salt and pepper to taste. Garnish with watercress if desired.

FRESH SIDE PORK FRY

*1   pound fresh side pork, sliced
¼   cup all-purpose flour
¼   cup cornmeal
½   teaspoon salt
¼   teaspoon pepper

1. Choose lean side slices. Rind need not be trimmed. Coat slices with mixture of flour, cornmeal, salt and pepper.

2. Fry coated slices slowly in 10-inch skillet until some fat cooks out of the meat. Increase heat to medium and fry until crisp.

*TIP: *Fresh side pork is uncured bacon. If fresh side pork is not available, serve bacon or ham cooked in the traditional manner.*

FRIED APPLES

4   cooking apples
½   teaspoon salt

2   tablespoons butter or margarine

¼   cup sugar
½   teaspoon ground cinnamon,
     nutmeg or cardamom

1. Core apples; cut into rings and place in glass bowl or dish. Sprinkle with salt.

2. Melt butter in 12-inch skillet over medium heat. Cook apples in butter, stirring frequently, until apple rings are partially cooked and appear slightly transparent.

3. Sprinkle sugar over apples. Cook and stir 1 to 2 minutes over medium heat until apples are evenly coated with sugar. Remove from heat; cover to keep warm. Sprinkle with cinnamon before serving. Garnish with watercress if desired.

KNEADED BREAKFAST BISCUITS *Makes about thirty-six 1½-inch biscuits or about twenty 2-inch biscuits*

1   cup shortening
*3   cups self-rising flour
⅔   cup milk

Heat oven to 450°

1. Cut shortening into flour until it has the consistency of cornmeal. Make "well" in center and pour in milk. Mix until dough holds together.

2. Round up dough on lightly floured cloth-covered board. Knead lightly 150 times, about 4 minutes. Roll ½ inch thick; cut with 1½- or 2-inch floured cutter. Place close together in ungreased 8- or 9-inch round layer pan.

3. Bake until light brown, 12 to 15 minutes.

*TIPS: *If using all-purpose flour, add 3 teaspoons baking powder and 1½ teaspoons salt.*

To freeze biscuits, cool, then wrap in foil. To reheat, place wrapped biscuits in 450° oven until warm, about 20 minutes.

Light Luncheon

SWISS CHEESE PIE MENU

•SWISS CHEESE PIE
•SWEET AND SOUR LETTUCE
FRENCH BREAD AND BUTTER
FRESH FRUIT
COFFEE

•Recipes included

Flavors of cheese, onion and bacon are blended in creamy Swiss Cheese Pie.

Not a quiche, not a soufflé, the Swiss Cheese Pie has a character all of its own. Whipping cream, Swiss cheese, onion and bacon are blended into a creamy mixture, then baked in a pie crust.

With the pie, serve a lettuce salad tossed with a hot sweet and sour dressing. The delicious dressing is made with leeks or green onions, brown sugar, vinegar and caraway seeds.

A crusty loaf of French bread and lots of butter go well with this luncheon and seasonal fresh fruit completes the meal. Serves 6.

Wine Suggestion: Keep your wine on the lighter side, and white, of course. From Alsace a Sylvaner Hugel or from Portugal a Vinho Verde, Casal Garcia, will do.

PARTY PLAN FOR SWISS CHEESE PIE MENU

3 Hours Before Serving:	Prepare Sweet and Sour Lettuce through step 1 in recipe; refrigerate.
1 Hour 30 Minutes Before Serving:	Make Swiss Cheese Pie. Prepare fresh fruit.
10 Minutes Before Serving:	Complete Sweet and Sour Lettuce.

SWISS CHEESE PIE

Pastry for one-crust pie

2   slices bacon, cut into ¼-inch
    pieces
2   tablespoons finely chopped
    onion

1   cup milk
½   cup whipping cream
3   tablespoons cornstarch
3   tablespoons milk

3   eggs
⅛   teaspoon nutmeg
½   teaspoon salt
    Dash white pepper
1½ cups shredded Swiss cheese

Heat oven to 400°

1. Prepare pastry for one-crust pie. Fit pastry into greased 8-inch pie plate; trim edge. Prick crust with fork.

2. Cook bacon over medium heat until limp. Add onion; cook and stir until onion is tender but not brown. Reserve.

3. Heat 1 cup milk and the cream in saucepan over low heat. Mix cornstarch and 3 tablespoons milk; stir into milk-cream mixture. Cook, stirring constantly, until sauce is smooth and thick. Remove from heat and cool slightly.

4. Beat eggs until very light and fluffy. Brush about 1 tablespoon beaten egg on pastry. Mix nutmeg, salt, pepper, cheese and the cooled cream sauce into eggs. Stir in bacon and onion (with any fat that is in the pan). Mix and turn into pastry-lined pan.

5. Bake on top rack of oven until nicely browned, about 35 minutes.

TIPS: The pie will shrink as it cools. It can be served piping hot, warm or cold.

The pie can be made in advance; cook completely, cool, wrap securely in aluminum foil and freeze. To reheat, place foil-wrapped frozen pie in 350° oven and heat until hot, about 1 hour.

SWEET AND SOUR LETTUCE

1   large head lettuce or
    2 small heads lettuce

1   cup sliced leeks or green onions
¼   cup butter or margarine
⅓   cup packed brown sugar
1   teaspoon caraway seed
1   teaspoon salt
¼   cup vinegar
    Cherry tomatoes

1. Cut lettuce crosswise in half. Place cut sides down on board and shred coarsely across heart. Refrigerate.

2. Cook and stir leeks in butter in saucepan over medium heat 1 minute. Stir in brown sugar, caraway seed, salt and vinegar. Cook, stirring constantly, until bubbly. Pour over lettuce; toss and drain. Garnish with tomatoes.

5

Holiday Favorites

The calendar records holidays throughout the year, yet sometimes it seems that all of them merge as the year comes to an end. The weeks between Thanksgiving Day and New Year's Day invariably overflow with social and family activities. It's a festive season, and it's a time when you'll be entertaining often, in many different ways. Brunches, dinners small and large, buffets and open houses—a menu for each of these is included in this chapter.

Smörgåsbord is the attraction in a Scandinavian-style buffet that's perfect for holiday-week entertaining. At a true Swedish smörgåsbord, it is customary to eat cold dishes first, those at room temperature next, then hot foods and finally dessert. But don't restrain your guests from loading their plates any way they want—that's part of the fun.

Celebrate a holiday morning with the Italian Omelet Menu. Omelets are another of those versatile egg dishes that become whatever you want them to be. Like crêpes and soufflés, omelets can be both main dishes and desserts. This is a main-dish omelet, served with fruit and coffee cake.

Recreate the aura of Merrie Olde England with dinner this Christmas by serving a handsome roast beef. In place of plum pudding there are plum-stuffed dumplings, and a Hazelnut Yule Log makes a fitting Christmas dessert. New Year's Eve is an excellent time to serve the Stuffed Leg of Lamb Menu. Unusually striking food and a flaming dessert are just right for ringing out the old year.

Thanksgiving Day is a time for families and friends. And since Thanksgiving is an annual celebration of thanks for a fruitful harvest, it's the one day when your board should be truly groaning. The Autumn Harvest Dinner offers an appropriate wealth of holiday foods, some traditional, some new and unique.

Duplicate the ancient Roman method of cooking in clay with the Capon Dinner Menu. The clay pot is used almost like a Dutch oven—it cooks meat by a combination of braising and roasting. Most gourmet cookshops have at least one kind available; the cover is usually made to look like a chicken or fish.

An open house can be an almost effortless way to entertain large groups of people. The task of preparing the food can be all but completed ahead of time, and the food can be set out buffet style. These two delightful open house menus are certain to please everyone. The Jambalaya Menu provides lots of appetizers, one hot dish, a salad and Irish Coffee for a winter-warming finish. At our second open house, good friends may celebrate the season by breaking bread together—in seven tasty varieties. They're all attractive to see and delicious to eat, and most of them can be baked in advance.

This Scandinavian-Style Menu includes Pickled Cucumbers, Potatoes Anchovy, Liver Paste and Herring Salad (see menu on page 80).

Christmas Week Buffet

Jul Ham, baked with bread crumbs, can be served hot or cold.

SCANDINAVIAN-STYLE MENU

- •GLÖGG
- •HERRING SALAD WITH SOUR CREAM-MUSTARD SAUCE
- •PICKLED CUCUMBERS
- •TOSSED SALAD
- •CHRISTMAS EVE SALAD
- •LIVER PASTE
  ASSORTED BREADS AND CRACKERS
- •JUL HAM
- •SMÖRGÅSBORD MEATBALLS
- •POTATOES ANCHOVY
- •BROWN BEANS
- •ALMOND-RICE CREAM
  COFFEE

•Recipes included

Pictured on page 79.

A typical smörgåsbord begins with hot spiced Glögg, set aflame just before serving. Our version of Glögg, a popular Swedish drink, combines wine, vodka and brandy, flavored with almonds, fruit and spices.

The lavish assortment of dishes appearing on the table includes a platter of scalloped potatoes with anchovies and two molded salads. Herring Salad with Sour Cream-Mustard Sauce has a base of herring and chicken, and when unmolded is an appetizing red and pink. Rings of chopped egg white, egg yolks and diced beets make an attractive garnish. Christmas Eve Salad is made with tartly flavored gelatin combined with raw apples, cabbage and celery.

In addition, there is a simple Tossed Salad with a mustard dressing, homemade Pickled Cucumbers and a delicious made-from-scratch Liver Paste to spread on bread or crackers. The Liver Paste is baked in a loaf and festively decorated.

Meat dishes include a glazed Jul Ham served hot or cold, and hot beef and pork meatballs served with a cardamom-spiced pot of Swedish Brown Beans (pinto or Mexican pink beans may also be used). The final course is a variation on traditional Scandinavian Christmas Eve porridge—cold Almond-Rice Cream with Raspberry Sauce. One whole almond is hidden in the pudding—the Swedes say that whoever finds it is guaranteed good luck. Serves 12.

Wine Suggestion: I like to give a choice of wines with smörgasbord. Here I suggest these particularly good ones from Hungary: Lake Balaton white, rosé or Cabernet.

PARTY PLAN FOR SCANDINAVIAN-STYLE MENU

5 Days Before:
Make Smörgåsbord Meatballs except do not bake; wrap, label and freeze.
Make Liver Paste; wrap tightly and refrigerate.

4 Days Before:
Make Almond-Rice Cream and Raspberry Sauce; cover and refrigerate separately.
Make Pickled Cucumbers; refrigerate.
Prepare Glögg through step 2 in recipe; cover and refrigerate.

2 Days Before:
Make Dressing for Tossed Salad; refrigerate.
Make Brown Beans; cover and refrigerate.
Prepare Herring Salad through step 1 in recipe. Make sauce. Cover and refrigerate separately.
Prepare Christmas Eve Salad through step 2 in recipe; refrigerate.

1 Day Before:
Bake Jul Ham (if you are serving it cold); refrigerate.
Prepare greens and vegetables for Tossed Salad; cover and refrigerate.

4 Hours Before Serving:
Bake Jul Ham (if serving hot).

1 Hour 45 Minutes Before Serving:
Heat meatballs in oven.
Make Potatoes Anchovy.
Heat Brown Beans.
Unmold Herring and Christmas Eve Salads.
Complete Tossed Salad.
Garnish Liver Paste.

10 Minutes Before Guests Arrive:
Complete Glögg.

GLÖGG

Makes about 3 quarts

10   whole cloves
2   cinnamon sticks
1   piece fresh ginger root, ½-inch square
7   whole cardamom
10   blanched almonds, cut in half lengthwise
1¾   cups raisins
1   cup pitted large prunes
1   orange, cut into fourths
2   cups water
2   bottles (⁴/₅ quart each) port wine
1¾   cups brandy
1¾   cups vodka
⅓   cup sugar

1. Tie cloves, cinnamon sticks, ginger root and cardamom in cheesecloth bag. Place spice bag, almonds, raisins, prunes, orange sections and water in 2-quart saucepan. Heat to boiling; reduce heat and cover. Simmer 45 minutes.

2. Remove orange sections, prunes and spice bag. (Set prunes aside for eating if desired.)*

3. Pour juice mixture into Dutch oven; pour in wine and cover. Heat until mixture begins to bubble. Remove from heat. Pour in brandy and vodka carefully; cover. Heat until mixture begins to bubble. Remove from heat. Let stand 5 minutes. Uncover; ignite carefully. Cover to smother flame. Uncover and stir in sugar.

4. Serve warm. Ladle almond half and a few raisins into each cup before filling with Glögg.

*TIPS: *Glögg can be prepared to this point 3 or 4 days before serving; cover and refrigerate.*

Leftover Glögg can be bottled for further use. Heat but do not boil before serving.

HERRING SALAD WITH SOUR CREAM-MUSTARD SAUCE

1   jar (12 ounces) herring in wine sauce
1   cup finely chopped cooked chicken or veal
1   cup finely chopped pared tart apples
*1   cup finely chopped pickled beets (reserve liquid)
1   cup finely chopped cooked potatoes
⅔   cup finely chopped no-garlic dill pickles
⅓   cup finely chopped candied dill pickle sticks
    Dash pepper

Diced pickled beets
Sieved hard-cooked egg yolks
Diced hard-cooked egg whites
Snipped parsley
Sour Cream-Mustard Sauce (recipe follows)

1. Rinse herring; drain on paper toweling. Chop herring; mix herring and remaining chopped ingredients. Stir in ¼ cup of the reserved beet liquid and the pepper; pack in 1½-quart glass bowl (6¾ inches in diameter). Refrigerate before serving to blend flavors at least 24 hours, no longer than 48 hours.

2. Dip bowl in hot water. Place serving dish on top of bowl; invert to unmold. Garnish with diced pickled beets, hard-cooked egg yolks and whites and snipped parsley. Serve with Sour Cream-Mustard Sauce.

*TIP: *1 jar (16 ounces) pickled beets will provide sufficient beets and beet liquid for both the salad and sauce. Dice remaining beets for garnish.*

SOUR CREAM-MUSTARD SAUCE

2   cups dairy sour cream
⅓   cup prepared mustard
2   tablespoons sugar
⅓   cup reserved beet liquid

Mix all ingredients in glass bowl; cover. Refrigerate.

PICKLED CUCUMBERS

4   medium unpared cucumbers
1   tablespoon salt

1½   cups white wine vinegar
2   tablespoons sugar
2   teaspoons salt
½   teaspoon white pepper
*2   tablespoons coarsely snipped fresh dill or parsley
    Fresh dill or parsley

1. Score cucumbers lengthwise with tines of fork; cut into paper-thin slices. Arrange slices in layers on large plate; sprinkle with 1 tablespoon salt. Cover cucumbers with another plate; weight down with heavy object to press out excess liquid. Let stand at room temperature about 3 hours.

2. Pour off liquid; drain cucumbers on paper toweling. Arrange in bowl. Mix vinegar, sugar, 2 teaspoons salt and the pepper; pour over cucumbers. Sprinkle with 2 tablespoons dill; cover. Refrigerate at least 24 hours, no longer than 4 days. Garnish with fresh dill.

*TIP: *2 teaspoons dill weed may be substituted for fresh dill; mix dill weed into vinegar mixture.*

TOSSED SALAD

    Dressing (recipe follows)
1   small head lettuce, torn into large pieces
½   medium head endive, torn into large pieces
1   cup sliced radishes
1   small onion, thinly sliced, separated into rings

1. Prepare Dressing.

2. Toss torn lettuce, endive, radishes and onion in salad bowl.* Pour dressing over salad; toss. Arrange in lettuce-lined bowl if desired. Garnish with reserved finely chopped egg white.

*TIP: *Tossed Salad can be prepared to this point 24 hours in advance. Store covered in refrigerator.*

| | | **DRESSING** | *Makes about 1 cup* |

2	hard-cooked egg yolks (reserve whites for garnish)
¼	cup vegetable oil
2	teaspoons sugar
¼	cup white vinegar
½	teaspoon salt
¼	teaspoon white pepper
1	teaspoon dry mustard
¼	cup light cream

DRESSING *Makes about 1 cup*

Place all ingredients in blender container; cover. Blend on medium speed, about 10 seconds. (If blender is not available, mash egg yolks and shake with remaining ingredients in tightly covered jar.)* Finely chop reserved egg whites.

TIP: *Dressing can be stored covered in refrigerator no longer than 3 days.*

CHRISTMAS EVE SALAD

2	envelopes unflavored gelatin
½	cup sugar
½	teaspoon salt
2½	cups water
¼	cup lemon juice
2	tablespoons white vinegar
½	cup finely chopped celery
3	cups finely chopped unpared tart red apples
1	cup finely shredded cabbage

Endive
Apple slices
Walnut halves

1. Mix gelatin, sugar and salt in saucepan. Add 1 cup of the water. Cook and stir over low heat until gelatin is dissolved. Remove from heat; stir in remaining 1½ cups water, the lemon juice and vinegar. Refrigerate until slightly thickened but not set.

2. Fold celery, chopped apples and cabbage into gelatin mixture. Pour into 5-cup mold. Refrigerate until firm, at least 5 hours.*

3. Unmold onto plate lined with endive. Garnish with apple slices and walnut halves.

TIP: *Salad can be made 48 hours in advance; unmold just before serving.*

LIVER PASTE

1	pound fresh pork liver, membrane removed
3	eggs
¼	cup milk
¼	cup all-purpose flour
1	teaspoon salt
½	teaspoon white pepper
½	teaspoon ground cloves
¼	cup butter or margarine, softened
2	slices white bread, cubed
1	small onion, chopped
6	anchovy fillets, drained
¼	pound pork fat, ground or chopped
1	cup whipping cream
12	slices bacon

Endive
Pimiento
Assorted breads and crackers

1. Place liver in large saucepan; cover with cold water. Heat to boiling; reduce heat. Simmer uncovered 5 minutes. Drain liver and cool. Cut into cubes, removing any veins or membrane; set aside.

2. Beat eggs, milk, flour, salt, pepper and cloves in large bowl until smooth. Stir in butter, bread, onion, anchovies, pork fat and cubed liver.

3. Place ¼ cup of the cream and ¼ liver mixture in blender container;* cover. Blend until smooth. Repeat 3 times with remaining cream and liver mixture.

4. Heat oven to 325°. Line bottom and sides of loaf pan, 8½ x 4½ x 2½ inches, with slices of bacon, overlapping slightly. (Reserve several slices for top of loaf.) Pour liver mixture into pan and cover with remaining bacon slices. Seal pan tightly with heavy-duty aluminum foil. Place in baking dish; fill dish with 1 to 2 inches boiling water.

5. Bake until knife inserted halfway between center and edge comes out clean, 1¾ to 2 hours. Cool at least 30 minutes before unmolding.** Garnish with endive and pimiento. Serve with assorted breads.

TIPS: *If blender is not available, put through food grinder twice and mix with cream.*

**Liver Paste can be prepared 5 days in advance. Unmold; cover. Refrigerate.*

JUL HAM

1   **fully cooked bone-in ham**
      (12 to 16 pounds)

1   **egg white**
1   **tablespoon dry mustard**
1   **tablespoon sugar**
½   **cup fine dry bread crumbs**

    Heat oven to 325°

1. Place ham fat side up on rack in open shallow roasting pan. Insert meat thermometer so tip is in center of thickest part of meat and does not touch bone or fat. Bake uncovered about 2½ hours. Remove from oven. Pour drippings from pan; cut away skin and loose fat.

2. Beat egg white, mustard and sugar; spread on top and sides of ham. Sprinkle with bread crumbs. Return to oven.

3. Bake until thermometer registers 140°, about 1 hour. If bread crumbs begin to brown too much, cover lightly with tent of aluminum foil. Allow ham to stand 15 minutes before carving.*

*TIPS: *Ham can also be served cold. Refrigerate immediately after baking. Store no longer than 24 hours.*

Traditionally the Jul Ham is decorated with the greeting Glad Jul *or "Merry Christmas." Inscribe greeting with cream cheese that has been thinned with cream and pressed through decorating tube. Garnish with parsley. Ham is especially attractive for the buffet if it is carved but the slices left in place, giving the appearance of a whole ham.*

SMÖRGÅSBORD MEATBALLS

Makes about 7 dozen meatballs

1   **pound ground beef**
½   **pound lean ground pork**
¾   **cup dry bread crumbs**
½   **cup finely chopped onion**
1   **tablespoon snipped parsley**
2   **teaspoons salt**
¼   **teaspoon pepper**
1   **egg**
½   **cup milk**
    About 2 tablespoons butter
      or margarine

    Heat oven to 350°

Mix all ingredients except butter. Shape into 1-inch balls. Melt butter in large skillet; brown meatballs, a few at a time, over medium-high heat 5 to 8 minutes.* Bake uncovered until done, 20 to 25 minutes.

*TIPS: *At this point, meatballs can be placed on tray in freezer 15 minutes. Wrap partially frozen meatballs in aluminum foil; seal, label and freeze. To serve, heat wrapped, frozen meatballs in 325° oven 1¼ to 1½ hours.*

These small meatballs are served without gravy for a smörgåsbord.

POTATOES ANCHOVY

2   **packages (5.5 ounces each)**
      scalloped potatoes
4   **medium onions, thinly sliced**
4   **cans (2 ounces each)**
      anchovy fillets, chopped
5   **cups boiling water**
1⅓ **cups light cream**
2   **tablespoons dry bread**
      crumbs

    Snipped parsley

    Heat oven to 325°

1. Mix all ingredients except bread crumbs and snipped parsley in ungreased 3-quart casserole. Sprinkle bread crumbs on top.

2. Bake uncovered until potatoes are tender, 70 to 75 minutes. Sprinkle with parsley.

Raspberry Sauce is the special topping for Almond-Rice Cream.

BROWN BEANS

*16 ounces (about 2⅓ cups) Swedish brown beans
6 cups cold water
1 tablespoon salt
¼ teaspoon ground cardamom
3 tablespoons butter or margarine
¾ cup dark corn syrup
⅓ cup packed light brown sugar
¾ cup white vinegar
¼ cup cornstarch
¼ cup cold water

1. Rinse beans. Place in Dutch oven; add 6 cups cold water and the salt. Heat to boiling; boil 2 minutes. Remove from heat; cover and let stand 1 hour.

2. Heat beans to boiling over low heat; stir in cardamom. Cover and cook until soft, 4 to 5 hours.** Add water, 1 cup at a time, if beans become dry.

3. Stir in butter, corn syrup, brown sugar and vinegar. Mix cornstarch and ¼ cup cold water; stir into beans. Cook uncovered, stirring frequently, about 30 minutes. Serve hot.

*TIPS: *Pinto beans or Mexican pink beans can be substituted for Swedish brown beans.*

**Beans should be very tender before beginning step 3 as vinegar stops the tenderizing process.*

ALMOND-RICE CREAM   *Makes 1½ quarts*

1 tablespoon butter or margarine
1 cup water
1 cup uncooked long-grain rice
1 quart milk
3 tablespoons sugar
½ teaspoon salt
1 cinnamon stick
1 cup finely chopped almonds
1 cup chilled whipping cream
2 teaspoons vanilla
1 unblanched almond
Raspberry Sauce (recipe follows)

1. Heat butter, water and rice to boiling in Dutch oven; reduce heat. Simmer uncovered until water is absorbed, about 12 minutes.

2. Stir milk, sugar, salt and cinnamon stick into rice mixture. Heat to boiling; reduce heat and cover. Simmer, stirring occasionally, until milk is absorbed, 50 to 60 minutes. Remove cinnamon stick; cool. Stir chopped almonds into cooled rice mixture.

3. Beat cream in chilled bowl until soft peaks form. Add vanilla; beat until stiff. Gently fold whipped cream into cooled rice mixture. Tuck the good luck almond into the pudding; divide among dessert dishes. Refrigerate. (Pudding can be stored covered in refrigerator no longer than 5 days.) To serve, top with Raspberry Sauce. Serve with your favorite cookie if desired.

RASPBERRY SAUCE   *Makes about 1⅓ cups*

*1 package (10 ounces) frozen raspberries, thawed
½ cup sugar

Mix raspberries (with syrup) and sugar in small bowl; let stand 2 hours. Sieve raspberry mixture. (Sauce can be stored covered in refrigerator no longer than 5 days.)

A Perfect Holiday Brunch

Combine artichoke hearts and mushrooms in a filling for plump omelets.

A basic omelet consists of beaten eggs quickly cooked and then folded over. The finished product will have a browned outside surface and a moist middle. Although omelet comes from a Latin word meaning "thin plate," some omelets are medium thin, others puffy and high. This recipe is the former version, folded over an Italian-style filling of artichoke hearts, mushrooms, onion and Parmesan cheese.

Open this holiday brunch with a hot fruit cup. Serve sherried orange and pineapple segments in zigzagged orange cups, topped with a sprinkling of pistachio nuts. A versatile recipe, Holiday Fruit Cup can be made with any fruit; try peaches and frozen strawberries as an alternative.

Thick slices of Canadian bacon glazed with a brown sugar and mustard mixture and studded with cloves go well with the omelet. Then add Sour Cream Coffee Cake, unusually good with its ribbon of nuts, currants and spices. Served warm from the oven, it's a delicious snack as well—serve it with coffee whenever guests drop in. Serves 6.

Wine Suggestion: Only a simple wine fits this: Rosatello Ruffino of Italy.

Begin brunch with fruit cups and Sour Cream Coffee Cake.

PARTY PLAN FOR ITALIAN OMELET MENU

1 Day Before:	Prepare Holiday Fruit Cup through step 1 in recipe; wrap orange shells and segments separately. Refrigerate.
1 Hour 10 Minutes Before Serving:	Make Glazed Canadian Bacon. Make Sour Cream Coffee Cake. Complete Holiday Fruit Cup. Make Omelets with Italian Filling.

HOLIDAY FRUIT CUP

4   **large oranges**

1   **can (13¼ ounces) pineapple tidbits in heavy syrup, undrained**

2   **tablespoons lemon juice**

¼   **cup dry sherry**

2   **tablespoons coarsely chopped pistachio nuts**

1. Cut zigzag lines around middle of each orange, cutting through center each time; separate carefully. Segment oranges with grapefruit knife, reserving juice and orange segments and leaving shells intact. Clean 6 half-shells; reserve for fruit cups.*

2. Cut up orange segments; mix with orange juice, pineapple tidbits and lemon juice. Heat to boiling; reduce heat. Simmer over medium heat, stirring occasionally, until thick and syrupy, about 25 minutes. Stir in sherry.

3. Heat oven to 350°. Place shells in muffin cups. Spoon about ⅓ cup fruit mixture into each reserved shell. Garnish each with 1 teaspoon chopped nuts. Bake 20 minutes.

*TIP: *Recipe can be prepared to this point 24 hours in advance. Wrap shells securely in plastic wrap and cover segments. Refrigerate.*

OMELETS WITH ITALIAN FILLING

1   **package (9 ounces) frozen artichoke hearts, thawed, cut in half**

5   **ounces fresh mushrooms, sliced (about 1½ cups)**

½   **cup finely chopped onion**

2   **tablespoons olive oil**

1   **teaspoon flour**

½   **teaspoon salt**

½   **cup light cream or half-and-half**

2   **tablespoons grated Parmesan cheese**

2   **tablespoons chopped pimiento**

10   **eggs**

½   **teaspoon salt**

2   **tablespoons butter or margarine**

1. Cook and stir artichokes, mushrooms and onion in olive oil until onion is tender. Stir in flour and ½ teaspoon salt; add cream. Cook, stirring constantly, until thickened. Stir in cheese and pimiento. Keep filling warm while preparing omelets.

2. Beat 5 of the eggs and ¼ teaspoon of the salt. Melt 1 tablespoon butter in 10-inch skillet over medium heat. Pour eggs into skillet. As omelet begins to set at bottom and side, gently lift cooked portions with spatula so thin uncooked portions can flow to bottom. Cook until eggs are set and bottom browns.

3. Spoon half of the artichoke mixture onto center of omelet. Fold portion of omelet nearest you just to center with fork. Turn omelet onto warm plate, flipping folded portion of omelet over so far side is on bottom. Keep warm while preparing second omelet. Cut each omelet into 3 sections to serve.

GLAZED CANADIAN BACON

2½- pound piece Canadian-style
     bacon

    Whole cloves
¼ cup packed brown sugar
1 tablespoon water
½ teaspoon dry mustard

    Heat oven to 350°

1. Remove any casing from bacon; place bacon fat side up on rack in shallow roasting pan. Bake 45 minutes; remove from oven.

2. Score bacon in diamond shapes; stud with cloves. Mix brown sugar, water and dry mustard; pour mixture over bacon. Bake until brown, about 15 minutes. (Meat thermometer should register 160°.)

SOUR CREAM COFFEE CAKE

¾ cup packed brown sugar
1 tablespoon flour
1 teaspoon ground cinnamon
½ teaspoon ground nutmeg
¼ teaspoon ground cloves
2 tablespoons butter or
     margarine
½ cup currants
½ cup chopped walnuts

½ cup butter or margarine
1 cup packed brown sugar
2 eggs
2 cups all-purpose flour
1 teaspoon baking powder
1 teaspoon baking soda
½ teaspoon salt
1 cup dairy sour cream

    Heat oven to 350°

1. Mix ¾ cup brown sugar, 1 tablespoon flour, the cinnamon, nutmeg and cloves. Cut in 2 tablespoons butter until crumbly. Stir in currants and walnuts; reserve.

2. Measure ½ cup butter, 1 cup brown sugar and the eggs into large mixer bowl. Beat 2 minutes on medium speed or 300 vigorous strokes by hand. Beat in 2 cups flour, the baking powder, baking soda and salt alternately with sour cream.

3. Spread half of the batter evenly in greased square pan, 9 x 9 x 2 inches. Sprinkle with half of the reserved nut mixture. Repeat with remaining batter and nut mixture.

4. Bake until wooden pick inserted in center comes out clean, 40 to 45 minutes.

A Merry Christmas Dinner

Surround the roast with plum dumplings.

Drizzle sauce over vegetable medley.

Complete the main course with Avocado-Citrus Salad.

CHRISTMAS ROAST MENU

- **ROAST BEEF WITH HORSERADISH SAUCE**
- **PORTLY PLUM DUMPLINGS**
- **VEGETABLE PLATTER**
- **AVOCADO-CITRUS SALAD**
  DINNER ROLLS AND BUTTER
  CURRANT JELLY
  OLIVES AND PICKLES
- **HAZELNUT YULE LOG**
  COFFEE

- Recipes included

A large beef rib roast is an uncomplicated entrée for holiday dinners. Sour cream sauce, snappy with horseradish and dill, is served with the meat. Let the sauce stand in the refrigerator for several hours so that the flavors can blend. Portly Plum Dumplings stuffed with wine-marinated prunes can be prepared a day in advance, ready for final simmering at serving time.

Bring out the hot Vegetable Platter when you bring out the beef. Nuggets of carrots and celery surround a whole, cooked cauliflower in a butter, sesame seed and chive sauce. For a pleasant contrast, a salad made of smooth avocado slices alternating with orange and grapefruit sections is excellent. A homemade tart-sweet dressing goes over it.

For dessert, bring out what many will call the *pièce de résistance*— Hazelnut Yule Log. Chocolate cake baked in a shallow jelly roll pan is spread with apricot preserves and hazelnut filling. Then it is rolled, chocolate-glazed and liberally studded with toasted whole hazelnuts. Use a different kind of preserves if you prefer, and almonds make a fine substitute for hazelnuts. This handsome cake can be made ahead, ready to serve anytime during the holidays. Serves 8.

Wine Suggestion: For this Christmastime menu, may I suggest a sturdy Châteauneuf-du-pape from P. Avril, or a similar wine from California, Petite Sirah by Parducci. Serve a beautiful, sweet wine, with deep fire in it, with this great dessert: a Hungarian Tokay Aszú.

Hazelnut Yule Log is richly filled then decorated with hazelnuts.

PARTY PLAN FOR CHRISTMAS ROAST MENU

2 Days Before:	Prepare Portly Plum Dumplings through step 1 in recipe.
1 Day Before:	Make Horseradish Sauce. Prepare Portly Plum Dumplings through step 3 in recipe; cover and refrigerate. Make Fruit French Dressing; cover and refrigerate. Make Hazelnut Yule Log; refrigerate.
3 Hours 30 Minutes to 4 Hours Before Serving:	Make Roast Beef with Horseradish Sauce. Prepare celery and cauliflower for Vegetable Platter; cover and refrigerate. Prepare avocados, oranges and grapefruit for Avocado-Citrus Salad; cover and refrigerate.
45 Minutes Before Serving:	Complete Vegetable Platter. Complete Portly Plum Dumplings. Complete Avocado-Citrus Salad.

ROAST BEEF WITH HORSERADISH SAUCE

**Horseradish Sauce
(recipe follows)**
1 **beef rib roast (8 pounds)
or 1 beef rib roast
boneless, rolled (5 pounds)**

Heat oven to 325°

1. Prepare Horseradish Sauce. Season meat with salt and pepper if desired. Place fat side up on rack in open shallow roasting pan. Insert meat thermometer so tip is in center of thickest part of meat and does not touch bone or fat. Do not add water.

2. Roast uncovered until thermometer registers 140° (rare) or 160° (medium), 2¾ to 3¼ hours for rolled roast, 3 to 3¾ hours for standing rib roast. Allow roast to stand 15 to 20 minutes before carving. Serve with Horseradish Sauce.

HORSERADISH SAUCE

1   cup dairy sour cream
⅓   cup prepared horseradish, drained
1   teaspoon dried dill weed
1   teaspoon salt
¼   teaspoon pepper

Mix all ingredients; cover. Refrigerate at least 3 hours.

PORTLY PLUM DUMPLINGS   *Makes 16*

⅔   cup port wine or grape juice
16 pitted large prunes

⅓   cup farina (uncooked wheat cereal)
⅔   cup milk
1   egg
1   teaspoon salt
⅔   cup all-purpose flour

3   tablespoons butter or margarine, melted
    Snipped parsley

1. Pour wine over prunes; cover and let stand 24 hours.

2. Cook farina and milk over medium heat, stirring constantly, until farina is thickened and all moisture absorbed, about 5 minutes. Cool to room temperature. Stir in egg and salt; mix until smooth. Stir in ⅓ cup flour; turn onto heavily floured board. Knead in remaining ⅓ cup flour.

3. Divide dough into 4 equal parts. Roll each part ⅛ inch thick. Cut into 4 circles with 3¼-inch cutter. Place 1 prune in center of each circle; gather dough around fruit. Pinch dough together; half twist top and snip off excess dough. Place in buttered baking dish, 10 x 6 x 1¾ inches; cover. Refrigerate no longer than 24 hours.

4. Drop dumplings into simmering water; cover. Cook, stirring occasionally, until dough puffs, about 20 minutes. Remove with slotted spoon to serving dish. Drizzle with melted butter; sprinkle with parsley.

VEGETABLE PLATTER

1   bunch green celery

1   medium head cauliflower
*3 cups beef bouillon
¾   teaspoon salt

2   packages (10 ounces each) frozen carrot nuggets in butter sauce

2   tablespoons toasted sesame seed
2   tablespoons snipped chives
2   tablespoons lemon juice

1. Wash celery; trim off root end. Do not separate stalks. Remove coarse outer strings and leaves. Cut celery bunch crosswise once so bottom section is 5 inches long (refrigerate top section for later use). Cut 5-inch portion crosswise into 4 sections, each 1¼ inches thick; tie each section with string. Set aside.

2. Remove outer leaves and stalk from cauliflower; cut off any discoloration and wash thoroughly. Heat beef bouillon and salt to boiling in 3-quart saucepan; add cauliflower. Heat to boiling; cover and reduce heat. Simmer 10 minutes. Put celery bundles under cauliflower; cover. Simmer until cauliflower is tender, 15 to 20 minutes.

3. While cauliflower and celery cook, prepare carrots according to package directions. Drain carrots, reserving butter sauce; keep carrots warm.

4. Heat butter sauce in small skillet. Add sesame seed, chives and lemon juice; cook and stir until hot, about 5 minutes. Place cauliflower in center of serving platter; remove string from celery bundles. Arrange celery and carrots attractively around cauliflower. Drizzle sauce over top.

*TIP: *3 cups boiling water and 1 tablespoon instant beef bouillon can be substituted for bouillon.*

AVOCADO-CITRUS SALAD

Fruit French Dressing
   (recipe follows)
2 ripe avocados
   Lemon juice
   Salt

2 oranges
2 grapefruit
   Bibb lettuce

½ cup vegetable oil
2 tablespoons vinegar
2 tablespoons lemon juice
½ teaspoon salt
¼ teaspoon dry mustard
¼ teaspoon paprika
3 tablespoons powdered sugar

1. Make Fruit French Dressing. Cut avocados in half crosswise; remove pits. Peel each half; cut into ¼-inch slices. Sprinkle slices with lemon juice and salt.

2. Pare and section oranges and grapefruit. Arrange avocado slices and fruit sections on bibb lettuce on salad plates. Serve with Fruit French Dressing.

FRUIT FRENCH DRESSING   *Makes ¾ cup*
Shake all ingredients well in tightly covered jar. Refrigerate at least 1 hour. Shake again just before serving.

HAZELNUT YULE LOG

¾ cup all-purpose flour
¼ cup cocoa
1 teaspoon baking powder
¼ teaspoon salt
3 eggs
1 cup granulated sugar
⅓ cup water
1 teaspoon vanilla

   Powdered sugar

½ cup apricot preserves
1 tablespoon rum or apricot
   nectar
¼ cup butter or margarine,
   softened
¼ teaspoon salt
3 cups powdered sugar
3 tablespoons light cream
¾ teaspoon vanilla
⅓ cup ground hazelnuts or
   almonds

1 square (1 ounce)
   unsweetened chocolate
1½ tablespoons butter or
   margarine
½ cup powdered sugar
½ teaspoon vanilla
4 teaspoons hot water
   About 2 dozen blanched
   hazelnuts or almonds, toasted

   Heat oven to 375°

1. Line jelly roll pan, 15½ x 10½ x 1 inch, with aluminum foil; grease. Stir together flour, cocoa, baking powder and ¼ teaspoon salt; set aside. Beat eggs in small mixer bowl until very thick and lemon colored, about 5 minutes. Pour eggs into large mixer bowl; gradually beat in granulated sugar. Blend in ⅓ cup water and 1 teaspoon vanilla on low speed. Add flour mixture gradually, beating just until batter is smooth. Pour into pan, spreading batter to corners.

2. Bake until wooden pick inserted in center comes out clean, 13 to 14 minutes. Loosen cake from edges of pan; invert onto towel sprinkled with powdered sugar. Remove foil carefully; trim off stiff edges with knife if necessary. While hot, roll cake and towel from narrow end. Cool on wire rack.

3. Unroll cake; remove towel. Mix preserves and rum; spread on cake. Beat ¼ cup butter, ¼ teaspoon salt, 3 cups powdered sugar, the cream and ¾ teaspoon vanilla in small mixer bowl until fluffy; stir in ground hazelnuts. Spread over apricot preserves mixture. Carefully roll cake; place on wire rack over waxed paper.

4. Melt unsweetened chocolate and 1½ tablespoons butter over low heat. Remove from heat; stir in ½ cup powdered sugar and ½ teaspoon vanilla. Mix in 4 teaspoons water, 1 teaspoon at a time, until glaze is proper consistency. Spread over cake. Decorate with toasted hazelnuts. Refrigerate no longer than 24 hours.

New Year's Eve Celebration

Enjoy the flavor blend of pork and lamb in this superb main course.

STUFFED LEG OF LAMB MENU

- OYSTER BISQUE

- STUFFED LEG OF LAMB
  BUTTERED RICE
- GREEN BEANS WITH CASHEWS
  TOSSED SALAD
  ROLLS AND BUTTER

- HOLIDAY JUBILEE
  COFFEE

- Recipes included

Bisque, a rich cream soup, starts off this impressive holiday offering. For this recipe, use fresh oysters and mushrooms, though canned substitutes are perfectly acceptable. If you prefer, the sherry can be omitted.

The lamb entrée looks and tastes truly sumptuous. A boned leg of lamb (your butcher will do the boning) is seasoned with herbs and then stuffed with pork tenderloin. The pork fits snugly into the lamb, and the meat flavors blend during roasting. Green beans combined with butter and cashews are an easy-to-make accompaniment, though asparagus, broccoli or any other green vegetable could provide a good color contrast, too. Add your favorite tossed salad and buttered rice.

Holiday Jubilee, our treatment of cherries jubilee, is a spectacular finale. Dark sweet cherries marinated in rum or brandy are set aflame and served over vanilla ice cream. The cherries may be prepared far in advance for this dessert. A little last-minute heating and stirring in a chafing dish is all that's left to do before flambéing. Also included is an easy same-day recipe for the cherries in case time is at a premium. Serves 6.

Wine Suggestion: The elegance and simplicity of Cabernet-type wines is a fine choice. From Bordeaux: Mouton Cadet Rouge. From California: Cabernet from Paul Masson.

A spectacular finale—flaming cherries.

The meal begins with sherried Oyster Bisque and salad.

PARTY PLAN FOR STUFFED LEG OF LAMB MENU

3 Weeks Before:
Make Celebration Cherries
(or make Quick Celebration Cherries day of party).

1 Day Before:
Prepare Holiday Oyster Bisque through step 1 in recipe; refrigerate.

4 to 4 Hours 30 Minutes Before Serving:
Make Stuffed Leg of Lamb.
Make tossed salad; cover and refrigerate.

30 Minutes Before Serving:
Complete Oyster Bisque.
Make rice.
Make Green Beans with Cashews.

15 Minutes Before Dessert:
Make Holiday Jubilee.

OYSTER BISQUE

½   **pound fresh mushrooms, sliced**
¼   **cup butter or margarine**
1   **cup water**
3   **egg yolks**
2   **teaspoons instant chicken bouillon**
1   **cup half-and-half or light cream**
¼   **teaspoon salt**
1   **pint fresh oysters, undrained**
2   **to 4 tablespoons dry sherry**
6   **pats butter**
    Oyster crackers

1. Cook and stir mushrooms in ¼ cup butter until tender. Pour mushrooms (with liquid) and water into blender container; cover. Blend on medium speed until mushrooms are coarsely chopped; blend in egg yolks.

2. Return mixture to saucepan. Stir in chicken bouillon, half-and-half and salt. Heat, stirring constantly, until thickened; remove from heat.

3. Cook oysters in another saucepan over low heat just until edges curl. Stir oysters into mushroom mixture. Stir in sherry; heat just until hot. Ladle into bowls; float butter pat in each. Serve with oyster crackers.

STUFFED LEG OF LAMB

1   **tablespoon dry mustard**
1   **tablespoon lemon juice**
2   **teaspoons salt**
½   **teaspoon dried thyme leaves, crushed**
½   **teaspoon dried rosemary leaves, crushed**
½   **teaspoon dried marjoram leaves, crushed**
¼   **teaspoon pepper**
1   **clove garlic, crushed**
1   **lamb leg roast, boneless (about 8 pounds), not tied**
1   **pork tenderloin, whole (about 1 pound)**

¼   **cup water**
2   **tablespoons flour**

    Heat oven to 325°

1. Mix mustard, lemon juice, salt, thyme, rosemary, marjoram, pepper and garlic. Brush mixture inside lamb. Place tenderloin inside lamb. Wrap lamb around tenderloin; tie securely. Insert meat thermometer so tip is in center of pork tenderloin. Place meat on rack in open shallow roasting pan.

2. Roast uncovered until thermometer registers 170°, 3½ to 4 hours. Remove roast from oven; let stand while preparing gravy.

3. Skim off fat. Add enough water to meat juice to measure 1¾ cups. Shake ¼ cup water and the flour until smooth; stir into drippings gradually. Heat to boiling, stirring constantly. Boil and stir 1 minute.

TIP: Refrigerate leftovers as soon as possible. This roast is very good cold.

GREEN BEANS WITH CASHEWS

2   **packages (9 ounces each) frozen cut green beans**
1   **tablespoon butter or margarine, softened**
¼   **cup cashews**

Cook green beans according to package directions. Toss beans with butter and cashews.

HOLIDAY JUBILEE

1   cup syrup from Celebration
     Cherries (recipe follows)
2   teaspoons cornstarch
1   tablespoon water
1½ cups Celebration Cherries

¼   cup light rum or brandy
     Vanilla ice cream

2   packages (20 ounces each)
     frozen unsweetened
     loose-pack pitted dark
     sweet cherries
2   cups sugar
1   bottle (⁴/₅ quart) light
     rum or brandy

1   can (17 ounces) pitted
     dark sweet cherries in extra
     heavy syrup
½   cup light rum

1. Heat syrup in chafing dish or saucepan just to simmering. Mix cornstarch and water; stir gradually into syrup. Cook and stir over medium heat until thickened; reduce heat. Simmer 2 minutes. Stir cherries into syrup.

2. Heat rum in small saucepan. Ignite and pour over cherries. Serve hot over ice cream.

CELEBRATION CHERRIES   *Makes 2¼ cups syrup, 2½ cups cherries*
Place cherries in large glass jar. Pour sugar over cherries; add rum and cover. Refrigerate, shaking occasionally until sugar dissolves, at least 3 weeks. Leftover Celebration Cherries can be served as an after-dinner liqueur. Serve picks with the cherries. Good served cold over ice cream.

TIP: For a quicker version of Celebration Cherries follow recipe below.

QUICK CELEBRATION CHERRIES
Drain cherries, reserving ½ cup syrup. Mix reserved syrup and rum; stir in cherries and cover. Refrigerate 3 hours.

A New Year's Day Buffet

Miniature quiches and sauerkraut balls are ideal fare for New Year's Day.

JAMBALAYA MENU

- •BIG-RED COCKTAILS
- •QUARTERBACK QUICHES
- •BACKFIELD BITES
- •REFEREE STICKS

- •JAMBALAYA
  WALDORF SALAD
  FRENCH BREAD

  IRISH COFFEE

•Recipes included

The football season is an entrenched part of the holiday season, so this menu is aimed at all armchair quarterbacks. But don't ignore it if you're not a football fan—it's an imaginative array of foods for any holiday open house.

Mugs of Big-Red Cocktails, a tangy mix of tomato juice and beer with green onions for stirrers, make bracing icebreakers. Pass trays loaded with three tasty appetizers: Quarterback Quiches, individual tartlets baked with a bacon, Swiss cheese and onion filling; pungent Backfield Bites, small balls of sauerkraut, potato, bacon and parsley, fried crisp and hot; and curry-flavored deviled ham Referee Sticks with a crunchy consistency.

Then serve a steaming pot of Jambalaya, a likable wintertime dish that's different for the holidays. Originally a Creole specialty, Jambalaya gets its name in part from the French word for ham, *jambon*. A popular Louisiana food, it incorporates chicken, sausage, ham and rice in a spicy tomato sauce. Provide a pleasantly cool contrast with Waldorf salad. Finally, set out hot coffee, Irish whiskey, sugar and whipped cream and let your guests make their own Irish coffee. Serves 12.

Wine Suggestion: Beer, only, all the way.

Delicious Jambalaya contains chicken, sausage, ham, tomatoes and spices.

PARTY PLAN FOR JAMBALAYA MENU

1 Day Before:	Prepare Quarterback Quiches through step 2 in recipe; cover pastry and filling separately. Refrigerate. Make Backfield Bites; cover and refrigerate. Make Referee Sticks; store in airtight container. Prepare Jambalaya through step 2 in recipe; cover chicken and tomato mixtures separately. Refrigerate.
That Afternoon:	Make Waldorf salad; cover and refrigerate.
45 Minutes Before Guests Arrive:	Heat oven to 425°; complete Quarterback Quiches. Return oven temperature to 425°; heat Backfield Bites until hot, about 10 minutes.
As Guests Arrive:	Make Big-Red Cocktails.
45 Minutes Before Serving:	Complete Jambalaya.

BIG-RED COCKTAILS

Makes 3 quarts

1 quart tomato juice, chilled
4 cans (16 ounces each) beer,
 chilled
12 green onions
 Red pepper sauce
 Salt
 Pepper

Pour ⅓ cup tomato juice into each of 12 chilled glasses. Divide each can of beer among 3 glasses; mix beer and tomato juice. Serve cocktails with green onion stirrers. Pass red pepper sauce, salt and pepper.

QUARTERBACK QUICHES

Makes about 30 appetizers

Pastry for two-crust pie

12 slices bacon, crisply
 fried, crumbled
1 cup shredded natural
 Swiss cheese (about 4 ounces)
⅓ cup finely chopped green
 onions
2 tablespoons snipped parsley
4 eggs
2 cups whipping cream
¾ teaspoon salt
¼ teaspoon sugar
¼ teaspoon red pepper
 sauce

 Paprika

1. Prepare pastry. Divide pastry in half. Roll each half into 14-inch circle; cut into smaller circles with 3-inch cutter. Fit small circles into 2½-inch tartlet pans. Press pastry to fit into pans.

2. Heat oven to 425°. Sprinkle bacon, cheese, onions and parsley in pastry-lined pans. Beat eggs slightly; beat in cream, salt, sugar and red pepper sauce.*

3. Pour egg mixture carefully over bacon-cheese mixture in pastry-lined pans; sprinkle with paprika. (Do not allow egg-cream mixture to fill beyond pastry.)

4. Bake 5 minutes. Reduce oven temperature to 300°. Bake until knife inserted toward center comes out clean, about 20 minutes. Remove from pans. Serve warm.

*TIP: *Recipe can be prepared to this point in advance; tightly cover and refrigerate pastry and filling separately no longer than 48 hours.*

BACKFIELD BITES

Makes about 60 appetizers

8 slices bacon
½ cup finely chopped onion
1 clove garlic, finely
 chopped
1 can (16 ounces) sauerkraut,
 drained
½ cup mashed potatoes
1 tablespoon snipped parsley

1½ cups finely crushed corn
 flake cereal
2 teaspoons caraway seed
2 eggs, beaten
 Oil

1. Fry bacon in large skillet until crisp; drain and crumble. Pour off all but 2 tablespoons fat. Cook and stir onion and garlic in fat until onion is tender. Remove from heat; stir in bacon, sauerkraut, mashed potatoes and parsley.

2. Drop by rounded teaspoonfuls onto waxed paper-lined baking sheet; gently form ball shapes with spoon. Cover with waxed paper or plastic wrap. Refrigerate until firm.*

3. Mix cereal and caraway seed. Dip sauerkraut balls in eggs; roll in cereal mixture. Heat oil (3 to 4 inches) to 375° in deep fat fryer or kettle. Fry sauerkraut balls until golden brown, about ½ minute. Drain on paper toweling;** serve hot.

*TIPS: *Appetizers can be refrigerated no longer than 48 hours before frying.*

**Appetizers can be fried 24 hours in advance. Cover and refrigerate. Reheat uncovered in 425° oven about 10 minutes.

Serve Jambalaya and Waldorf salad with French bread and Irish coffee.

REFEREE STICKS

Makes about 6 dozen appetizers

1 can (4½ ounces) deviled
  ham
1 teaspoon instant minced
  onion
1 package (11 ounces) pie
  crust mix
1 teaspoon curry powder
½ cup dairy sour cream

1. Mix deviled ham and onion; set aside.

2. Mix pie crust mix (dry) and curry powder; stir in sour cream. Divide pastry in half; shape each half into ball. Roll each on lightly floured cloth-covered board into rectangle, 18 x 12 inches. Spread ¼ cup deviled ham mixture lengthwise on half of each rectangle; fold top half over ham mixture, matching edges. Cover. Refrigerate 15 minutes.

3. Heat oven to 425°. Cut pastry crosswise into ½-inch strips. Twist to form 5-inch sticks.

4. Bake 8 minutes. Immediately remove from baking sheet. Cool on wire rack.

JAMBALAYA

2 broiler-fryer chickens
  (2½ to 3 pounds each),
  cut up
2 tablespoons salt
½ teaspoon pepper
1 pound sausage links
2 cups diced smoked ham
2 cans (28 or 29 ounces each)
  tomatoes
1 can (12 ounces) tomato paste
3 tablespoons instant minced
  onion
3 tablespoons green pepper
  flakes
2 bay leaves
½ teaspoon chili powder
¼ teaspoon instant minced
  garlic
¼ teaspoon ground thyme
¼ to ½ teaspoon red pepper
  sauce
2 cups uncooked long-grain
  rice
  Snipped parsley

1. Place chickens in Dutch oven; add water to cover. Season with salt and pepper. Heat to boiling; reduce heat and cover. Simmer 45 minutes.

2. Remove chicken from broth; reserve. Strain broth; reserve 4 cups.* Brown sausages and ham in Dutch oven; remove sausages and ham. Spoon off fat; reserve ¼ cup. Measure into each of 2 Dutch ovens or large saucepans, 2 tablespoons of the reserved fat, half the sausage links, half the ham, 2 cups reserved broth, 1 can tomatoes, half the tomato paste, 1½ tablespoons instant minced onion, 1½ tablespoons green pepper flakes, 1 bay leaf, ¼ teaspoon chili powder, ⅛ teaspoon instant minced garlic, ⅛ teaspoon thyme and ⅛ to ¼ teaspoon red pepper sauce.**

3. Heat to boiling; stir 1 cup rice into each Dutch oven. Reduce heat and cover. Simmer 25 minutes. Stir in reserved chicken. Heat until hot. Serve in large bowls; sprinkle with parsley.

*TIPS: *Remaining broth can be frozen for use in other dishes.*

***Recipe can be prepared in advance to this point; cover chicken and tomato mixtures separately. Refrigerate no longer than 24 hours.*

Harvest Dinner

Spicy Applesauce Mold.

Pumpkin Squares and Mincemeat Pie.

Combine lima beans, green pepper strips and tomatoes for an interesting flavor.

ROAST DUCK MENU

- ROAST DUCK AND DUMPLINGS
- FRIED SWEET POTATOES
- RUTABAGAS WITH BROWN BUTTER
- PEPPER-BEAN CASSEROLE
- SPICY APPLESAUCE MOLD
- CORN RELISH
- BUTTERMILK BUNS
- GRAPE JELLY
- MINCEMEAT PIE
- PUMPKIN SQUARES

• Recipes included

Carve yourself a new Thanksgiving tradition with tender roast ducklings instead of turkey. Sage, for centuries a favorite holiday seasoning, appears unexpectedly in dumplings cooked in the roasting pan.

Sweet potatoes fried in brown sugar and butter, and rutabagas with a butter sauce, provide only two of the wealth of vegetable options. Rutabagas are quite similar to turnips.

The green pepper and lima bean casserole in this menu would be an asset to any meal. Cinnamon-candy-flavored applesauce mold, home-made Corn Relish, Grape Jelly and Buttermilk Buns can all be made days in advance.

Dessert on Thanksgiving Day ought to be lavish, so offer not one but two choices: make an old-fashioned Mincemeat Pie using packaged mincemeat plus freshly chopped apples and ground beef. Along with it, serve Pumpkin Squares that are fluffy with beaten egg whites and have an easy graham cracker crust. Serves 8.

Wine Suggestion: There are taste combinations which are unforgettable for the rest of our lifetimes. One of them is the combination of Roast Duck and Chambertin from Burgundy.

Ducklings, roasted to perfection, are served with dumplings and spiced crab apples.

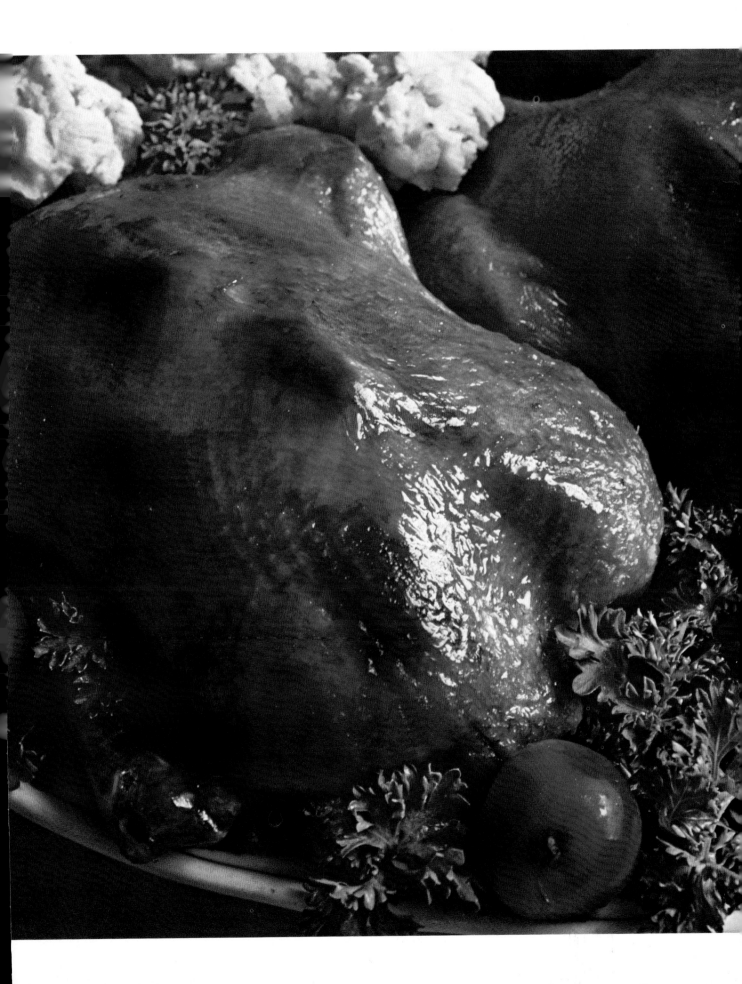

PARTY PLAN FOR ROAST DUCK MENU

1 Week Before:	Make Corn Relish and Grape Jelly; store in dark, dry place. Make Buttermilk Buns; cool, wrap in aluminum foil. Freeze.
1 Day Before:	Prepare Pepper-Bean Casserole through step 3 in recipe; cover and refrigerate. Prepare Spicy Applesauce Mold through step 1 in recipe; refrigerate. Prepare Pumpkin Squares through step 4 in recipe; cover and refrigerate. Make Mincemeat Pie; cool, cover loosely with aluminum foil and refrigerate. Thaw ducklings if frozen.
3 Hours Before Serving:	Prepare ducklings through step 3 in recipe. Prepare relishes and garnishes for menu; wrap separately and refrigerate.
50 Minutes Before Serving:	Make Fried Sweet Potatoes. Make Rutabagas with Brown Butter.
40 Minutes Before Serving:	Heat oven to 325°. Make dumplings. Bake Pepper-Bean Casserole and heat Buttermilk Buns. Unmold Spicy Applesauce Mold and garnish.
30 Minutes Before Dessert:	Place pie in oven to reheat if desired. Complete Pumpkin Squares.

ROAST DUCK AND DUMPLINGS

4   **ducklings (5 pounds each)**
    Salt and pepper

    Water
1   **tablespoon chicken-flavored instant bouillon**

1½ **cups all-purpose flour**
2   **teaspoons baking powder**
¾   **teaspoon ground sage**
¾   **teaspoon salt**
    Dash pepper
3   **tablespoons shortening**
¾   **cup milk**
¾   **cup chopped onion**

    Parsley
    Spiced crab apples

    Heat oven to 325°

1. Season insides of ducklings generously with salt and pepper. Place ducklings on rack in deep roasting pan, about 16½ x 11½ x 4 inches.*

2. Roast uncovered until done, about 2½ hours. (Ducklings are done when drumstick meat feels very soft.)

3. Remove ducklings from roasting pan and place on serving platter; cover with aluminum foil to retain heat while preparing dumplings. Place roasting pan on two burners on range. Spoon off excess fat; add water just to the bottom of rack. Stir in chicken bouillon; heat to boiling.

4. Measure flour, baking powder, sage, salt and pepper into bowl. Cut in shortening until mixture looks like cornmeal. Stir in milk and onion. Drop dough by tablespoonfuls onto rack. Cook uncovered 10 minutes. Cover; cook 10 minutes longer or until dumplings are fluffy.

5. Arrange dumplings on platter with ducklings. Garnish with parsley and crab apples.

TIP: *Do not use a lightweight pan for roasting ducklings.*

FRIED SWEET POTATOES

4	pounds sweet potatoes (10 to 12 medium)
½	cup butter or margarine
¼	cup packed brown sugar

1. Place potatoes in enough salted water (½ teaspoon salt to 1 cup water) to cover. Heat to boiling. Cook until tender, about 30 minutes; drain. Slip off skins; cut potatoes into ½-inch slices and set aside.

2. Melt butter in heavy 10-inch skillet. Stir in 2 tablespoons of the brown sugar. Cook over low heat, stirring constantly, 1 minute; add sweet potato slices. Sprinkle sweet potato slices with remaining 2 tablespoons brown sugar.

3. Cook over low heat, turning occasionally, until hot, about 10 minutes.

RUTABAGAS WITH BROWN BUTTER

*2	rutabagas (2 pounds each)
2	tablespoons sugar
	Brown Butter (recipe follows) Freshly ground black pepper

1. Wash rutabagas and pare thinly. Cut into ¼-inch cubes or pieces. Heat 1 inch salted water (½ teaspoon salt to 1 cup water) to boiling. Add rutabagas and sugar; cover. Heat to boiling.

2. Cook until tender, about 25 minutes; drain. Pour Brown Butter over rutabagas. Sprinkle with pepper.

*TIP: *Kohlrabi, parsnips or turnips can be substituted for rutabagas. Cooking times might vary slightly.*

BROWN BUTTER

½	cup butter
1	tablespoon plus 1 teaspoon cider vinegar

Cook butter in heavy small skillet over low heat until brown. Stir in vinegar.

PEPPER-BEAN CASSEROLE

1½	cups water
1	teaspoon salt
3	packages (10 ounces each) frozen fordhook lima beans
3	medium green peppers, cut into ¼-inch julienne strips
¼	pound bacon, cut into ½-inch pieces
1	tablespoon packed brown sugar
1	teaspoon dry mustard
1	tablespoon molasses
1	can (16 ounces) stewed tomatoes

1. Heat water and salt to boiling. Add lima beans and green pepper strips. Heat to boiling; reduce heat. Cover and simmer until tender, about 8 minutes. Drain vegetables and set aside.

2. Cook bacon pieces in medium skillet until limp but not brown. Stir in brown sugar, mustard, molasses and stewed tomatoes. Cook over low heat 5 minutes.

3. Heat oven to 325°. Mix tomato and vegetable mixtures. Pour into buttered 2-quart casserole; cover.* Bake until hot, 35 to 45 minutes.

*TIP: *Casserole can be prepared to this point 24 hours in advance. Store covered in refrigerator.*

SPICY APPLESAUCE MOLD

½	cup red cinnamon candies
1	cup water
1	package (6 ounces) raspberry-flavored gelatin
2	cans or jars (15 ounces each) applesauce
2	tablespoons vinegar
	Endive Orange slices, cut in half

1. Cook candies in 1 cup water, stirring frequently, until candies melt. Heat to boiling; pour over gelatin in large bowl, stirring until gelatin is dissolved. Stir in applesauce and vinegar. Pour into 6-cup mold. Refrigerate until firm.

2. Unmold onto serving plate; garnish with endive and orange slices. Top with dollop of mayonnaise or salad dressing if desired.

CORN RELISH

*8 cups fresh whole kernel corn (about 18 ears)
3 cups chopped onions
2 medium green peppers, chopped (about 1 cup)
1 medium sweet red pepper, chopped (about ½ cup)
1 cup unpared cucumber, chopped
1 cup packed light brown sugar
2 tablespoons salt
1 tablespoon dry mustard
1 teaspoon ground turmeric
2 teaspoons celery seed
¼ cup all-purpose flour
3 cups cider vinegar
½ cup light corn syrup

1. Prepare vegetables; set aside.

2. Mix sugar, salt, mustard, turmeric, celery seed and flour in Dutch oven. Stir in vinegar and corn syrup. Heat to boiling, stirring constantly. Add vegetables; reduce heat. Simmer 30 minutes, stirring frequently.

3. Check jars for nicks, cracks or sharp edges on sealing surfaces. Wash jars in hot soapy water. Rinse. Cover with hot water until ready to use. Prepare lids and bands according to manufacturer's directions. Fill water-bath canner half full with hot water about 10 minutes before ready to use; heat. (Water should be hot but not boiling when jars are placed in canner.)

4. Pour boiling hot relish into hot jars, leaving 1-inch headspace. Wipe top and screw-threads of jar with damp cloth; seal immediately according to manufacturer's directions. Place each jar on rack in water bath as it is sealed, allowing enough space for water to circulate. (Jars should not touch each other or fall against side of canner during processing.)

5. Add boiling water to cover all jars to depth of 1 to 2 inches. (Do not pour boiling water directly on jars.) Cover canner. Heat water to boiling; reduce heat to hold water at steady but gentle boil. Start counting process time; process pints 20 minutes. Remove jars; place upright, a few inches apart, on several thicknesses of cloth and out of draft to cool. Test for seal when cool. (Metal caps or lids will be depressed in the centers; lids with wire clamps and rubber seals will not leak when inverted.) If the seal is incomplete, reheat the produce to boiling and repack in sterilized jars with sterilized lids or store in refrigerator for immediate use. Store sealed jars in cool, dark, dry area.

*TIP: *2 packages (20 ounces each) frozen whole kernel corn or 4 cans (16 ounces each) whole kernel corn can be substituted for the fresh.*

BUTTERMILK BUNS

4½ cups all-purpose flour
2 packages active dry yeast
¾ cup warm water (105° to 115°)
2 teaspoons baking powder
1¼ teaspoons salt
¼ cup sugar
½ cup butter or margarine
1¼ cups buttermilk

1. Heat oven to 350°; turn off and let cool for 10 minutes. Place flour in warm oven for 15 minutes. Dissolve yeast in warm water; set aside.

2. Place heated flour, baking powder, salt and sugar in large bowl. Cut in butter until mixture looks like cornmeal. Make "well" in center and pour in buttermilk and dissolved yeast. Stir, then knead to blend well. Add more flour if necessary until dough does not adhere to side of bowl (dough should be soft and slightly sticky). Knead gently in bowl for about 2 minutes; cover. Let rise in warm place until double, about 1 hour. (Dough is ready if impression remains when touched with finger.)

3. Punch down dough; divide into 24 equal pieces. Shape each piece into smooth ball. Place about 3 inches apart on lightly greased baking sheet; cover. Let rise until double, about 45 minutes.

4. Heat oven to 375°. Bake until light brown, 15 to 20 minutes.

TIP: To freeze buns, cool, then wrap in aluminum foil. To serve, heat wrapped buns in 325° oven until warm, about 30 minutes.

GRAPE JELLY

6½ cups sugar
2 cups water
⅓ cup lemon juice
1 bottle (6 ounces) liquid
    pectin
2 cans (6 ounces each) frozen
    grape juice concentrate,
    thawed

1. Heat sugar and water in Dutch oven until sugar is dissolved. Heat to boiling, stirring constantly. Add lemon juice. Boil and stir 1 minute; remove from heat and immediately stir in pectin and grape juice concentrate.

2. Pour jelly into hot sterilized glasses, leaving ½-inch headspace. Cover hot jelly with ⅛-inch layer melted paraffin.* Cover glasses with metal or paper lids when paraffin hardens. Store in dark dry place.

*TIP: *To ensure a good seal, paraffin must touch side of glass and be even. Prick any bubbles that appear on paraffin as they may allow spoilage.*

MINCEMEAT PIE

½ pound lean ground beef
2 packages (9 ounces each)
    condensed mincemeat
1 cup chopped pared apple
¼ cup sugar
2½ cups water

    Pastry for 9-inch two-crust
    pie

1. Brown ground beef in small skillet; drain. Break mincemeat into small pieces. Mix ground beef, mincemeat, apple and sugar; add water. Heat to boiling. Boil and stir 3 minutes; cool.

2. Heat oven to 425°. Prepare pastry. Pour mincemeat mixture into pastry-lined 9-inch pie pan. Cover with top crust which has slits cut in it; seal and flute. Cover edge with 2- to 3-inch strip aluminum foil to prevent excessive browning.

3. Bake until pie is bubbly and crust is brown, 35 to 45 minutes. Remove foil last 15 minutes of baking. Best served warm.

TIP: Mincemeat pie can be made 24 hours in advance. Cool pie slightly; cover with foil. Refrigerate. To serve pie, heat oven to 350°. Heat pie with foil covering about 30 minutes.

PUMPKIN SQUARES

24 single graham crackers,
    crushed (about 1¾ cups)
⅓ cup sugar
½ cup butter or margarine,
    melted

2 eggs
¾ cup sugar
1 package (8 ounces) cream
    cheese, softened

1 can (16 ounces) pumpkin
    (about 2 cups)
3 egg yolks
½ cup sugar
½ cup milk
½ teaspoon salt
2 teaspoons ground cinnamon
1 envelope unflavored gelatin
¼ cup cold water

3 egg whites
¼ cup sugar

1 cup chilled whipping cream
1 tablespoon sugar
1 teaspoon vanilla

1. Mix graham cracker crumbs and ⅓ cup sugar. Stir in melted butter; pat in buttered baking dish, 13½ x 9 x 2 inches.

2. Heat oven to 350°. Beat 2 eggs, ¾ cup sugar and the cream cheese until light and fluffy. Pour over graham cracker crust. Bake 20 minutes.

3. Beat pumpkin, egg yolks, ½ cup sugar, the milk, salt and cinnamon in top of double boiler. Cook over boiling water, stirring frequently, until thick, about 5 minutes. Sprinkle gelatin on water in small sauce-pan. Stir over low heat just until dissolved; stir into pumpkin mixture. Cool.

4. Beat egg whites until foamy. Gradually beat in ¼ cup sugar; beat until stiff and glossy. Gently fold beaten egg whites into pumpkin mixture. Pour over baked mixture; refrigerate.

5. Just before serving, beat whipping cream and 1 tablespoon sugar in chilled bowl until stiff. During last minute of beating, add vanilla. To serve, cut dessert into squares; garnish with whipped cream.

Festive Dinner

Capon is baked in a clay pot.

CAPON DINNER MENU

- CAPON IN CLAY POT
- PILAF AND BRUSSELS SPROUTS
- CRANBERRY RELISH SALAD
  PICKLED FRUITS
  RELISH TRAY
- HOLIDAY POPOVERS

- PUMPKIN SPICED BAKED
  ALASKA
  COFFEE

• Recipes included

A plump capon baked with herbs and vegetables in a clay pot is the entrée in this holiday menu for four. Capons tend to be meatier, juicier and more tender than ordinary fowl.

Molded rice pilaf made with giblets and raisins, ringed by Brussels sprouts, is an excellent accompaniment for the capon. Cranberry Relish Salad supplies crunch and color—it is a mélange of chopped apples, carrots, celery and walnuts.

Pickled fruits and an assortment of relishes round out the meal, along with Holiday Popovers, surprise-flavored with poultry seasoning.

Dessert offers a dramatic twist to traditional pumpkin pie. A fresh treatment of Baked Alaska, the dessert can be made and frozen the day before, all ready for last-minute browning. Homemade sponge cake forms a base for vanilla ice cream stirred with pumpkin pie spice. It is covered with rum-laced meringue and lightly browned. The Step-By-Step Recipe shows exactly how it's done. Serves 4.

Wine Suggestion: One of the first peoples to bake fowl in clay were the Romans. Their wines go perfectly with this dish. So how about a Chianti Reserva?

Poultry seasoning adds subtle flavor to popovers.

Brussels sprouts complement this raisin-rich molded pilaf.

PARTY PLAN FOR CAPON DINNER MENU

1 Day Before:	Prepare Pilaf and Brussels Sprouts through step 1 in recipe; cover giblets and broth separately. Refrigerate. Prepare Pumpkin Spiced Baked Alaska through step 5 in recipe; freeze.
2 Hours Before Serving:	Make Capon in Clay Pot.
50 Minutes Before Serving:	Make Holiday Popovers. Complete Pilaf and Brussels Sprouts. Make Cranberry Relish Salad.
15 Minutes Before Dessert:	Complete Pumpkin Spiced Baked Alaska.

CAPON IN CLAY POT

1   capon (5 to 6 pounds)
1   tablespoon salt
4   small leeks
4   large stalks celery, cut in half crosswise
4   carrots, cut in half lengthwise
*2   cups hot beef bouillon
2   tablespoons butter or margarine, softened
¼   teaspoon dried basil leaves
¼   teaspoon dried tarragon leaves
¼   teaspoon dried thyme leaves

¼   cup all-purpose flour

Heat oven to 450°

1. Prepare clay pot according to manufacturer's directions;** line with parchment or heavy brown paper.

2. Rub capon with salt. Place breast side up in clay pot. Arrange vegetables around and on top of capon. Mix bouillon, butter and herbs; stir until butter melts. Pour over capon; cover.

3. Bake until capon is done, about 1½ hours. Remove cover during last 10 minutes of baking. Pour juices into bowl; discard leeks and celery.

4. Skim ¼ cup drippings from juices; place in large skillet. Stir in flour. Cook over low heat, stirring constantly, until mixture is smooth and bubbly. Remove from heat. Add enough water to reserved juices to measure 2 cups; stir into flour mixture. Heat to boiling, stirring constantly. Boil and stir 1 minute. Season to taste. Pass gravy.

*TIPS: *Dissolve 2 teaspoons instant beef bouillon or 2 beef bouillon cubes in 2 cups boiling water.*

**A Dutch oven can be substituted for a clay pot.*

PILAF AND BRUSSELS SPROUTS

Giblets (gizzard, heart, neck and liver from capon)

Chicken bouillon
1   tablespoon lemon juice
1   tablespoon butter or margarine
1   bay leaf
½   teaspoon salt
½   cup raisins
1   cup uncooked long-grain rice

1   or 2 packages (10 ounces each) frozen Brussels sprouts
Pimiento strips

1. Cook gizzard, heart and neck in salted water (1 quart water and 2 teaspoons salt) 1¼ hours. Add liver; cook until gizzard is tender, about 15 minutes. Reserve broth. Remove meat from neck; finely chop giblets.

2. Add enough chicken bouillon to reserved broth to measure 2½ cups. Heat broth, lemon juice, butter, bay leaf, salt and raisins to boiling in large saucepan. Stir in rice and chopped giblets; cover. Heat to boiling, reduce heat. Simmer over low heat until all liquid is absorbed, about 30 minutes. Remove bay leaf.

3. Cook Brussels sprouts according to package directions. Lightly pack rice mixture in buttered 4-cup mold or loaf pan. Unmold onto serving plate; garnish with pimiento strips. Place Brussels sprouts around rice.

CRANBERRY RELISH SALAD

Makes 4 or 5 servings

*1   cup fresh or frozen cranberries
⅓   cup sugar
1   medium apple, chopped
½   cup shredded carrot
½   cup finely chopped celery
2   tablespoons chopped walnuts
¼   cup mayonnaise or salad dressing
Salad greens

Measure cranberries and sugar into blender container; cover. Blend 30 seconds.** Toss with remaining ingredients except salad greens. Serve on salad greens on individual salad plates.

*TIPS: *If frozen cranberries are used, blend about 1 minute, scraping down sides of blender container frequently. Allow mixture to stand 10 minutes before combining with remaining ingredients.*

**Cranberry Relish Salad can be prepared to this point 24 hours in advance. Store covered in refrigerator.*

Pumpkin and rum flavorings make this Baked Alaska something special.

HOLIDAY POPOVERS
Makes 6

2	eggs
1	cup milk
1	cup all-purpose flour
½	teaspoon salt
1	teaspoon poultry seasoning
	Heat oven to 450°

1. Grease 6 deep custard cups (6 ounces each), popover pan cups or 8 medium muffin cups. Beat eggs slightly with rotary beater. Add remaining ingredients; beat just until smooth. Fill cups about ⅔ full.

2. Bake 25 minutes. Reduce heat to 350°; bake until deep golden brown, 15 to 20 minutes longer. Remove from cups immediately. Serve hot.

PUMPKIN SPICED BAKED ALASKA
See STEP-BY-STEP RECIPE on page 112.

1.

2.

3.

4.

5.

Sponge Cake (recipe follows)

1   **quart vanilla ice cream**
2   **teaspoons pumpkin pie spice**

5   **egg whites**
½   **teaspoon cream of tartar**
¾   **cup sugar**
1   **tablespoon light rum or**
     1½ teaspoons rum flavoring

Pistachio nuts, halved

Grapes, if desired

1. Make Sponge Cake; cool.

2. Soften ice cream slightly in chilled 1½-quart bowl 2 to 3 inches smaller than cake diameter; stir in pumpkin pie spice. Pack mixture in chilled bowl (photo 1); freeze.

3. Place cake right side up on serving board or freezer-to-ovenware platter. Loosen ice cream slightly (dip bowl quickly into hot water); invert onto cake (photo 2). Return to freezer.

4. Beat egg whites and cream of tartar until foamy. Beat in sugar, 1 tablespoon at a time; beat until stiff and glossy (photo 3). Fold in rum.

5. Cover cake and ice cream completely with meringue, sealing it to board or platter (photo 4). Sprinkle with nuts and return to freezer. Store no longer than 24 hours.

6. Just before serving, heat oven to 500°. Bake on lowest rack in oven until meringue is light brown, 3 to 5 minutes. Serve immediately. Attractive garnished with grapes (photo 5).

2 eggs
½ cup sugar
3 tablespoons water
½ teaspoon vanilla
⅔ cup cake flour
½ teaspoon baking powder
⅛ teaspoon salt

Powdered sugar

Heat oven to 375°

SPONGE CAKE
Makes one 9-inch layer

1. Line one 9-inch round layer pan with aluminum foil or waxed paper; grease. Beat eggs in small mixer bowl until very thick and lemon-colored, about 5 minutes.

2. Pour eggs into large mixer bowl; gradually beat in sugar. Blend in water and vanilla on low speed. Add flour, baking powder and salt gradually, beating just until batter is smooth. Pour into pan, spreading to edges.

3. Bake until wooden pick inserted in center comes out clean, 12 to 15 minutes. Loosen cake from edges of pan; invert onto towel-covered rack sprinkled with powdered sugar. Carefully remove foil; trim off stiff edges if necessary. Cool.

A Holiday Open House

Breads, doughnuts and kuchen are flavorful fare for a holiday open house.

114

Tom and Jerrys, made with hot milk, brandy, rum and spices, are a timely beverage for the holiday season, and go well with the many-flavored breads of this menu. This foamy drink, enriched with beaten eggs, dates back to 19th-century England.

Breads, each one enticingly different, are the main offerings in this open-house menu. The best way for guests to enjoy this broad choice of tasty breads is to wander around the table trying one after another. Sugar-glazed Potato Doughnuts are an especially delicious sample to start with. They would be good to serve anytime during the year. Danish Puffs with cream pufflike tops and kolacky-styled Cheese Delights run a close second. Brown Breads, nut-rich and bran-flavored, are best with whipped cream cheese spread on top.

The Almond Crusted Loaf has a crunchy glaze; a Black Walnut Kuchen is served warm, garnished with greens. And last, but not at all least, there is an impressive Cardamom Christmas Crown, braided and sprinkled with chopped pecans and sugar. Serves 16 to 20.

Wine Suggestion: The wine should be simple—Zinfandel by Christian Brothers.

PARTY PLAN FOR BREAD PARTY MENU

3 Days Before:	Prepare Potato Doughnuts through step 2 in recipe; cover and refrigerate. Make Brown Breads. Wrap in aluminum foil; refrigerate.
2 Days Before:	Make Cardamom Christmas Crown. Wrap in aluminum foil.
1 Day Before:	Make Cheese Delights and Almond Crusted Loaf; cool. Wrap separately in aluminum foil. Make Danish Puffs through step 4 in recipe; cool. Wrap in aluminum foil.
5 Hours Before Guests Arrive:	Complete Potato Doughnuts.
1 Hour Before Guests Arrive:	Make Powdered Sugar Glaze for Danish Puffs. Make Black Walnut Kuchen.
30 Minutes Before Guests Arrive:	Heat oven to 350°. Heat Danish Puffs and Cardamom Christmas Crown wrapped in foil until hot, 15 to 20 minutes. Complete Danish Puffs.
As Guests Arrive:	Make Tom and Jerrys.

TOM AND JERRYS
Makes about 2 quarts

2   eggs, separated
¼   cup sugar
    Dash ground cinnamon
    Dash ground cloves
    Dash salt
1   cup brandy
1   cup dark rum
5⅓ cups hot milk
    Ground nutmeg

1. Beat egg whites until foamy. Add sugar gradually; beat until stiff but not dry. Add egg yolks; beat until soft peaks form. Fold in cinnamon, cloves and salt.

2. Measure 3 tablespoons egg mixture into each mug. Add 1 tablespoon each brandy and rum. Stir in ⅓ cup hot milk. Sprinkle with nutmeg.

POTATO DOUGHNUTS
Makes about 3 dozen doughnuts

1   cup sieved cooked potatoes
      (warm or cold)
1   cup liquid (reserved from
      cooking potatoes)
¾   cup shortening
½   cup sugar
1   tablespoon salt
1   package active dry yeast
¾   cup warm water
      (105° to 115°)
2   eggs, beaten
5   to 6 cups all-purpose flour

    Oil

    Glaze, if desired
      (recipe follows)

1. Mix potatoes, potato liquid, shortening, sugar and salt. Dissolve yeast in warm water; stir into potato mixture. Stir in eggs and enough flour to make dough easy to handle.

2. Turn dough onto lightly floured surface; knead until smooth and elastic, 5 to 8 minutes. Place in greased bowl; turn greased side up and cover. Let rise until double, 1 to 1½ hours. (Don't punch down.)*

3. Pat out dough on lightly floured surface to ¾-inch thickness. Cut doughnuts with floured 2½-inch cutter. Let rise until double, about 1 hour.

4. Heat oil (3 to 4 inches) to 375° in heavy pan. Fry doughnuts until golden, 2 to 3 minutes on each side. Drain on paper toweling.

5. Glaze doughnuts while warm. Store doughnuts at room temperature covered with towel. (Doughnuts are best when eaten same day they are fried.)

TIP: *Dough can be stored in refrigerator 3 days before using. Refrigerate in greased bowl immediately after kneading. Grease top of dough generously and cover with damp towel. If dough rises in refrigerator, punch down and cover with damp towel.

GLAZE

6   cups powdered sugar
1   cup boiling water

Mix powdered sugar and boiling water until consistency of gravy.

BROWN BREADS   *Makes 4 loaves*

2   cups whole bran cereal
2   cups buttermilk
2   teaspoons baking soda
2   eggs, beaten
2¼   cups all-purpose flour
¼   teaspoon salt
1   cup chopped pecans
1   cup raisins
1   cup packed dark brown sugar

Heat oven to 350°

1. Mix cereal, buttermilk and baking soda in large bowl. Let stand until liquid is absorbed, about 5 minutes. Stir in remaining ingredients; mix until moistened.

2. Divide among 4 greased 1-pound cans. Place cans on baking sheet. Bake until wooden pick inserted in center comes out clean, about 55 minutes. Remove loaves from cans and cool on wire rack. Serve with whipped cream cheese if desired.

DANISH PUFFS   *Makes 2*

¼   cup butter or margarine,
       softened
1   cup all-purpose flour
¼   cup chopped black walnuts
       or English walnuts
2   tablespoons water

1   cup water
½   cup butter or margarine,
       softened
1   cup all-purpose flour
1   teaspoon almond extract
⅛   teaspoon salt
3   eggs

     Powdered Sugar Glaze
       (recipe follows)
2   tablespoons finely chopped
       black walnuts or English
       walnuts

Heat oven to 350°

1½   cups powdered sugar
1½   tablespoons milk
1   tablespoon butter or
       margarine, softened
½   teaspoon vanilla

1. Cut ¼ cup butter into 1 cup flour; stir in ¼ cup chopped nuts. Sprinkle 2 tablespoons water over mixture; stir until moistened. Round into ball; divide in half.

2. Pat each half into strip, 12 x 3 inches, on ungreased baking sheet. (Strips should be about 3 inches apart.)

3. Heat 1 cup water and ½ cup butter in medium saucepan to rolling boil. Remove from heat; quickly stir in 1 cup flour, the almond extract and salt. Stir vigorously over low heat until mixture forms a ball, about 1 minute. Remove from heat. Beat in eggs until smooth and glossy. Divide mixture in half; spread each half evenly over pastry strips.

4. Bake until topping is crisp and brown, about 1 hour; cool. (Topping will shrink and fall, forming the custardy tops of these puffs.)

5. Spread puffs with Powdered Sugar Glaze and sprinkle each puff with 1 tablespoon finely chopped walnuts. Best served warm. Garnish with greens if desired.

POWDERED SUGAR GLAZE
Mix all ingredients until smooth and spreading consistency.

CHEESE DELIGHTS

1	package active dry yeast
¼	cup warm water (105° to 115°)
¼	cup lukewarm milk (scalded, cooled)
¼	cup granulated sugar
½	teaspoon salt
1	egg
¼	cup shortening
2½	to 3 cups all-purpose flour
1	package (8 ounces) cream cheese, softened
¼	cup packed light brown sugar
1	egg yolk
1	tablespoon shredded lemon peel
½	cup golden raisins

1. Dissolve yeast in warm water in large bowl. Stir in milk, granulated sugar, salt, egg, shortening and 1¼ cups of the flour. Beat until smooth. Mix in enough remaining flour to make dough easy to handle.

2. Turn dough onto lightly floured surface. Knead until smooth and elastic, about 5 minutes. Place in greased bowl; turn greased side up and cover. Let rise in warm place until double, about 1½ hours. (Dough is ready if impression remains.)

3. Beat cream cheese, brown sugar, egg yolk and lemon peel until light and fluffy. Stir in raisins; reserve.

4. Punch down dough. Roll dough into rectangle, 18 x 12 inches. Cut into twenty-four 3-inch squares. Place 1 level tablespoon reserved cheese mixture on center of each square. Bring 2 diagonally opposite corners to center of each square; moisten edges. Overlap slightly; pinch to seal. Place on greased baking sheets. Let rise until double.

5. Heat oven to 375°. Bake until golden brown, about 15 minutes. Cool on wire rack.

ALMOND CRUSTED LOAF

1	package active dry yeast
1¼	cups warm water (105° to 115°)
2	tablespoons granulated sugar
2	tablespoons shortening
2	teaspoons salt
2⅔	cups all-purpose flour
⅓	cup butter or margarine, softened
½	cup packed light brown sugar
½	cup sliced almonds
½	cup almond paste, cut up
2	tablespoons butter or margarine
1	egg yolk

1. Dissolve yeast in warm water in large mixer bowl. Add granulated sugar, shortening, salt and 2 cups of the flour. Blend on low speed, scraping bowl constantly, ½ minute. Beat on medium speed, scraping bowl occasionally, 2 minutes. Stir in remaining flour. Scrape batter from side of bowl; cover. Let rise in warm place until double, about 30 minutes. (Dough is ready if impression remains.)

2. Mix ⅓ cup butter and the brown sugar; stir in almonds. Spread and pat mixture evenly on bottom and halfway up sides of loaf pan, 9 x 5 x 3 inches. Mix almond paste, 2 tablespoons butter and the egg yolk; reserve.

3. Stir down batter by beating about 25 strokes. Carefully spread and pat ½ the batter evenly on almond mixture in loaf pan. Spread reserved almond paste mixture over batter to within ½ inch of edges. Spread and pat remaining batter over almond paste mixture; cover. Let rise until double, about 50 minutes.

4. Heat oven to 375°. Bake until loaf sounds hollow when tapped, about 35 minutes. Invert on wire rack; cool.

Tom and Jerrys are served hot with a sprinkle of nutmeg.

CARDAMOM CHRISTMAS CROWN

2 packages active dry yeast
½ cup warm water
  (105° to 115°)
½ cup lukewarm milk
  (scalded, cooled)
½ cup sugar
1 teaspoon crushed cardamom
  seed
1 teaspoon salt
2 eggs
½ cup butter or margarine,
  softened
4½ to 5 cups all-purpose
  flour

Melted butter or margarine
½ cup sugar
1 teaspoon crushed cardamom
  seed

Melted butter or margarine
¼ cup finely chopped pecans

1. Dissolve yeast in warm water in large bowl. Stir in milk, ½ cup sugar, 1 teaspoon cardamom, the salt, eggs, ½ cup butter and 2½ cups of the flour. Beat until smooth. Mix in enough remaining flour to make dough easy to handle.

2. Turn dough onto lightly floured surface. Knead until smooth and elastic, about 5 minutes. Place in greased bowl; turn greased side up and cover. Let rise in warm place until double, about 1½ hours. (Dough is ready if impression remains.)

3. Punch down dough; shape into ball and cover. Let rest 5 minutes. Roll dough into rectangle, 24 x 12 inches, on lightly floured surface. Cut into 3 long strips, 24 x 4 inches. Brush center of each strip with melted butter. Mix ½ cup sugar and 1 teaspoon cardamom; sprinkle 2 tablespoons mixture down center of each strip. Reserve remaining sugar mixture. Fold one long side of each strip to meet second side; press edges to seal.

4. Place strips seam sides down close together on greased baking sheet. Beginning from center, braid strips toward one end, stretching slightly to keep braid from becoming uneven in center. Turn pan and braid toward other end. Shape into circle, pinching ends to seal; cover. Let rise until double, about 45 minutes.

5. Heat oven to 375°. Brush braid with melted butter. Mix chopped pecans into remaining sugar mixture; sprinkle over braid. Bake until golden brown, about 30 minutes.

BLACK WALNUT KUCHEN

2 cups all-purpose flour
1 cup sugar
1 tablespoon baking powder
1 teaspoon salt
1 cup milk
⅓ cup butter or margarine, softened
1 egg
Topping (recipe follows)

Heat oven to 350°

¼ cup packed brown sugar
2 tablespoons flour
2 tablespoons butter or margarine, softened
1 teaspoon ground cinnamon
¼ cup flaked coconut
¼ cup finely chopped black walnuts or English walnuts

1. Mix all ingredients except Topping; beat vigorously 1 minute. Spread batter in greased baking pan, 13 x 9 x 2 inches. Sprinkle Topping over batter.

2. Bake until wooden pick inserted in center comes out clean, 35 to 40 minutes. Serve warm. Garnish with greens if desired.

TOPPING
Mix brown sugar, flour, butter and cinnamon; stir in coconut and walnuts.

6 A Foreign Flair

Ever since the earliest explorers sailed through uncharted seas to discover new worlds, travelers have returned to home port carrying souvenirs of their trips. Often the souvenirs were food, or new ways of preparing food.

One of the first known importers of foreign cookery was Marco Polo, 13th-century visitor to ancient China. He is credited with transporting both pasta and the innovative notion of ice cream from the Orient to his native Italy. American Indians introduced English voyagers to strange new vegetables and fruits—corn, pumpkins, cranberries—and recipes such as succotash and Indian pudding.

Among the most treasured imports were spices. Throughout the ages, these berries, leaves and bits of bark or roots have played a romantic and vital role in the history of cooking. More than a luxury or form of barter, until the advent of refrigeration spices were a necessity. Foods spoiled rapidly and spices could work miracles in disguising tainted fare. The particular combination of spices used eventually became characteristic of an individual country's cuisine.

Nearly everyone has roots in the Old World; ethnic foods are as much a part of our heritage as the family tree. Today the wide world of foreign cookery is open to all. Cities and many towns throughout the United States offer an astonishing range of restaurants specializing in ethnic cuisines. And good cooks everywhere are discovering the excitement of preparing foreign foods in their own homes. Surprising tastes and textures, unusual combinations of flavors and foods, new methods of cooking—all are part of the fun of ethnic cookery.

Menus from eight cuisines are included in this chapter. Northern China's mandarin cooking, the ancient Aztec foods of Mexico, an Indian curry dinner, a colorful array of Serbian dishes and an African buffet introduce novel, sometimes exotic new realms of cookery. France, Italy and Greece are represented by traditional foods arranged into typical menus that might be served in those countries.

The epicurean specialties of far-flung nations can be reproduced in your own kitchen with ease. Gourmet shops and supermarkets carry all manner of prepared and fresh ethnic foods, and when these are not available, local products may usually be used with excellent results. Suggestions for substitutes are given whenever possible. Many of the recipes can be made ahead—see the Party Plans included with each menu. Five Step-By-Step Recipes are also included.

Shrimp with dips and Buttermilk Soup are the beginnings of this African Menu (see menu on page 122).

An African Sampling

Chicken in Groundnut Sauce, a vegetable medley and rice and accompaniments

AFRICAN BUFFET MENU

- •COCONUT COCKTAILS
- •SHRIMP AND CELERY STICKS
- •BUTTERMILK SOUP
  Pictured on page 121.
- •AVOCADO BROTH
- •CHICKEN IN GROUNDNUT SAUCE
- •OKRA-CORN-TOMATO MEDLEY
- •HONEY-LIME STRAWBERRIES
- •SPICE NUT COOKIES
  MINT TEA
- •Recipes included

This African menu is a kind of Thanksgiving feast that can be celebrated anytime of the year. The recipes for this menu come from the Ivory Coast, in West Africa.

Coconut is a staple of life for West Africans, and dinner begins with creamy rum-coconut cocktails. Shrimp are dipped into a choice of sauces—pink, made with mayonnaise, or red, with chili sauce. These are variations on a popular African red pepper paste called *berbere*. There are two soups to try, too—smooth Buttermilk Soup served icy cold and a clear, beef-chili broth with slices of avocado floating on top.

Chicken in Groundnut Sauce is a hot, peppery dish. If you prefer a milder taste, use less chilies. It is served with saffron rice and a diverse array of accompaniments. Add a vegetable medley including fresh corn, okra and tomatoes.

Fruit and spices are a typical African combination. Fresh strawberries drenched in lime juice and honey and sprinkled with toasted coconut, plus crisp Spice Nut Cookies, carry on the tradition. Minted tea, hot or iced, is a popular beverage in the warm-climate countries. Serves 8.

Wine Suggestion: How about beer or a simple Sangría—all the way?

Coconut Cocktails are blended with brandy.

PARTY PLAN FOR AFRICAN BUFFET MENU

2 Days Before:	Bake Spice Nut Cookies; cool and store in airtight container. Make Red and Pink Dips; refrigerate.
1 Day Before:	Clean and cook shrimp; cover and refrigerate. Prepare celery sticks; refrigerate in cold water. Make Buttermilk Soup; cover and refrigerate.
That Day:	Mix honey and lime juice for Honey-Lime Strawberries; refrigerate. Wash and hull strawberries; refrigerate. Prepare Chicken in Groundnut Sauce through step 2 in recipe; refrigerate. Prepare Accompaniments, cover and refrigerate, except peanuts. Measure and label ingredients for final preparation of recipes; refrigerate perishables.

As Guests Arrive:	Make Coconut Cocktails; serve with appetizers.
40 Minutes Before Serving:	Heat Chicken in Groundnut Sauce; complete recipe. Make saffron rice according to package directions. Make Okra-Corn-Tomato Medley. Make Avocado Broth and garnish Buttermilk Soup.
10 Minutes Before Dessert:	Assemble Honey-Lime Strawberries.

COCONUT COCKTAILS
Makes 1 quart

*2 cups coconut milk
1 cup brandy or light rum
1 cup crushed ice

Measure all ingredients into blender container; cover. Blend 1 minute. Serve immediately.

*TIP: *Canned coconut milk, powdered coconut mix, canned coconut cream or canned squeezed coconut can be substituted. Prepare according to package directions. To serve 16, make the recipe twice.*

SHRIMP AND CELERY STICKS WITH RED AND PINK DIPS

1 pound fresh or frozen jumbo shrimp (16 to 20)
4 stalks celery

Red Dip (recipe follows)
Pink Dip (recipe follows)

1. Clean shrimp and cook according to package directions; refrigerate. Cut celery into sticks. Refrigerate in cold water.

2. Prepare dips. Serve in bowls with shrimp and celery.

2 tablespoons Red Pepper Paste (recipe follows)
1 cup chili sauce

RED DIP *Makes about 1 cup*
Mix all ingredients.

2 tablespoons Red Pepper Paste (recipe follows)
⅔ cup mayonnaise or salad dressing
1 tablespoon lemon juice

PINK DIP *Makes about ¾ cup*
Mix all ingredients.

TIP: Red and Pink Dips can be prepared 48 hours in advance. Store covered in refrigerator.

¼ cup dry red wine
1 teaspoon cayenne pepper
¾ teaspoon salt
¼ teaspoon ground ginger
⅛ teaspoon ground cardamom
⅛ teaspoon ground coriander
⅛ teaspoon ground nutmeg
⅛ teaspoon ground cloves
⅛ teaspoon ground cinnamon
⅛ teaspoon ground allspice
⅛ teaspoon black pepper
⅛ of a medium onion
1 small clove garlic

¼ cup paprika

RED PEPPER PASTE *Makes ¼ cup*
1. Measure 2 tablespoons wine and remaining ingredients except paprika into blender container; cover. Blend until smooth, scraping sides of blender frequently. With remaining wine, wash spices down sides of blender.

2. Heat paprika in saucepan 1 minute. Add spice mixture in small amounts, stirring until smooth. Cook until hot, about 3 minutes, stirring occasionally. Cool.

BUTTERMILK SOUP

Makes about 1 quart

3   cups buttermilk
Juice of 2 lemons (about
    ⅔ cup)
2   cloves garlic
1½ teaspoons salt
6   or 7 drops red pepper sauce
Dash cayenne pepper

10 slices bread (crusts
    removed)
Snipped parsley

1. Measure buttermilk, lemon juice, garlic and seasonings into blender container; cover. Blend.

2. Add bread and cover. Blend until thickened slightly. Refrigerate. Serve icy cold garnished with snipped parsley.

TIPS: To serve 16, make the recipe twice. Can be combined when refrigerated.

This recipe can be prepared 24 hours in advance. Store covered in refrigerator.

AVOCADO BROTH

Makes about 1¼ quarts

2   cans (10½ ounces each) beef
    broth
2   soup cans water
*4 crumbled dried chilies
Juice of 1 lemon
1   ripe avocado, thinly sliced

Mix beef broth, water, chilies and lemon juice. Heat to just below boiling. Stir in avocado. Serve immediately.

*TIP: *2 teaspoons crumbled dried chilies can be substituted.*

CHICKEN IN GROUNDNUT SAUCE

2   cans (2 ounces each)
    anchovies
⅓ cup peanut oil
2   broiler-fryer chickens
    (3 pounds each), cut up

2   medium onions, cut into
    rings
4   large firm ripe tomatoes,
    chopped
2   cloves garlic, finely
    chopped
*4 to 6 crumbled dried chilies
    (caution—these are hot!)
1   tablespoon chili powder
2   tablespoons chopped candied
    ginger or ½ teaspoon grated
    fresh ginger root
¼ cup tomato paste
2   cups hot water
1   teaspoon salt

2   to 3 cups chunky peanut
    butter
Whole chilies
4   cups cooked saffron or
    plain rice
Accompaniments

1. Drain oil from anchovies into 6-quart Dutch oven. Add peanut oil; heat. Brown chicken in hot oil, setting aside pieces as they brown. Drain excess fat from pan.

2. Mix anchovies, onions, tomatoes, garlic, dried chilies, chili powder, ginger, tomato paste, water and salt in Dutch oven. Heat to boiling; reduce heat and cover. Simmer 10 minutes. Return chicken to Dutch oven; cover. Simmer 45 minutes.**

3. Mix some of the hot liquid into 2 cups of the peanut butter and add to Dutch oven. Taste and add more peanut butter if you like. Mix sauce; turn chicken to coat with sauce. Cover. Cook until chicken is tender, 15 to 20 minutes. Garnish with whole chilies. Serve with saffron rice and a variety of accompaniments.

ACCOMPANIMENTS:
Fried sliced plantains, chopped raw peanuts, chutney, chopped tomatoes, diced green pepper, chopped onion, diced cucumber.

*TIPS: *1 tablespoon crumbled dried chilies can be substituted.*

***Chicken can be prepared to this point 24 hours in advance. Store covered in refrigerator. To serve, heat until chicken is hot. Proceed with step 3.*

To serve 16, make the recipe twice and cook in two 6-quart Dutch ovens.

OKRA-CORN-TOMATO MEDLEY

*6 ears fresh corn

2 cups cut-up okra (about 1 pound)

⅓ cup butter or margarine

2 tablespoons butter or margarine

3 medium tomatoes, chopped (about 2 cups)

1 tablespoon sugar

1½ teaspoons salt

¼ teaspoon pepper

Whole okra

1. Cut corn from cobs (about 1 quart).

2. Cook and stir 2 cups cut-up okra in ⅓ cup butter in large skillet over medium heat until tender, about 7 minutes. Add corn and 2 tablespoons butter. Cook until tender, about 7 minutes.

3. Stir in tomatoes and seasonings. Cook until tomatoes are hot, about 3 minutes. Garnish with whole okra.

*TIPS: *2 cans (16 ounces each) whole kernel corn can be substituted for fresh corn.*

To serve 16, make the recipe twice and cook in 2 large skillets.

HONEY-LIME STRAWBERRIES

1½ quarts strawberries, hulled

1 cup honey

¼ cup lime juice

1⅓ cups toasted coconut

1. Place strawberries in dessert dishes. Refrigerate. Mix honey and lime juice. Refrigerate until slightly thickened.

2. Spoon 1 tablespoon of lime-honey mixture on strawberries at serving time. Top with toasted coconut.

SPICE NUT COOKIES

Makes about 7 dozen cookies

1 cup butter or margarine, softened

2 cups packed light brown sugar

¼ cup red wine

1 egg

4 cups all-purpose flour

¾ teaspoon baking soda

1½ teaspoons cinnamon

½ teaspoon ginger

1 cup finely chopped almonds

1. Mix butter, sugar, wine and egg. Stir in remaining ingredients.

2. Divide dough into 3 equal parts; shape each into a roll 1½ inches in diameter and about 8 inches long. Wrap and refrigerate at least 4 hours, no longer than 1 month.

3. Heat oven to 400°. Cut rolls into ¼-inch slices; place on ungreased baking sheet. Bake until golden brown, 6 to 8 minutes. Cool 1 minute on baking sheet. Remove and cool on wire rack.

Serve Honey-Lime Strawberries and Spice Nut Cookies with minted tea.

A Mandarin Dinner

Dip fruits first in hot syrup, then in ice water for a crystalline dessert.

MANDARIN DINNER MENU

- •HOT-SOUR SOUP
- •STEAMED DUMPLINGS
- •SWEET AND HOT SAUCES
- •GINGER SHRIMP WITH
  FLOATING ISLANDS
- •MOO SHU PORK WITH
  MANDARIN PANCAKES
- •CHICKEN AND VEGETABLES
  OVER SIZZLING RICE
- •GLACEED FRUIT
  TEA
- •Recipes included

The exotic mandarin cuisine of northern China has only recently become known in America. It is a tantalizingly different way of cooking which originated with the aristocracy of ancient China; a "mandarin" was a Chinese official. Mandarin cooking uses seasonings which create pungent, piquant flavors, spicier than the more familiar Cantonese.

Dinner begins with Hot-Sour Soup, a spicy mix of mushrooms, chicken, bamboo shoots and bean curd. Bean curd is made from soy beans; firm and white with a smooth texture and bland taste, it is used as an ingredient in many Chinese recipes. Steamed Dumplings filled with pork and vegetables are picked up whole (with chopsticks, if possible). They are dipped into two sauces—one sweet, the other spicy-hot. Ginger-sauced shrimp are served over light Floating Islands.

Mandarin Pancakes are fun to eat. Just spoon the pork filling onto the pancakes, roll them up and eat them with your fingers. Another traditional Chinese specialty is bits of chicken and vegetables served over specially prepared rice so hot it really sizzles. Fruit chunks dipped in a hot sugar syrup, then plunged into ice water, form a unique do-it-yourself dessert. The result is a crystalline treat, brittle-crisp outside, tender and juicy inside. Serves 6.

Wine Suggestion: It is difficult to choose a wine for Chinese type of food but a lively species of Gewürztraminer from Alsace or California is marvelous.

Guests roll a spicy pork filling in Mandarin Pancakes.

PARTY PLAN FOR MANDARIN DINNER MENU

1 Week Before:

Make Mandarin Pancakes; wrap in aluminum foil and freeze.
Prepare Sizzling Rice through step 2 in recipe. Store in refrigerator in tightly covered container.

1 Day Before:

Make Sweet and Hot Sauces; store at room temperature.
Prepare Hot-Sour Soup through step 2 in recipe; cover and refrigerate.
Prepare Ginger Shrimp through step 3 in recipe; cover and refrigerate.
Prepare Moo Shu Pork through step 4 in recipe; cover and refrigerate.

That Day: Morning

Prepare Steamed Dumplings through step 4 in recipe; cover and refrigerate.
Prepare Chicken and Vegetables through step 3 in recipe; cover and refrigerate.

That Day: Afternoon

Deep fry Sizzling Rice (step 3 in recipe); drain and store in airtight container.
Prepare syrup for Glacéed Fruit through step 1 in recipe; let stand at room temperature.
Measure and label ingredients for final preparation of recipes; refrigerate perishables.

20 Minutes Before Guests Arrive:

Cook Steamed Dumplings.

10 Minutes Before Guests Arrive:

Make Floating Islands.
Complete Hot-Sour Soup recipe; keep warm over very low heat.
Make tea.
Heat Mandarin Pancakes in 325° oven 30 minutes.

After Guests Arrive:

Serve Hot-Sour Soup and tea.
Complete Ginger Shrimp recipe; if Floating Islands are finished, lower oven temperature to 200° to keep warm.
Serve Steamed Dumplings.
Heat Moo Shu Pork over medium-high heat.
Serve Ginger Shrimp with Floating Islands.
Turn oven to 350°; place Sizzling Rice in oven. Complete Chicken and Vegetables recipe; keep hot.
Serve Moo Shu Pork and Mandarin Pancakes.
Start to heat syrup for Glacéed Fruit.
Heat platter and bowl; serve Chicken and Vegetables over Sizzling Rice.
Slice fruit and arrange on tray. Serve Glacéed Fruit.

Note: Substitution of ingredients—¼ to ½ teaspoon ground ginger can be substituted for 1 tablespoon finely chopped peeled fresh or canned ginger root.

1 cup canned sliced mushrooms can be substituted for ½ cup dried Chinese mushrooms. Drain canned mushrooms; do not soak.

HOT-SOUR SOUP

Makes 1½ quarts

½ ounce dried Chinese mushrooms (about ½ cup)

1 pound chicken breasts, boned, skinned, cut into julienne strips

2 tablespoons sesame or vegetable oil

*1 quart chicken broth

½ cup sliced canned bamboo shoots, cut into julienne strips

¼ cup white vinegar

2 tablespoons soy sauce

1 teaspoon sugar

1 tablespoon finely chopped peeled fresh or canned ginger root

¼ teaspoon cayenne pepper

¼ teaspoon black pepper

1 tablespoon cornstarch

3 tablespoons water

4 egg yolks, slightly beaten

1½ cups fresh or canned bean curd cake, cut into julienne strips (about 8 ounces)

Sliced green onions

Sweet and Hot Sauces (recipes follow)

1. Place mushrooms in large bowl; cover with cold water. Place weighted plate on top to keep mushrooms under water. Let stand 30 minutes; drain and cut into julienne strips.

2. Cook and stir chicken in sesame oil in 3-quart saucepan until chicken is tender, about 5 minutes; stir in chicken broth. Heat to boiling. Stir in mushrooms, bamboo shoots, vinegar, soy sauce, sugar, ginger, cayenne and black pepper.**

3. Mix cornstarch and water; stir slowly into soup, stirring constantly, until sauce thickens slightly and all ingredients are hot, about 5 minutes.

4. Remove from heat; add egg yolks gradually, stirring constantly. Stir in bean curd. Serve in small bowls. Garnish with sliced green onions. Pass Sweet and Hot Sauces in separate bowls.

*TIPS: *1 quart water plus ¼ cup chicken seasoned stock base can be substituted for chicken broth.*

***Hot-Sour Soup can be prepared to this point 24 hours in advance. Store covered in refrigerator. To serve, heat soup just until it simmers and proceed with step 3.*

SWEET SAUCE
Makes about ⅓ cup

2 tablespoons sugar

3 tablespoons white vinegar

1 tablespoon soy sauce

Stir sugar, vinegar and soy sauce until sugar is dissolved. Store covered at room temperature no longer than 48 hours. Pass sauce with Hot-Sour Soup, Steamed Dumplings and Moo Shu Pork.

HOT SAUCE
Makes about ¼ cup

1 tablespoon cayenne pepper

2 tablespoons sesame or vegetable oil

½ teaspoon sesame seed

Stir pepper, oil and sesame seed. Store covered at room temperature no longer than 48 hours. Stir just before serving. Pass sauce with Hot-Sour Soup, Steamed Dumplings and Moo Shu Pork.

STEAMED DUMPLINGS
See STEP-BY-STEP RECIPE on page 135.

GINGER SHRIMP WITH FLOATING ISLANDS

1 pound cleaned fresh or frozen raw small shrimp

¾ cup chopped green onions

3 tablespoons sesame or vegetable oil

1¾ cups water

1½ tablespoons light dry sherry

1½ tablespoons finely chopped peeled fresh or canned ginger root

1. Cut shrimp according to diagram, making diagonal cut halfway through shrimp at tail end. Turn shrimp over and make diagonal cut halfway through shrimp at head end.

Cut here

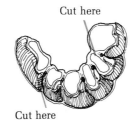

Cut here

1½ teaspoons sugar
1½ teaspoons monosodium glutamate
1½ teaspoons curry powder
1 teaspoon salt

Floating Islands (recipe follows)

2 tablespoons cornstarch
2 tablespoons water

4 egg whites
¼ teaspoon salt
¼ teaspoon cream of tartar

6 cups boiling water

Heat oven to 325°

2. Cook shrimp in boiling water until shrimp turn pink, about 4 minutes; drain. Rinse with cold water.*

3. Cook and stir green onions in sesame oil in 1½-quart saucepan until tender, about 3 minutes. Stir in 1¾ cups water, the sherry, ginger, sugar, monosodium glutamate, curry powder and salt.*

4. Make Floating Islands 20 minutes before serving time.

5. Heat ginger sauce until hot. Mix cornstarch and 2 tablespoons water; stir into ginger sauce. Heat to boiling, stirring constantly, until sauce thickens; mix in shrimp. Cook over low heat until hot, about 5 minutes.

6. Place Floating Islands on platter or serving plates; spoon about ½ cup Ginger Shrimp over each.

TIP: *Shrimp and ginger sauce can be prepared 24 hours in advance. Cover separately and store in refrigerator.*

FLOATING ISLANDS

1. Beat egg whites and salt until foamy; add cream of tartar and continue beating until stiff but not dry.

2. Pour boiling water into baking pan, 13 x 9 x 2 inches. Drop meringue by six ½ cupfuls onto water. Bake 15 minutes. Remove with slotted spoon. (Floating Islands can remain in low oven 15 minutes if desired.)

MOO SHU PORK WITH MANDARIN PANCAKES

Mandarin Pancakes (recipe follows)
1½ ounces dried Chinese mushrooms (about 1½ cups)

2 eggs, beaten
3 tablespoons sesame or vegetable oil

¾ pound pork shoulder, boneless, cut into julienne strips
½ cup water
½ cup soy sauce
1 tablespoon sugar
1 tablespoon finely chopped peeled fresh or canned ginger root
½ cup sliced peeled fresh or canned bamboo shoots, cut into julienne strips
¼ cup sliced green onions

1 teaspoon cornstarch
1 tablespoon water

1. Make Mandarin Pancakes. While pancakes cook, place mushrooms in large bowl; cover with cold water. Place plate and water-filled bowl on top to keep mushrooms under water. Let stand 30 minutes; drain and cut into julienne strips.

2. Scramble eggs in 1 tablespoon of the sesame oil; break into very small pieces and reserve.

3. Brown pork in remaining 2 tablespoons sesame oil in wok or 2-quart saucepan. Stir in mushrooms, ½ cup water, the soy sauce, sugar, ginger, bamboo shoots and green onions. Heat to boiling.

4. Mix cornstarch and 1 tablespoon water; stir slowly into pork mixture. Mix gently but rapidly until sauce thickens and all ingredients are very hot. Stir in scrambled eggs.*

5. Serve Moo Shu Pork in bowl and hot Mandarin Pancakes on a plate. Guests serve themselves. Spoon pork filling (about ¼ cup) on each pancake and roll; fold bottom end over to contain filling. Pick up and eat.

TIP: *Moo Shu Pork can be prepared to this point 24 hours in advance. Store covered in refrigerator. To serve, heat over medium-high heat until hot.*

1.

3.

4.

5.

Moo Shu Pork will be rolled in these thin Mandarin Pancakes.

MANDARIN PANCAKES

Makes 12 pancakes

⅓ cup boiling water
1 cup all-purpose flour

Sesame or vegetable oil

1. Stir water into flour until crumbly; shape into ball. Knead on lightly floured board until smooth and satiny, about 10 minutes (photo 1). Cover; let rest 30 minutes.

2. Shape dough into roll 6 inches long. Cut into twelve ½-inch pieces. (Keep pieces well covered at all times as dough dries out very quickly.)

3. Roll each of two pieces of dough into 3-inch circles. Lightly brush one circle with sesame oil; cover with remaining circle (photo 2). Roll together into 6-inch circle (photo 3). (Do not wrinkle circles when rolling.) Make only 1 or 2 pancakes at a time, then cook. Repeat to make each pancake.

4. Place pancake in ungreased skillet over medium-high heat; turn frequently with tongs or cooking chopsticks. Cook until pancake blisters and is parchment-colored (photo 4). Remove from skillet; separate with small pointed knife into two pancakes (photo 5). Stack and cover pancakes. Keep warm until all pancakes are cooked.

TIP: Mandarin Pancakes can be prepared in advance. Stack and cover pancakes until completely cool. Wrap in aluminum foil and freeze no longer than 2 weeks. To serve, heat frozen wrapped pancakes in 325° oven 30 minutes.

CHICKEN AND VEGETABLES OVER SIZZLING RICE

Sizzling Rice (recipe follows)

¾ ounce dried Chinese mushrooms (about ¾ cup)

¼ cup sesame or vegetable oil
1 pound chicken breasts, boned, skinned, cut into julienne strips
1 can (13¼ ounces) chicken broth

1. Make Sizzling Rice up to 1 week in advance.

2. Place mushrooms in large bowl; cover with cold water. Place plate and water-filled bowl on top to keep mushrooms under water. Let stand 30 minutes; drain and cut into julienne strips.

3. Heat oil in wok or large skillet; cook chicken in oil until tender, about 5 minutes. Stir in chicken broth, mushrooms, green onions,

¼ cup sliced green onions
1 tablespoon finely chopped peeled fresh or canned ginger root
¼ teaspoon salt
3 carrots, cut with crinkle cut vegetable cutter into 3-inch julienne strips

1 tablespoon cornstarch
1 tablespoon water
1 cup thinly sliced canned bamboo shoots
1 cup fresh or frozen snow peas

1½ cups uncooked regular rice (not converted)
6 cups water
1 tablespoon salt

Vegetable oil

ginger, salt and carrots. Heat to boiling; reduce heat. Simmer uncovered until carrots are tender, about 10 minutes.*

4. Mix cornstarch and water; stir slowly into chicken mixture. Stir rapidly until sauce thickens. Stir in bamboo shoots and snow peas. Cook until snow peas are crisp-tender, about 2 minutes. Serve in oven-warmed bowl; pass Sizzling Rice separately.

TIP: *Chicken mixture can be prepared to this point 24 hours in advance. Store covered in refrigerator. To serve, heat chicken mixture until hot and proceed with step 4.

SIZZLING RICE

1. Mix rice, water and salt in saucepan; let stand 30 minutes. Heat to boiling; reduce heat. Simmer covered 30 minutes. (Rice will be slightly wet.) Heat oven to 250°.

2. Pat rice in well-greased jelly roll pan, 15½ x 10½ x 1 inch. Bake 2 hours. Cut rice into 4-inch pieces; turn pieces over. Bake 5 hours, turning occasionally. Cool completely.*

3. Heat oil (3 to 4 inches) to 400° in deep-fat fryer or kettle. Slide a few rice pieces into hot oil with wide spatula. Fry until light golden brown, about 1½ minutes each side. Drain on paper toweling.** Cool completely. Store in airtight container no longer than 24 hours.

4. Heat oven to 350°. Place rice on ungreased baking sheet. Bake 20 to 25 minutes. Serve immediately on oven-heated platter (rice must be very hot so that it "sizzles" when chicken and vegetables are poured over top).

TIPS: *The size of pan and timing are important in this step. Store rice in tightly covered container no longer than 1 week.

**To serve immediately, place fried rice on ungreased baking sheet. Keep warm in 350° oven until all rice is fried. Serve immediately on oven-heated platter.

GLACEED FRUIT

½ cup sesame oil
2 cups water
4 cups sugar
2 tablespoons light corn syrup
1 teaspoon vanilla

2 bananas, peeled, cut into 1-inch pieces
1 apple, thinly sliced
Fresh or canned litchi nuts
Ice water

1. Mix sesame oil, water, sugar, corn syrup and vanilla in 6-cup electric fondue pot. Cook on range until candy thermometer registers 280°, stirring just until sugar is dissolved.

2. Place fondue pot on warmer on table over medium-low heat.* Place plate of fruit and bowl of ice water on table. Let guests dip fruits into glacé, using fondue forks. Immediately plunge coated fruit into bowl of ice water.

TIP: *Let syrup stand in fondue pot no longer than 45 minutes. Syrup can be prepared through step 1 early in the day. Let stand at room temperature. Reheat to 280° before serving.

1.

2.

3.

*Dumpling Dough (recipe follows)
¼   ounce dried Chinese mushrooms (about ¼ cup)
¼   pound ground uncooked pork
2   tablespoons finely chopped Chinese or green cabbage
1   tablespoon finely chopped green onion
1   tablespoon finely chopped water chestnuts
¼   teaspoon finely chopped peeled fresh or canned ginger root
1   teaspoon cornstarch
2   teaspoons soy sauce
4   or 5 large cabbage leaves Sweet and Hot Sauces (recipes on page 131), if desired

1. Make Dumpling Dough. While making dough, place mushrooms in large bowl; cover with cold water. Place plate and water-filled bowl on top to keep mushrooms under water. Let stand 30 minutes; drain and chop finely.

2. Mix mushrooms, pork, chopped cabbage, onion, water chestnuts and ginger. Stir together cornstarch and soy sauce; stir into pork mixture. Shape by slightly rounded tablespoonfuls into balls (photo 1); place on waxed paper and refrigerate.

3. Shape Dumpling Dough into roll 6 inches long. Cut into twelve ½-inch pieces. (Keep pieces well covered at all times as dough dries out very quickly.) Roll each piece on lightly floured board into 3-inch circle. Place pork ball on center of each circle; fold dough over filling and twist to seal (photo 2).

4. Place dumplings in shallow baking dish; cover. Refrigerate no longer than 24 hours.**

5. Pour water to depth of 1 inch in wok or deep saucepan. Place steamer over water so that rack is above water.*** Arrange single layer of cabbage leaves on steamer rack; arrange dumplings on leaves (photo 3). Heat water to boiling. Cover steamer; keep water boiling over low heat. Steam dumplings 40 minutes. Serve dumplings in steamer or arrange on cooked cabbage leaves on platter. Pass Sweet and Hot Sauces.

*TIPS: *Commercially prepared egg roll wrappers can be substituted for the Dumpling Dough. Cut each wrapper into 4 squares. Place pork ball in center of each square; fold dough over pork ball to make triangle. Moisten edges; pinch well to seal.
**To serve dumplings immediately, do not refrigerate. Proceed with step 5.
***If you do not have a steamer, a Dutch oven can be used. Place 3 or 4 custard cups upside down in Dutch oven; balance rack on top of custard cups and steam dumplings as directed.*

DUMPLING DOUGH
Stir water into flour until mixed. Knead on lightly floured board until smooth and satiny, about 10 minutes; cover. Let rest 30 minutes. (Keep covered until ready to use.)

2   tablespoons boiling water
¼   cup all-purpose flour

A Serbian Repast

A many-layered pecan torte.

Cut Cheese Pudding into diamond shapes and serve with Slivovitz Tea.

SERBIAN DINNER MENU

- •GIBANICA (Cheese Pudding)
- •SUMADIJSKI CAJ (Slivovitz Tea)
- •MUCKALICA (Pork with Onions)
- •MUSAKA OD PRAZILUKA (Leek Moussaka)
- •PREBRANAC (Lima Bean Casserole)
- •SRBSKA SALATA (Raw Salad of Onions, Green Peppers and Tomatoes)
- •KAJMAK I AJVAR (Creamed Cheese and Roasted Peppers)
- HLEB (Bakery Bread)
- •VASINA TORTA (Vasa's Pecan and Chocolate Torte)
- SLIVOVITZ (Plum Brandy)
- TURSKA KAVA (Turkish Coffee)

•Recipes included

Serbia, one of the six republics of Yugoslavia, is a land of rugged mountains, deep valleys and broad rivers. Its people are earthy, creative and wonderfully hospitable—its food a fascinating blend of peasant and poet. Pork is predominant in Serbian cooking; beans, onions and sweet peppers also appear in countless dishes.

Gibanica, a unique cheese pudding cut into diamond shapes, is a delicious hot appetizer. Traditionally it is served with a pot of Slivovitz Tea—hot plum brandy and water sweetened with caramelized sugar. You might prefer to serve Slivovitz Tea as an after-dinner drink. The main course of the Serbian menu is a dish of pork and onions, snappy with red peppers. With it come large leek-flavored pancakes layered with ground pork, onion and sour cream, covered with thick cream and cheese. There are also a peppery Lima Bean Casserole and a refreshing salad of raw onion, green pepper and tomatoes.

An excellent feta and cream cheese spread, beaten fluffy, goes with roasted pepper relish on warm slices of bread. Dessert, a four-layered torte of ground pecans and chocolate crowned with whipped cream, would be good served anytime; it's not too sweet. Small glasses of strong Turkish coffee and Slivovitz—Serbia's national drink—provide an ideal finish. Serves 8.

Wine Suggestion: The Serbians like their food spicy, sometimes hot and have husky and full-bodied wines from Hungary or their own Yugoslavian wines. They drink Villanyi Burgundy. Here one can match it with a red from Bully Hill Vineyards, New York State.

Pepper and tomato salad, Lima Bean Casserole, Leek Moussaka and Pork with Onions are Serbian specialties.

PARTY PLAN FOR SERBIAN DINNER MENU

1 Day Before:

Make salad; cover and refrigerate.
Make Creamed Cheese and Roasted Peppers; cover separately and refrigerate.
Prepare Vasa's Pecan and Chocolate Torte through step 4 in recipe; cover and refrigerate.
Make chocolate curls for torte; refrigerate.

That Day:

Measure and label ingredients for final preparation of recipes; refrigerate perishables.

3 Hours 15 Minutes Before Serving:

Make Lima Bean Casserole.

1 Hour 10 Minutes Before Guests Arrive:

Make Cheese Pudding.
Prepare Leek Moussaka through step 2 in recipe; cover.
Bring Creamed Cheese and Roasted Peppers to room temperature.

As Guests Arrive:

Make Slivovitz Tea.
Serve Cheese Pudding and Slivovitz Tea.

45 Minutes Before Serving:

Complete Leek Moussaka and Pork with Onions.

5 Minutes Before Dessert:

Complete torte.

GIBANICA (Cheese Pudding)

1	pound feta cheese, finely chopped
1	pint creamed cottage cheese (small curd)
6	eggs, beaten
½	cup carbonated water
½	pound fillo strudel leaves
	Heat oven to 400°

1. Mix feta cheese, cottage cheese, eggs and carbonated water in large bowl.

2. Cover bottom of buttered baking pan, 13 x 9 x 2 inches, with one fillo leaf.

3. Dip each remaining fillo leaf into cheese mixture. Crumble and place in pan in rows. Spoon excess cheese mixture over fillo leaves.

4. Bake until knife inserted near center comes out clean, 35 to 40 minutes. Cut into diamonds to serve.

SUMADIJSKI CAJ (Slivovitz Tea)

Makes 2 cups

1	cup plum brandy (slivovitz)
1	cup water
*¼	cup sugar

1. Mix brandy and water; reserve. Melt sugar in heavy 2-quart saucepan, stirring constantly, until an even amber color. Remove from heat; stir in brandy mixture.

2. Heat, stirring constantly, over medium heat until caramel melts. Serve hot in small mugs.

*TIP: *For a sweeter drink, use ⅓ cup sugar.*

MUCKALICA (Pork with Onions)

6	medium onions, coarsely chopped (about 3 cups)
¼	cup vegetable oil
2	teaspoons salt
1	teaspoon paprika
¾	teaspoon pepper
¼	teaspoon crushed red peppers
2	pork tenderloins (about 1 pound each), cut into julienne strips
¼	cup vegetable oil
1	red pepper, cut into 8 pieces
8	cubes (about 1 inch) feta cheese

1. Cook and stir onions in ¼ cup oil until crisp-tender. Stir in salt, paprika, pepper and crushed peppers; keep warm.

2. While onions are cooking, brown pork in ¼ cup oil; cook thoroughly. Top with red pepper pieces and cover. Cook until peppers are crisp-tender, about 3 minutes; remove peppers and reserve.

3. Stir onion mixture into meat; spoon meat into serving dish or individual casseroles. Garnish with cubes of feta cheese and reserved strips of cooked red pepper.

MUSAKA OD PRAZILUKA (Leek Moussaka)

1	vegetable bouillon cube
½	cup hot water
1½	cups chopped leeks (about 2)
1	cup all-purpose flour
1	egg, beaten
¼	teaspoon salt
½	pound ground fresh pork
⅓	cup chopped onion
½	teaspoon paprika
½	teaspoon salt
¼	teaspoon pepper Dash crushed red peppers
⅓	cup dairy sour cream
¼	cup whipping cream
¼	cup shredded Swiss cheese

1. Dissolve bouillon cube in hot water in saucepan; stir in leeks. Heat to boiling; reduce heat. Simmer 5 minutes, stirring occasionally. Cool to lukewarm. Drain; reserve liquid. Add enough water to reserved liquid to measure 1 cup.

2. Mix flour, reserved liquid, egg and ¼ teaspoon salt. Stir in leeks. Pour ¾ cup batter onto lightly greased hot griddle; spread into 8-inch circle. Turn when light brown on bottom. Repeat to make 2 more cakes.

3. Cook and stir ground pork and onion in large skillet until onion is tender. Stir in paprika, ½ teaspoon salt, the pepper and red peppers; stir in sour cream.

4. Heat oven to 375°. Place a leek cake in greased 9-inch pie plate. Spread with about ¾ cup meat mixture. Place second leek cake on top and repeat for second layer. Top with remaining leek cake. Pour whipping cream over top; sprinkle with cheese.

5. Bake until top is lightly browned, about 20 minutes. Cut into wedges to serve.

PREBRANAC (Lima Bean Casserole)

1	pound dried lima beans, washed, drained
½	teaspoon salt
4	medium onions, chopped (about 2 cups)
½	cup vegetable oil
1	tablespoon flour
2	teaspoons salt
1½	teaspoons paprika
½	teaspoon pepper

1. Place beans in large saucepan; add water to cover. Heat to boiling; boil 2 minutes. Remove from heat; cover and let stand 1 hour. Heat to boiling; reduce heat and cover. Simmer until beans are tender, about 45 minutes. (Add water if necessary.) Drain beans, reserving ¾ cup liquid. Mix beans and ½ teaspoon salt.

2. Cook and stir onions in oil over low heat until tender and light brown, about 25 minutes. Stir in flour, 2 teaspoons salt, the paprika and pepper. Stir reserved bean liquid into onion mixture gradually. Cook and stir until thick.

3. Heat oven to 375°. Layer half of the beans in 1½-quart casserole. Spread with half of the onion mixture; repeat with remaining beans and onion mixture. Bake 45 minutes.

TIP: Can be served as an entrée (for four) or as an accompaniment for other meats such as lamb.

SRBSKA SALATA (Raw Salad of Onion, Green Pepper and Tomatoes)

1   large onion
1   large green pepper, cut into
     1½-inch pieces
2   large tomatoes, cut into
     eighths
¼   cup white vinegar
2   tablespoons vegetable oil
1   tablespoon snipped parsley
1   clove garlic, crushed
½   teaspoon salt
⅛   teaspoon pepper

1. Cut onion into rings; cut rings in half. Place onion, green pepper and tomatoes in glass bowl. Shake vinegar, oil, parsley, garlic, salt and pepper in tightly covered jar.

2. Pour dressing over vegetables; stir until coated and cover. Refrigerate at least 3 hours, no longer than 24 hours.

KAJMAK I AJVAR (Creamed Cheese and Roasted Peppers)   *Makes about 2 cups cheese and 1⅔ cups peppers*

1   cup butter or margarine,
     softened
4   ounces feta cheese, diced
     (about 1 cup)
½   package (3-ounce size)
     cream cheese, softened
     Bread
     Roasted Peppers
     (recipe follows)

Beat butter and cheeses in small bowl until light and fluffy. Serve with bread and Roasted Peppers.

TIP: Kajmak can be stored covered in refrigerator no longer than 1 week. To serve, bring Kajmak to room temperature.

ROASTED PEPPERS

2   large green peppers
1   large red pepper

2   tablespoons Italian salad
     dressing
2   cloves garlic, crushed
1   teaspoon salt
½   teaspoon sugar
⅛   teaspoon crushed red peppers

    Heat oven to 450°

1. Place peppers on oven rack. Bake until light brown, 10 to 12 minutes. Plunge peppers into cold water. Remove outer skins, seeds and stems.

2. Chop peppers finely. Mix remaining ingredients; stir in peppers and cover. Refrigerate at least 1 hour, no longer than 24 hours.

VASINA TORTA

See STEP-BY-STEP RECIPE on page 141.

1.   2.   3.

4.   5.   6.

6	egg yolks
1½	cups granulated sugar
1½	cups all-purpose flour
1	teaspoon baking powder
½	teaspoon salt
⅓	cup cold water
2	teaspoons vanilla
1	cup ground pecans
6	egg whites (about ¾ cup)
½	teaspoon cream of tartar
	Chocolate Filling (recipe follows)
1	cup chilled whipping cream
2	tablespoons powdered sugar
	Chocolate curls

Heat oven to 325°

1. Beat egg yolks in small mixer bowl until very thick and lemon colored, about 5 minutes (photo 1). Pour into large mixer bowl; beat in granulated sugar gradually. Mix in flour, baking powder and salt alternately with water and vanilla on low speed (photo 2). Fold in pecans.

2. Beat egg whites and cream of tartar in another large bowl until stiff. Fold egg yolk mixture gradually into egg whites (photo 3). Pour into 2 greased layer pans, 9 x 1½ inches.

3. Bake until wooden pick inserted in center comes out clean, 45 to 55 minutes. Loosen edges of layers with spatula. Cool 10 minutes; remove from pans. Cool thoroughly.

4. Prepare Chocolate Filling. Split layers to make 4 layers (photo 4). Fill each split layer with about 1 cup Chocolate Filling, leaving top of cake plain* (photo 5).

5. Before serving, beat whipping cream and powdered sugar in chilled bowl until stiff; spread on top of cake (photo 6). Garnish with chocolate curls.

TIP: *Filled layers can be stored covered in refrigerator no longer than 24 hours.

CHOCOLATE FILLING
Mix all ingredients except egg yolks. Beat egg yolks until very thick and lemon colored. Fold into chocolate mixture. Refrigerate until of spreading consistency, about 1 hour.

½	cup butter or margarine, softened
2	cups ground pecans
1	cup powdered sugar
¼	cup milk
4	squares (1 ounce each) unsweetened chocolate, melted, cooled
1	tablespoon plus 1½ teaspoons orange juice
¼	teaspoon orange extract
4	egg yolks

A Greek Banquet

Wedges of Greek cheese are flamed with brandy.

The legendary gods of ancient Greece's Mount Olympus may have had their nectar and ambrosia, but today's Greek has roast lamb and good wine. Lamb is both popular and plentiful in Greece. On feast days even the poorest family dines on lamb. Olive oil is also abundant and is much used. Its distinctive taste, along with that of lemon, is found often in Greek cooking.

Two appetizers begin this menu—Saganaki, wedges of soft Greek cheese dramatically flamed with brandy, and Avgolemono, an elegant egg, lemon and rice soup. Entrées include Roast Spring Lamb, Dolmades—grape vine leaves stuffed with a minty beef and rice mixture—and Pastitsio, baked layers of macaroni, beef and cheese. The classic Greek salad, garnished with olives, anchovies and feta cheese, is good served with any meal. Feta cheese is made from goat or sheep milk; it is soft, white and crumbly.

Kourabiedes, sugar-coated Crescent Cookies, are a Christmas tradition in Greece, but are also served on other holidays. Candied almonds— Koufeta—are a special treat at weddings.

Greeks drink their coffee very strong and thick, Turkish-style, in demitasse cups, but any freshly brewed coffee would be fine.

Serves 6, 12 or 18 (see note following Party Plan).

Wine Suggestion: A refreshing fruity young wine will do marvels for this dinner: Verdicchio from Italy or Chenin Blanc, Chapellet from California will do it.

**Roast lamb, Spinach Cheese Pie and baked macaroni are served
with Greek Salad. Crescent Cookies are for dessert.**

•Recipes included

PARTY PLAN FOR GREEK BUFFET MENU

2 Days Before: Make Crescent Cookies; store in airtight container.

1 Day Before: Prepare Baked Macaroni with Beef and Cheese through step 2 in recipe; cover and refrigerate.
Prepare Stuffed Grape Vine Leaves through step 2 in recipe; cover and refrigerate.
Prepare Spinach Cheese Pie through step 3 in recipe; cover and refrigerate separately.
Prepare dressing for Salad; refrigerate.

3 Hours 30 Minutes Before Serving: Prepare Roast Spring Lamb; roast on middle rack of oven.

1 Hour 20 Minutes Before Serving: Complete Spinach Cheese Pie; place in oven on middle rack with lamb.
Complete Baked Macaroni with Beef and Cheese; place on lower rack of oven.

1 Hour Before Serving: Complete Stuffed Grape Vine Leaves.
Prepare Salad through step 2 in recipe; refrigerate.

30 Minutes Before Serving: Prepare Lemon Soup through step 1 in recipe; cover. Heat, if necessary; complete step 2 just before serving.
Toss Salad with dressing.

As Guests Arrive: Make Flaming Cheese.

This menu can be easily adapted to serve small or large groups. To serve 6 people, choose one of the appetizers and two of the entrées. To serve up to 18 people, increase the recipes for Saganaki, Avgolemono and Salata, accordingly. When planning for more than 18 people, increase the recipes proportionately; you'll need a second oven.

SAGANAKI (Flaming Cheese)

*1   pound soft kasseri or kefalotiri cheese
2   tablespoons butter or margarine, melted

2   tablespoons brandy
½   lemon

Heat oven to broil and/or 550°

1. Cut cheese into 3 wedges; arrange on buttered broiler pan. Pour melted butter on cheese. Broil 4 to 6 inches from heat until cheese is bubbly and light brown.**

2. Pour brandy quickly over hot cheese; ignite immediately. Squeeze juice from lemon over cheese as flame begins to die. Cut wedges in half to serve.

*TIPS: *Mozzarella cheese can be substituted.*

***Cheese and butter can be transferred to shallow chafing dish or heatproof serving dish at this point for flaming at the table. If cheese is transferred, brandy should be warmed.*

AVGOLEMONO (Lemon Soup)

Makes 3 cups

3	cups water
1	tablespoon instant chicken bouillon
¼	cup uncooked rice
2	tablespoons fresh lemon juice
2	eggs, beaten
	Parsley

1. Heat water and chicken bouillon in 2-quart saucepan to boiling; stir in rice and reduce heat. Simmer uncovered until rice is tender, 20 to 25 minutes. Remove from heat.

2. Stir lemon juice slowly into eggs. Gradually stir at least half the hot broth and rice into eggs; mix into hot mixture in pan. Garnish with parsley.

PSITO ARNI (Roast Spring Lamb)

1	lamb leg, whole (about 5 pounds)
2	or 3 cloves garlic, slivered
1	teaspoon salt
½	teaspoon pepper
¼	cup butter or margarine, melted
2	lemons
	Grape leaves, if desired
	Greek-style peppers, if desired

Heat oven to 325°

1. Make slits in meat with tip of sharp knife; insert slivers of garlic. Rub surface with salt and pepper.

2. Place meat fat side up on rack in open shallow roasting pan. Brush with melted butter; squeeze lemon juice over meat. Insert meat thermometer so tip is in thickest part of meat and does not touch bone or rest in fat.

3. Roast uncovered until thermometer registers 175°, about 3 hours. Allow meat to stand 15 to 20 minutes before carving. Line platter with grape leaves; arrange lamb and peppers on grape leaves.

DOLMADES (Stuffed Grape Vine Leaves)

Makes 36

1	jar (16 ounces) grape vine leaves
4	medium onions, finely chopped
1	teaspoon salt
½	cup olive oil
2	pounds ground beef
⅔	cup uncooked regular rice
½	teaspoon salt
¼	teaspoon pepper
1	teaspoon snipped mint leaves
3	cups water
6	eggs
⅓	cup lemon juice
	Lemon slices

1. Wash and drain grape vine leaves; lay flat in a single layer. Cook and stir onions and 1 teaspoon salt in olive oil until tender, about 5 minutes.

2. Mix ground beef, rice, ½ teaspoon salt, the pepper, mint leaves and half the cooked onions. Place a rounded measuring tablespoon of meat mixture in center of each grape leaf. Fold each leaf tightly; place seam side down in large skillet.

3. Add water and remaining cooked onions. Heat to boiling; reduce heat and cover. Simmer until tender, about 40 minutes.

4. Beat eggs until thick and lemon colored, about 5 minutes. Slowly beat in lemon juice. Gradually stir 1 cup hot broth from meat into egg mixture; pour over grape leaves. Simmer uncovered 10 to 15 minutes. Garnish with lemon slices.

TIP: Grape vine leaves can be stuffed, covered and refrigerated up to 24 hours before cooking.

PASTITSIO (Baked Macaroni with Beef and Cheese)

2 cups elbow macaroni
1½ pounds ground beef
1 small onion, chopped
1 can (6 ounces) tomato paste
⅓ cup water
2 teaspoons salt

¼ cup grated hard cheese
   (kefalotiri, Parmesan or
   Romano)
1 teaspoon salt
⅛ teaspoon ground nutmeg
⅛ teaspoon ground cinnamon

2⅓ cups milk
⅓ cup butter or margarine
4 eggs, beaten

1. Cook macaroni according to package directions; drain and set aside. Cook and stir meat and onion in large skillet until meat is brown and onion is tender. Stir in tomato paste, water and 2 teaspoons salt; set aside.

2. Heat oven to 325°. Mix cheese, 1 teaspoon salt, the nutmeg and cinnamon. Spread half of the macaroni in greased baking dish, 13½ x 9 x 2 inches. Cover macaroni with meat mixture. Sprinkle cheese-spice mixture on meat; cover with remaining macaroni.

3. Measure milk and butter into 2-quart saucepan. Cook and stir until butter is melted. Remove from heat. Gradually stir at least half of hot milk mixture into beaten eggs; mix into hot milk mixture in pan. Pour on macaroni.

4. Bake until bubbly, about 55 minutes. Garnish with parsley if desired.

SPANAKOPITA (Spinach Cheese Pie)

1 package (8 ounces) cream
   cheese, softened
1 cup butter or margarine,
   softened
2 cups all-purpose flour

1 large onion, finely chopped
3 tablespoons olive oil
1 package (10 ounces) frozen
   chopped spinach, thawed,
   drained
1 teaspoon salt
¾ cup crumbled feta cheese
   (about 4 ounces)
⅓ cup pot cheese
1 egg, slightly beaten

1. Mix cream cheese and butter; cut into flour until dough gathers together. Press into ball; cover and chill until firm enough to roll, about 3 hours.*

2. Divide dough in half and shape into 2 flattened rounds. On lightly floured board, roll one round 2 inches larger than inverted 9-inch pie plate. Fold pastry into quarters; unfold and ease into pie plate. Trim overhanging edge of pastry ½ inch from rim of plate. Roll second round of dough.

3. Cook and stir onion in olive oil until tender, about 5 minutes. Remove from heat. Stir in remaining ingredients.**

4. Heat oven to 325°. Pour filling into pastry-lined pie plate. Cover with top crust. Seal and flute edge; prick top with fork. Bake until golden brown, about 1 hour 10 minutes.

TIPS: *Dough can be refrigerated no longer than 24 hours. Let stand at room temperature about 30 minutes before rolling.

**Spinach filling can be prepared 24 hours in advance. Store covered in refrigerator.

SALATA (Salad)

½   head lettuce
½   unpared cucumber, thinly sliced
½   bunch radishes, thinly sliced
2   green onions, chopped
2   tomatoes, cut into wedges
12 calamata (Greek-style) olives
½   pound feta cheese, cut in ½-inch cubes
8   anchovy fillets

⅓   cup olive oil
¼   cup white wine vinegar
½   teaspoon dried oregano leaves
½   teaspoon salt

1. Tear lettuce into bite-size pieces; toss with cucumber, radishes and onions.

2. Arrange lettuce, vegetables and tomatoes in salad bowl. Garnish with olives, cheese and anchovies; refrigerate.

3. Shake remaining ingredients in tightly covered jar; refrigerate.

4. Shake dressing and pour over salad; toss to serve.

KOURABIEDES (Crescent Cookies)   *Makes about 11 dozen*

1   cup butter or margarine, softened
1   cup shortening
2   cups powdered sugar
1   egg
2   tablespoons ouzo or anisette liqueur
1½ teaspoons almond extract
5   cups all-purpose flour
    Powdered sugar

Heat oven to 350°

1. Measure butter, shortening, 2 cups sugar, the egg, liqueur, almond extract and 2 cups of the flour into large mixer bowl. Blend ½ minute on low speed, scraping bowl constantly. Beat 1 minute on medium speed, scraping bowl occasionally.

2. Stir in remaining flour. Knead until smooth. Shape 1-inch pieces of dough into crescent shapes. Place 1 inch apart on ungreased baking sheet.

3. Bake until cookies are light brown on bottoms, 15 to 20 minutes. Sprinkle powdered sugar on cookies while hot. Cool on wire racks. Flavor mellows after 2 or 3 days. Store cookies in airtight containers at room temperature no longer than 9 days or in freezer no longer than 2 months.

Dîner Français

The unique sauce for roast ducklings is made with green peppercorns.

FRENCH DINNER MENU

•QUENELLES SAUCE BOURSIN (Fish Dumplings with Boursin Sauce)

•CANETON ROTI AU POIVRE VERT (Roast Ducklings with Green Peppercorn Sauce)

ASPERGES DU BEURRE (Buttered Asparagus)

•ARTICHAUTS DIJONNAISE (Artichokes with Dijon Sauce)

FROMAGE (Cheese)

PAIN (Bread)

FRUIT

•GATEAU AU CHOCOLAT (Chocolate Torte)

CAFE (Coffee)

COGNAC

The exquisite cookery of France, justly renowned throughout the pages of history, has been translated into a dinner perfectly suited to the American kitchen. The ingredients used in this classic French menu are easily obtainable, and many of the dishes can be prepared in advance.

Fluffy quenelles—light dumplings with a delicate fish flavor baked in an herbed cheese sauce—start the meal with a fine French flair. Crisply crusted tender ducklings are enhanced with a piquant sauce spiced with green peppercorns (unripened black peppercorns pickled in vinegar). Fresh buttered asparagus is a good accompaniment to the ducks. A separate course of chilled artichokes follows; diners dip the leaves into a chived mustard sauce and nibble off the fleshy part.

At this point in the meal, refresh the palate with French bread and cheese; then the dessert will be properly appreciated. The French often serve salad after the entrée for the same reason. If you wish, make the Gâteau au Chocolat days ahead. It is a chocolate torte with a ricotta and cream cheese filling, chocolate-glazed and sprinkled with chopped filberts. Fresh fruit, coffee and Cognac bring the dinner to an elegant conclusion. Serves 4.

Wine Suggestion: This finely balanced classic French menu will call for a perfectly selected line of the best available French wines. With fish, a full-bodied white Burgundy—Corton-Charlemagne. With duck, of course, a Chambertin-Clos de Beze. With cheese, have the oldest, biggest and best of your Bordeaux. With dessert, a Mumm's Cordon. A Lucullan dinner, worth every penny.

•Recipes included

Fish dumplings in cheese sauce.

Dijon mustard sauce enhances artichokes.

Serve a selection of cheese as a separate course.

PARTY PLAN FOR FRENCH DINNER MENU

1 Day Before:

Make Chocolate Torte; cover loosely and refrigerate.
Prepare Fish Dumplings through step 3 in recipe; cover and refrigerate.

That Day: Morning

Prepare artichokes through step 2 in recipe; cover and refrigerate.
Make Dijon Mustard Sauce for artichokes; cover and refrigerate.
Clean asparagus (if fresh); cover and refrigerate.

3 Hours Before Serving:

Prepare ducklings through step 3 in recipe.
Complete artichoke recipe.
Arrange cheese and fruit on separate serving trays; refrigerate.
Prepare Green Peppercorn Sauce for ducklings through step 2.

Just Before Guests Arrive:

Complete Green Peppercorn Sauce (except for adding wine); keep warm.
Remove cheese tray from refrigerator.
Heat oven to 425°.

As Guests Arrive:

Bake Fish Dumplings 15 minutes.
Cook asparagus; keep warm.
Complete sauce for ducklings.

Quenelles are shaped with tablespoons, then cooked in boiling water.

QUENELLES SAUCE BOURSIN (Fish Dumplings with Boursin Sauce)

½	pound fresh or frozen (thawed, dried) pike or halibut steaks or fillets
½	cup water
¾	teaspoon salt
⅛	teaspoon white pepper
2	tablespoons butter or margarine
½	cup all-purpose flour
1	egg
1	egg white
	Boursin Sauce (recipe follows)

1. Remove any bones and skin from fish; cut fish into small pieces. Place in blender container; cover. Blend on medium speed, scraping down sides of blender frequently, until fish is a smooth puree.

2. Heat water, salt, pepper and butter over medium heat to boiling; remove from heat. Mix in flour all at once. Beat in egg, then egg white. Beat until smooth. Stir in fish puree.

3. Heat 1½ inches water to boiling in 10-inch skillet. Heat oven to 425°. Using about ¼ cup fish mixture for each quenelle, shape into ovals with 2 tablespoons (photo 1). Drop into boiling water (photo 2); reduce heat and cover. Simmer quenelles until almost double, about 10 minutes. Remove quenelles from water with slotted spoon, draining well. Place 2 quenelles in each of 4 individual au gratin dishes or ramekins. Spoon about ¼ cup Boursin Sauce over each serving.*

4. Bake uncovered until sauce is hot and bubbly and quenelles are heated through, about 10 minutes. Garnish with watercress if desired.

TIP: *Quenelles can be prepared to this point. Cover immediately and refrigerate no longer than 24 hours. Just before serving, heat oven to 425°. Bake uncovered until sauce is hot and bubbly and quenelles are heated through, about 15 minutes.*

1	tablespoon butter or margarine
1	tablespoon flour
¼	teaspoon salt
	Dash white pepper
1	cup half-and-half
*1	package (about 2 ounces) spiced French cheese with garlic and herbs

BOURSIN SAUCE
Melt butter in 2-quart saucepan. Stir in flour, salt and pepper; mix until smooth. Remove from heat. Stir in half-and-half gradually. Return to heat. Heat to boiling, stirring constantly. Boil and stir 1 minute. Stir in cheese; cook and stir until cheese is melted.

TIP: *This is known as a spiced triple-crème cheese and is packaged in aluminum foil (about 1½ x 1 inch). If it is not available, substitute 1 cup whipping cream for the 1 cup half-and-half. Stir in 1 package (3 ounces) cream cheese, softened, ½ teaspoon finely snipped parsley, 1 small clove garlic, crushed, ½ teaspoon snipped chives and dash cayenne pepper.*

Center cone of the artichoke is cut out before removing the choke.

CANETON ROTI AU POIVRE VERT (Roast Ducklings with Green Peppercorn Sauce)

2	ducklings (4 to 5 pounds each), reserve giblets
1	to 1½ teaspoons salt
½	cup herb-seasoned croutons
	Green Peppercorn Sauce (recipe follows)
	Heat oven to 450°

1. Cut ducklings lengthwise in half with poultry shears. Sprinkle cavities with salt. Place duckling halves skin sides up on rack in open shallow roasting pan. Place ducklings in oven.

2. Reduce oven temperature immediately to 350°. Roast uncovered until drumstick meat feels very soft when pressed between fingers, 2¼ to 2¾ hours. Measure croutons into blender container; cover. Blend until consistency of coarse bread crumbs.

3. Sprinkle ducklings with crouton crumbs during last 30 minutes of roasting. Keep ducklings warm.

4. Prepare Green Peppercorn Sauce and serve with ducklings.

GREEN PEPPERCORN SAUCE

	Giblets (hearts, necks and livers from ducklings)
	Celery leaves
	Parsley sprigs
4	black peppercorns
¾	cup red wine vinegar
*1	tablespoon green peppercorns, drained
3	tablespoons flour
3	tablespoons red wine

1. Simmer giblets with celery leaves, parsley sprigs and black peppercorns in enough salted water (1 teaspoon salt to 2 cups water) to cover, until giblets are fork-tender, about 1 hour (add water if necessary). Add enough water to broth to measure 3 cups.

2. Mix broth from giblets, wine vinegar and green peppercorns in saucepan. Heat to boiling. Boil until remaining liquid measures 2¼ cups.

3. Measure 3 tablespoons drippings from roasting pan into 1-quart saucepan. Stir in flour. Cook over low heat, stirring constantly, until mixture is smooth and bubbly. Remove from heat. Stir in broth-peppercorn mixture gradually. Heat to boiling. Boil and stir 1 minute. Remove from heat. At serving time stir in wine and heat.

*TIP: *Green peppercorns can be purchased in specialty and gourmet shops.*

ARTICHAUTS DIJONNAIS (Artichokes with Dijon Sauce)

4   large artichokes, about
        5 x 4 inches each

1   teaspoon salt
2   teaspoons lemon juice

       Dijon Mustard Sauce (recipe
       follows)

1. Wash artichokes under cold running water, gently spreading leaves. Drain upside down. Cut off stem ends of artichokes including first layer of small leaves. Cut about 1 inch off tops of artichokes. Snip off prickly tip of each leaf with kitchen shears.

2. Fill Dutch oven or large saucepans with water to depth of 2 inches. Add ¼ teaspoon salt and ½ teaspoon lemon juice for each artichoke. Heat to boiling. Add artichokes and cover; reduce heat. Simmer until leaves pull out easily, 35 to 40 minutes. (Do not overcook.) Remove artichokes carefully from water (use tongs or 2 large spoons); drain upside down. Refrigerate at least 3 hours.

3. Spread outer leaves of each artichoke apart gently. Cut or pull out center cone of pale yellow leaves in one piece (see photo page 151); reserve. (Exposed fuzzy, inedible layer is the choke.) Remove choke with melon ball cutter, spoon or small pointed knife to expose tender edible artichoke bottom; discard choke.

4. Turn reserved cone of leaves upside down; set in hollow formed in top of artichoke. Serve with Dijon Mustard Sauce.

TIP: The French place artichoke near top of rimmed dinner plate with knife under the plate to elevate top edge. Sauce is spooned onto plate near bottom edge. Rest of plate is used for inedible portions of leaves.

⅔   cup olive oil
⅓   cup red wine vinegar
¼   cup Dijon-style mustard
½   teaspoon salt
       Dash pepper
1   tablespoon snipped chives

DIJON MUSTARD SAUCE
Measure all ingredients except chives into blender container; cover. Blend on medium-high speed until smooth, about 30 seconds. Stir in chives; refrigerate until ready to serve.

GATEAU AU CHOCOLAT (Chocolate Torte)

¾   cup all-purpose flour
¼   cup cocoa
1   teaspoon baking powder
¼   teaspoon salt
3   eggs
1   cup sugar
⅓   cup water
1   teaspoon vanilla

       Cream Filling (recipe
       follows)
       Chocolate Glaze (recipe
       follows)

       About ¼ cup chopped filberts

       Heat oven to 375°

1. Line jelly roll pan, 15½ x 10½ x 1 inch, with aluminum foil or waxed paper; grease. Mix flour, cocoa, baking powder and salt; set aside. Beat eggs in small mixer bowl until very thick and lemon colored, about 5 minutes. Pour eggs into large mixer bowl; gradually beat in sugar. Mix in water and vanilla on low speed. Add cocoa mixture gradually, beating just until batter is smooth. Pour into pan, spreading batter to corners.

2. Bake until wooden pick inserted in center comes out clean, 13 to 14 minutes. Remove from pan; cool.

3. Prepare Cream Filling; refrigerate. Prepare Chocolate Glaze.

4. Cut cake crosswise into 4 equal parts. Spread about 1 cup Cream Filling on each of 3 layers. Stack layers (plain one on top). Frost top with Chocolate Glaze; sprinkle with chopped filberts. Refrigerate until serving time, no longer than 36 hours.

TIP: Leftover torte can be frozen no longer than 1 month.

Chocolate Torte is layered with cream-filbert filling.

1 cup ricotta cheese
⅓ cup light cream or
   half-and-half
¾ cup butter or margarine,
   softened
1 cup powdered sugar
2 teaspoons vanilla
1 cup ground or finely
   chopped filberts (about 4
   ounces)

1 square (1 ounce) unsweetened
   chocolate
1½ tablespoons butter or
   margarine
½ cup powdered sugar
½ teaspoon vanilla
1 tablespoon hot water

CREAM FILLING

1. Measure cheese and cream into blender container; cover. Blend until smooth; set aside.

2. Beat butter until light; gradually add sugar, beating until light and fluffy. Beat in cheese mixture and vanilla gradually. (Filling may appear curdled.) Stir in filberts.

CHOCOLATE GLAZE

Melt chocolate and butter over low heat. Remove from heat; mix in sugar and vanilla. Stir in water, 1 teaspoon at a time, until glaze is proper spreading consistency.

An Italian Feast

Shown are Insalata, Gnocchi, Fettucini, Fagiolini and Saltimbocca.

ITALIAN DINNER MENU

- •NEGRONI COCKTAILS
- •ANTIPASTO DI FUNGHI CRUDI
  (Appetizer of Raw Mushrooms)
- •FETTUCINI AL FORNO (Baked
  Noodles)
- •SALTIMBOCCA ALLA ROMANA
  (Veal or Beef Rolls)
- •GRANITA DI LIMONE (Lemon Ice)
- •FAGIOLINI ALLA MARINARA
  (Green Beans with Tomato Sauce)
- •GNOCCHI VERDI (Spinach
  Dumplings)
- •INSALATA MISTA (Mixed Salad)
- •PANE CALDO (Hot Crusty Bread)
- •FRUTTA E FORMAGGIO (Fruit
  and Cheese)
- •CAFFE ESPRESSO (Italian Coffee)

•Recipes included

The colorful, flavorful foods of Italy are not highly spiced as much as they are an imaginative blending of tastes. Italian food is basically simple, and uses the freshest of vegetables, fruits and meats wherever possible.

Negronis, cocktails made with bittersweet Campari, and a simple marinated mushroom antipasto begin the meal. Saltimbocca, thin slices of veal rolled around prosciutto ham, are served with squares of Fettucini al Forno—noodles baked with eggs and cheese. A cold lemon ice may accompany the entrée or follow as a separate course. Either way, it nicely revitalizes the taste buds.

Gnocchi Verdi (Spinach Dumplings) are a nice change from pasta. Instructions for making them are given in the Step-By-Step Recipe. Italian salads—insalata—are always splendid creations. Choose your own components from a lengthy list of possibilities.

Fresh fruit and cheese are a typical Italian dessert combination. If you are dining in true Italian style, eat all the fruit—except for grapes—with knife and fork. Then wind up the meal with Caffè Espresso or freshly brewed black coffee. Either is excellent at the end of this meal. Espresso is quite strong so use twists of lemon peel as an attractive garnish and also to help lighten the flavor. Serves 8.

Wine Suggestion: With Fettucini, Soave-Ruffino. With Saltimbocca, Orvieto Secco (dry). With cheese, Chianti Classico.

PARTY PLAN FOR ITALIAN DINNER MENU

3 Days Before:	Make Tomato Sauce; refrigerate in tightly covered container. Make Oil-and-Wine Vinegar Dressing; refrigerate. Make Lemon Ice; freeze following special directions. Prepare Hot Crusty Bread through step 2 in recipe; freeze.
1 Day Before:	Prepare Appetizer of Raw Mushrooms through step 2 in recipe; cover and refrigerate. Prepare Veal Rolls through step 1 in recipe; cover and refrigerate. Prepare Spinach Dumplings through step 2 in recipe; cool, place in single layer, cover and refrigerate. Prepare greens for Mixed Salad; cover and refrigerate.
That Day: Afternoon	Prepare remaining ingredients for salad; refrigerate in separate containers. Clean and cut green beans; cover and refrigerate.
1 Hour 30 Minutes Before Serving:	Chill glasses for Lemon Ice. Prepare fruit centerpiece and plate of fruit for dessert.
1 Hour Before Serving:	Complete Veal Rolls (complete 1½ hours before serving time if using beef). Assemble ingredients for Italian Coffee; set aside. Heat frozen bread in oven. Prepare Baked Noodles through step 1 in recipe.
30 Minutes Before Serving:	Complete appetizer of Raw Mushrooms. Arrange cheeses on tray; set out at room temperature. Complete Spinach Dumplings. Complete Green Beans with Tomato Sauce; keep warm in separate pans over very low heat. Combine before serving. Bake prepared noodles. Complete Mixed Salad.
As Guests Arrive:	Mix Negroni Cocktails and serve with appetizer.
10 Minutes Before Dessert:	Make Italian Coffee.

NEGRONI COCKTAILS

Makes 3 cups

	Ice cubes
8	ounces gin
8	ounces sweet Italian vermouth
8	ounces Campari
	Lemon peel twists

Place 12 ice cubes in tall pitcher. Add gin, vermouth and Campari; stir and refrigerate. Serve over ice in old-fashioned glasses; garnish with lemon peel twists.

TIP: Campari can also be served over ice, or mixed half and half with vodka and served over ice.

ANTIPASTO DI FUNGHI CRUDI (Appetizer of Raw Mushrooms)

Makes 4 to 5 cups

1	pound fresh mushrooms, sliced ⅛ inch thick
¼	cup fresh lemon juice (about 2 lemons)
½	cup olive oil or vegetable oil
2	green onions (with tops), thinly sliced
¼	cup snipped parsley
1	clove garlic, finely chopped
¾	teaspoon salt
¼	teaspoon freshly ground black pepper
	Parsley sprigs
	Paprika
	*Grissini

1. Toss mushrooms with lemon juice in large bowl.

2. Stir in remaining ingredients except parsley sprigs, paprika and grissini; toss to mix and cover. Refrigerate, tossing once or twice, at least 3 hours, no longer than 24 hours.

3. Transfer to shallow serving bowl. Bring mushrooms to room temperature for best flavor. Garnish with parsley sprigs and sprinkle with paprika. Serve with grissini.

*TIP: *Crunchy grissini (very long, very thin breadsticks) are available in Italian bakeries.*

FETTUCINI AL FORNO (Baked Noodles)

1	pound fettucini noodles
½	cup butter or margarine, softened
½	cup milk
4	eggs, beaten
¾	cup grated Parmesan cheese
¼	cup Italian-style seasoned bread crumbs

Heat oven to 325°

1. Cook noodles according to package directions; drain and return to pan. Stir in butter, milk, eggs and cheese until butter is melted.

2. Spoon into greased baking dish, 13½ x 9 x 2 inches. Sprinkle with bread crumbs. Bake 15 to 20 minutes. Cut into squares to serve.

SALTIMBOCCA ALLA ROMANA (Veal or Beef Rolls)

3½	pounds veal or beef round steak, ½ inch thick
½	teaspoon dried sage leaves, crushed
½	teaspoon freshly ground black pepper
¼	pound prosciutto, smoked ham or boiled ham, sliced paper thin
¼	pound sliced Swiss cheese
¼	cup butter or margarine
2	tablespoons olive oil or vegetable oil
3	tablespoons flour
*¾	cup dry white wine
1½	cups water
	Parsley sprigs

1. Cut bone and fat from meat; pound meat until ⅛ inch thick. Rub 1 side of meat with sage and pepper. Cut meat into 12 to 16 pieces, 4 or 5 inches square. Divide ham and cheese onto seasoned sides of meat pieces. Roll up each carefully from 1 side; secure with wooden picks.**

2. Heat butter and oil in large skillet; brown meat on all sides over high heat, 5 to 10 minutes. Remove from heat. Place meat (leave drippings in skillet) in baking dish, 13½ x 9 x 2 inches. Arrange meat in single layer; set aside.

3. Heat oven to 325°. Stir flour into drippings in skillet; stir in wine and water. Heat to boiling. Pour over meat rolls. Cover baking dish with aluminum foil. Bake until tender, veal 35 minutes, beef 70 to 75 minutes. Garnish with parsley. Meat rolls can also be served cold, sliced thinly.

*TIPS: *Marsala wine is traditional.*

***At this point, meat rolls can be refrigerated no longer than 24 hours. When meat is refrigerated, use the round wooden picks—they are stronger.*

GRANITA DI LIMONE (Lemon Ice)

2   cups water
1   cup sugar
½   cup slivered fresh lemon
     peel (½ x ⅛ inch)
1   cup fresh lemon juice

1. Measure water and sugar into 2-quart saucepan. Cook and stir over medium heat until sugar is dissolved. Heat to boiling; reduce heat. Simmer uncovered 5 minutes. Remove from heat; cool to room temperature.

2. Stir lemon peel and juice into cooled mixture; pour into 9 x 5 x 3-inch metal loaf pan. Freeze about 3 hours, stirring every ½ hour and scraping crystals from edges of pan. *Serve in chilled individual dishes.

*TIPS: *If granita is not served immediately, freeze as directed above. After 3 hours, chop mixture with spoon into ½-inch chunks; place in bowl. Cover with aluminum foil or plastic wrap; return to freezer.*

Granita can be served as a dessert but in this menu it is served as a meat accompaniment. Texture of granita is granular and slightly coarse.

FAGIOLINI ALLA MARINARA (Green Beans with Tomato Sauce)

     Salsa Marinara (recipe
     follows)
*2   pounds fresh green beans

Prepare Salsa Marinara. Cut beans into 1½-inch pieces. Place beans in 1 inch salted water (½ teaspoon salt to 1 cup water). Heat to boiling; reduce heat and cover. Simmer until crisp-tender, 12 to 15 minutes. Drain. Arrange in serving dish; spoon Salsa Marinara over beans.

*TIP: *3 packages (9 ounces each) frozen beans can be substituted for the fresh beans in this recipe. Cook according to package directions; drain.*

*SALSA MARINARA (Sailor-Style Sauce)

¼   cup olive oil or vegetable
     oil
¼   cup butter or margarine
4   cloves garlic, crushed or
     finely minced
⅓   cup finely chopped onion
1   carrot, finely chopped
⅓   cup snipped parsley

3   cans (16 ounces each)
     tomatoes, undrained
**½ teaspoon salt
½   teaspoon pepper
1   tablespoon dried oregano
     leaves, crushed
1   teaspoon dried basil leaves,
     crushed
1   bay leaf
     Anchovy fillets, finely
     chopped, if desired
3   tablespoons tomato paste

1. Heat olive oil and butter in 3-quart saucepan. Cook and stir garlic, onion, carrot and parsley over medium heat until onion and carrot are tender, about 5 minutes (do not brown).

2. Stir tomatoes, salt,** pepper, oregano leaves, basil leaves and bay leaf into vegetable mixture (break up tomatoes). Heat to boiling; reduce heat. Simmer 40 minutes, stirring occasionally. Remove bay leaf. Stir in anchovies and tomato paste. Cook and stir 2 minutes.

*TIPS: *Salsa Marinara can be prepared 3 days in advance, cooled and refrigerated in a tightly covered container. At serving time, heat to boiling; reduce heat. Simmer 5 minutes.*

***Omit salt if anchovy fillets are used.*

GNOCCHI VERDI (Spinach Dumplings)

See STEP-BY-STEP RECIPE on page 159.

INSALATA MISTA (Mixed Salad)

*4   cups salad ingredients

**8 cups bite-sized greens, chilled
     Oil-and-Wine Vinegar Dressing
     (recipe follows)

1. Prepare salad ingredients; refrigerate in separate containers until serving time.

2. Arrange salad greens in large salad bowl or large platter. Arrange salad ingredients on top. Drizzle with dressing. Serve immediately.

*TIPS: *Salad ingredients—choose 4 or more of the following: sliced green onions, red onion rings, marinated artichoke hearts, black olives, mild or medium-hot pickled peppers, anchovy fillets, julienne strips salami, capers, pimiento pieces and choose 4 or more of the following: cherry tomatoes, sliced cucumber, green pepper rings, sliced zucchini, parsley sprigs, sliced celery, canned or frozen artichoke hearts, sliced radishes, sliced mushrooms, raw cauliflower pieces, quartered hard-cooked eggs, canned chick peas (garbanzo beans), julienne strips cheese.*

***Salad greens—select 2 or 3 of the following: romaine, iceberg lettuce, Boston lettuce, bibb lettuce, endive, escarole, dandelion greens.*

OIL-AND-WINE VINEGAR DRESSING

1 cup olive oil	1. Measure all ingredients into jar with tight-fitting lid; shake to blend. Refrigerate,* no longer than 4 days.
⅓ cup red wine vinegar	
3 tablespoons fresh lemon juice	2. Allow dressing to come to room temperature. Remove garlic pieces from dressing and shake well just before tossing with salad.
2 teaspoons salt	
1½ teaspoons freshly ground black pepper	*TIP: *Salad greens can be prepared and refrigerated one day in advance. Salad (except for dressing) can be assembled in serving bowl, covered with plastic wrap and refrigerated 2 hours in advance.*
2 cloves garlic, peeled, halved	

PANE CALDO (Hot Crusty Bread)

1 one-pound loaf Italian or French bread (14 to 16 inches long)	1. Cut bread into ¾-inch slices, cutting just to the bottom crust.
	2. Mix crushed garlic clove and butter. Spread bread slices generously with butter. Wrap loaf completely but loosely with aluminum foil.*
1 clove garlic, crushed, if desired	
½ cup butter or margarine, softened	3. Heat 25 to 30 minutes. For a very crisp crust, open foil last 5 minutes of baking. Wrap hot bread in napkins and serve immediately from basket or breadboard, allowing each guest to pull his own portion from the loaf.
Heat oven to 325°	
	*TIP: *Bread can be sliced, buttered and wrapped in foil several hours in advance of heating. Or, at this point, bread can be frozen no longer than 1 month. Heat unthawed loaf in 325° oven 45 to 50 minutes.*

FRUTTA E FORMAGGIO (Fruit and Cheese)

4 crisp red apples (Red Delicious or Jonathan)	Refrigerate fruits. Allow cheeses to come to room temperature before serving. Arrange fruits and cheeses attractively on serving platter. Garnish with lemon leaves or endive if desired.
4 ripe pears (Bosc or D'Anjou)	
½ pound red grapes	
½ pound green grapes	
½ pound Bel Paese cheese	
½ pound blue cheese	
½ pound provolone cheese	

CAFFE ESPRESSO (Italian Coffee)

10 cups water	Make coffee in regular drip or percolator coffeepot, or in espresso coffeepot according to manufacturer's directions. Serve in demitasse cups. Garnish with lemon peel twists. Sugar can be used if desired.
1¼ cups finely ground Italian-roast coffee	
Lemon peel twists	
Sugar	*TIPS: Italian coffee is available in specialty and gourmet food stores and in many supermarkets. Instant espresso is also available; prepare according to package directions.*
	If desired, freshly brewed strong black coffee can be served instead of espresso and would be entirely appropriate with the menu.

1.

2.

3.   4.   5.

6	tablespoons butter or margarine
1	tablespoon finely chopped onion
3	packages (10 ounces each) frozen chopped spinach, thawed, drained
1	cup ricotta cheese or sieved cottage cheese
¾	cup all-purpose flour
½	cup grated Parmesan cheese
¾	teaspoon salt
½	teaspoon pepper
¼	teaspoon garlic powder
¼	teaspoon ground nutmeg or mace
2	tablespoons snipped parsley
2	eggs, slightly beaten Flour
3	quarts water
3	tablespoons instant chicken bouillon
¼	cup butter or margarine, melted
½	cup grated Parmesan cheese Parmesan cheese

1. Melt 6 tablespoons butter in large skillet; cook and stir onion in butter until tender. Add spinach; cook and stir over medium heat until spinach is quite dry, 4 to 5 minutes (photo 1). Mix in ricotta cheese; cook and stir 3 minutes. Transfer to large bowl.

2. Mix in flour, ½ cup Parmesan cheese, the salt, pepper, garlic powder, nutmeg and parsley. Cool mixture 5 minutes. Stir in eggs (photo 2). Drop spinach mixture, 2 tablespoons at a time, into small bowl of flour; roll to coat with flour (photo 3). Shape into balls.*

3. Measure water and chicken bouillon into 4-quart saucepan. Heat to boiling; reduce heat. Simmer, stirring to dissolve bouillon. Drop balls into broth; cook uncovered until gnocchi are quite firm and rise to top of broth, about 10 minutes (photo 4). (Avoid overcrowding; cook in several batches if necessary.) Remove from broth with slotted spoon.

4. Place gnocchi in serving dish; drizzle with ¼ cup butter. Sprinkle ½ cup Parmesan cheese on gnocchi (photo 5). Serve with additional grated Parmesan cheese. (Gnocchi can be kept warm in 200° oven 30 to 45 minutes. Often called Ravioli Verdi.)

*TIP: *Gnocchi can be prepared to this point 24 hours in advance. Cool and place in single layer in a covered glass or plastic container. Refrigerate.*

A Mexican Fiesta

Margarita Punch served with appetizers.   Flan, cookies and a liqueur are desse

Mexico's colorful cuisine is one of the world's oldest. Much of the country's cookery is more Aztecan than Spanish; it can be traced as far back as A.D. 900. This menu includes some new interpretations of Mexican cooking.

The Mexican custom of taking a lick of salt, a taste of fiery tequila and a bit of lime is translated into our Margarita Punch recipe. Rub the rim of the glass with fresh lime, then dip it into coarse salt.

Sesame seed-sprinkled turkey is served with legendary molé sauce. The strange-sounding ingredients of this sauce—pumpkin seeds, almonds, peanuts, cumin, anise, cinnamon and unsweetened chocolate—blend to make a dark and subtly different, yet not chocolaty, taste. The idea of using unsweetened chocolate in this way is said to have originated with Montezuma, the last Aztec emperor.

The accompaniments to this turkey are designed to provide visual drama and textural contrast. Rice Chile Verde is rice with cheese, sour cream and chilies. The unusual salad is made of whole cauliflowers and crowned with avocado.

Flan is a typical Mexican dessert. It's the south-of-the-border version of baked custard, in caramel sauce. Sugar-cookie Mexican Wedding Cakes complement Flan well. As a finale, make a tequila liqueur. It's delicious, and tasty anytime. Serves 10.

Wine Suggestion: Have a nice Chilean wine with the dinner—Undurraga Cabernet.

Turkey Molé, rice-cheese casserole, hot tortillas and cauliflower-avocado salad
are fiesta fare.

PARTY PLAN FOR MEXICAN DINNER MENU

3 Weeks Before: Prepare Berry Liqueur through step 1 in recipe; refrigerate.

1 Week Before: Make Mexican Wedding Cakes. Store in airtight container.

3 Days Before: Make Salted Pumpkin Seeds. Cool; store in airtight container.

1 Day Before: Prepare Turkey Molé through step 4 in recipe; refrigerate.
Make Chile Con Queso and Frijoles Dip. Store covered in refrigerator.
Make Mexican Coffee, strain, and store in refrigerator.

That Day: Morning Make Flan; refrigerate.
Roll Mexican Wedding Cakes second time in sugar.
Cook cauliflower; refrigerate.
Strain Berry Liqueur and pour into decanter.

That Day: Afternoon Make avocado topping for cauliflower. Store covered in refrigerator.
Prepare carrot and celery sticks; drain ripe olives.

2 Hours Before Serving: Prepare Margarita Punch through step 2 in recipe. Cover punch and refrigerate. Rim punch glasses with salt.
Prepare Rice Chile Verde through step 1 in recipe; cover and refrigerate.

1 Hour Before Serving: Heat oven to 300°. Put turkey, rice and tortillas in oven together.

20 Minutes Before Guests Arrive: Complete Cauliflower Ensalada; refrigerate.
Heat appetizer dips and put into servers.
Complete Margarita Punch.

15 Minutes Before Dessert: Heat coffee until hot.
Unmold Flan onto dessert dishes.

MARGARITA PUNCH

Makes 1¼ quarts

6   limes
1½ bottles (⁴/₅-quart size) tequila
1   bottle (⁴/₅ pint—about 1½ cups) orange-flavored liqueur

Salt

6   to 8 cups crushed ice
Lime slices

1. Squeeze limes, reserving rinds. Mix tequila, liqueur and lime juice; refrigerate.

2. Rub rims of glasses or punch cups with lime rind, then dip into a bowl of salt to coat rims.

3. Pour tequila mixture over crushed ice in pitcher or punch bowl. Garnish with lime slices. Ladle into glasses; sip through salt.

TIP: Increase recipe for number of drinks you will be serving. Additional Margaritas may be mixed and refrigerated, adding crushed ice just before serving.

FRIJOLES DIP

Makes about 2 cups

1 can (15 ounces) refried beans
2 tablespoons milk
*½ cup (2 ounces) shredded Monterey Jack cheese

Carrot and celery sticks
Snipped parsley

1. Mix beans and milk in small saucepan; heat, stirring constantly. Stir in cheese. Cook and stir until cheese is melted.

2. Serve in fondue pot or chafing dish with carrot and celery sticks for dipping. Garnish with parsley.

*TIPS: *Brick or mozzarella cheese can be substituted for Monterey Jack cheese.*

Dip can be prepared 24 hours in advance. Store covered in refrigerator. To serve, heat in double boiler until smooth.

CHILE CON QUESO

Makes about 3 cups

½ cup finely chopped onion
2 tablespoons butter or margarine
1 can (4 ounces) peeled green chilies, seeded, chopped
1 cup drained solid pack tomatoes
½ teaspoon salt
Pepper to taste
*½ pound Monterey Jack cheese, cubed
¾ cup light cream

Corn chips

1. Cook and stir onion in butter over medium heat about 5 minutes. Stir in chilies, tomatoes, salt and pepper.

2. Heat to boiling; reduce heat. Simmer 15 minutes; stir in cheese. Stir in cream when cheese begins to melt. Cook and stir until cheese is melted; cook 10 minutes longer.

3. Serve in fondue pot or chafing dish with corn chips for dipping.

*TIPS: *Brick or mozzarella cheese can be substituted for Monterey Jack cheese.*

Dip can be prepared 24 hours in advance. Store covered in refrigerator. To serve, heat in double boiler until smooth. Chile Con Queso is available in a canned mix in many areas.

SALTED PUMPKIN SEEDS

Makes 1 cup

1 cup (about 5 ounces) pumpkin seeds
2 tablespoons butter or margarine
1 teaspoon salt

Heat oven to 350°

1. Place seeds and butter in ungreased shallow baking pan.

2. Bake, stirring occasionally, until seeds are golden brown and skins begin to crack, about 12 minutes.

3. Drain on paper toweling. Toss seeds with salt. Serve warm or at room temperature.

TIP: Pumpkin seeds can be prepared 24 hours in advance. Store in airtight container.

TURKEY MOLE

1   turkey (8 to 10 pounds),
        cut into serving-size pieces

1¾   cups chopped onions
3   cloves garlic, finely chopped
¼   cup butter or margarine
4   tortillas, torn into
        pieces and dried

4   squares (4 ounces) unsweetened
        chocolate, chopped
⅓   cup slivered almonds
⅓   cup peanuts
*⅓   cup pumpkin seed
¼   cup sesame seed, toasted

½   to ¾ cup chili powder
2   to 3 tablespoons sugar
2   teaspoons ground cumin
1   teaspoon salt
¼   teaspoon anise seed
1   cinnamon stick (2-inch),
        broken into small pieces

1   teaspoon sesame seed,
        toasted

1. Place turkey pieces in large pan(s). Add salted water (1 tablespoon salt to 1 quart water) to cover turkey. Heat to boiling; reduce heat and cover. Simmer until thickest pieces are tender, about 1½ hours. Drain turkey, reserving 1 quart turkey broth. Place turkey pieces in ungreased baking dishes.

2. Cook onions and garlic in butter until onions are tender. Pour 1 cup of the reserved turkey broth, the tortilla pieces and onion mixture into blender container; cover. ** Blend until smooth, about 1 minute. Pour onion mixture into large bowl.

3. Pour 1½ cups of the reserved turkey broth, the chocolate, almonds, peanuts, pumpkin seed and ¼ cup sesame seed into blender container; cover. Blend until smooth, about 1 minute. Add to onion mixture in bowl.

4. Pour remaining 1½ cups reserved turkey broth, the chili powder, sugar, cumin, salt, anise and cinnamon into blender container; cover. Blend until smooth, about 1 minute. Add to onion mixture in bowl. Mix all ingredients. Mixture will be consistency of chocolate sauce. Pour sauce over turkey pieces; cover. Refrigerate no longer than 24 hours.

5. Heat oven to 300°. Bake turkey until hot, about 50 minutes. Before serving, sprinkle with 1 teaspoon toasted sesame seed.

*TIPS: *Sunflower seeds can be substituted for pumpkin seeds.*

***If blender is not available, ingredients can be finely ground in food grinder.*

Molé sauce is available in canned and mix forms in many areas. Our molé sauce recipe makes about 6 cups. Use this amount of canned sauce.

RICE CHILE VERDE

3   cups dairy sour cream
1   can (4 ounces) peeled green
        chilies, seeded, chopped
4½   cups cooked rice
*1   pound Monterey Jack cheese,
        cut into thin slices

¾   cup (3 ounces) shredded
        Cheddar cheese
        Whole chilies, canned or fresh

        Heat oven to 300°

1. Mix sour cream and chopped chilies. Layer 1½ cups rice, 1½ cups sour cream mixture and half of the cheese slices in buttered 3-quart casserole. Repeat, ending with 1½ cups rice on top.

2. Bake uncovered until hot, 45 minutes. Sprinkle with Cheddar cheese. Bake 5 minutes or until cheese is melted. Garnish with whole chilies.

*TIP: *Brick or mozzarella cheese can be substituted for Monterey Jack cheese.*

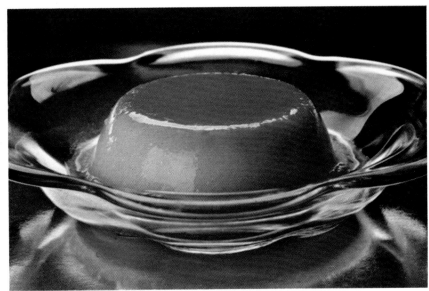

Flan forms its own caramel syrup as it bakes.

CAULIFLOWER ENSALADA

2	medium (about 2 pounds each) cauliflowers
6	ripe avocados, peeled, pitted
1	cup finely chopped onions
2	tablespoons vinegar
2	teaspoons salt
¼	teaspoon pepper
1	can (4 ounces) peeled green chilies, seeded, chopped
	Lettuce leaves
	Radish roses

1. Heat 1 inch salted water (½ teaspoon salt to 1 cup water) to boiling in each of 2 large saucepans; add cauliflowers and cover. Heat to boiling; reduce heat. Cook until tender, 20 to 25 minutes. Drain and refrigerate.

2. Mash avocados until smooth. Mix in onions, vinegar, salt, pepper and chilies; cover. Refrigerate until ready to use.

3. Place chilled cauliflowers on serving platter. Cut each cauliflower into 5 wedges; do not separate wedges. Spread avocado mixture over cauliflowers. Arrange lettuce leaves and radish roses around cauliflowers.

HOT BUTTERED TORTILLAS

20	tortillas
	Soft butter or margarine
	Heat oven to 300°

1. Stack and wrap tortillas tightly in 2 aluminum foil packets.

2. Heat 50 minutes. Remove aluminum foil. Wrap tortillas in a colorful napkin to keep warm. Serve in breadbasket with butter for spreading.

TIP: Freshly made tortillas are delightful to serve, if available in your area. Frozen or canned tortillas may also be used in this recipe.

FLAN

See STEP-BY-STEP RECIPE on page 167.

MEXICAN WEDDING CAKES

Makes about 4 dozen cookies

1   cup butter or margarine,
    softened
½   cup powdered sugar
1   teaspoon vanilla
2¼   cups all-purpose flour
¼   teaspoon salt
¾   cup finely chopped nuts

    Powdered sugar

    Heat oven to 400°

1. Mix butter, ½ cup powdered sugar and vanilla. Stir in flour, salt and nuts until dough holds together.

2. Shape dough into 1-inch balls. Place on ungreased baking sheet. Bake 10 to 12 minutes or until set, but not brown.

3. Roll in powdered sugar while warm. Cool. Roll in sugar again before serving.

TIP: Cookies can be stored in airtight container no longer than 1 week or frozen no longer than 2 months.

MEXICAN COFFEE

Makes about 3½ cups

4   cups water
½   cup packed dark brown sugar
1   cinnamon stick (2-inch)
4   whole cloves
¼   cup regular grind coffee

1. Heat water, sugar, cinnamon and cloves in saucepan, stirring until sugar is dissolved. Add coffee. Heat to boiling; reduce heat. Simmer uncovered 2 minutes. Stir; cover saucepan.

2. Heat on low heat a few minutes until grounds settle. Strain and serve in demitasse cups.

TIP: Coffee can be prepared 24 hours in advance. Strain and store covered in refrigerator.

BERRY LIQUEUR

Makes about 1¼ cups

4   cups strawberries, halved
    About 2 cups tequila

1. Place strawberries in jar with tight-fitting lid. Add enough tequila to cover strawberries. Cover tightly. Refrigerate at least 3 weeks.

2. Strain through cheesecloth. Pour liqueur into decanter. Serve in chilled liqueur glasses.

TIP: For a special treat some other time, use strawberries to prepare a sauce for ice cream. Heat 1 cup sugar and 1 cup water to boiling. Boil 5 minutes. Add strawberries and 1 teaspoon red food color; heat to boiling. Boil 5 minutes. Cover and chill.

1.

2.

3.

4.

½   **cup sugar**

5   **eggs**

⅓   **cup sugar**

1   **can (13½ ounces) evaporated milk**

1   **cup water**

1   **tablespoon vanilla**

1   **teaspoon almond extract**

   Heat oven to 350°

1. Heat ½ cup sugar in small skillet over medium heat, stirring occasionally, until syrup turns an even amber color, about 5 minutes. Divide into ten 6-ounce custard cups, about 1 teaspoonful for each cup (photo 1). Set cups aside.

2. Beat eggs with fork until well mixed and bubbly. Stir ⅓ cup sugar gradually into eggs (photo 2). Mix in remaining ingredients.

3. Divide custard into prepared cups. Place cups in shallow baking pan on oven rack; pour very hot water into pan to within ½ inch of tops of cups (photo 3).

4. Bake until table knife or small spatula inserted halfway between center and edge comes out clean, about 15 minutes (photo 4). Remove cups from water with spatula. Cool at room temperature 45 minutes.

5. Chill at least 2 hours, but no longer than 18 hours. Loosen edges of custard with spatula. Invert onto dessert dishes with rims.

An Indian Table

Deep-fried pastries have a choice of two fillings.

Carrot Pudding is served warm.

INDIAN DINNER MENU

- •SAMOSAS (Deep-fried Filled Pastries)
- •DAL SHORBA (Lentil Soup)
- •PATRANI MACHLI (Fish Stuffed with Chutney)
- •MURGHI KARI (Chicken Curry)
- •MASSALE DAR PILAU (Spicy Rice)
- •SAME KI BHAJI (Green Beans with Coconut)
- •CHATNI (Chutney)
- •SIDE DISHES
- •PAPPADAMS (Bread)
- •GAJAR HALVA (Carrot Pudding) TEA

•Recipes included

168

India's cuisine is as fascinatingly varied as its multitudes of people and the awesome diversity of its land. The magic blend of spices called curry is the keynote of Indian cooking and this menu includes several flavorful curry dishes.

Because the cow is held sacred in India, you will not find beef used in an authentic Indian menu. Tiny, crisp pastries called Samosas make a tasty appetizer course. They are filled with curried lamb or shrimp and served piping hot. Dal Shorba is a thick, smooth soup containing pureed lentils and spices, again with curry.

Whole fish stuffed with freshly made chutney is the hot and spicy main dish. Murghi Kari, Chicken Curry, is mildly hot, and goes well with spiced rice pilau. Place small dishes of chopped hard-cooked eggs, nuts, onion, toasted coconut, cucumbers and chutney on the table, ready for sprinkling on top of the curry or eating on the side. Gingered green beans cooked with coconut are the vegetable accompaniment and Pappadams, spicy thin bread wafers fried crisp and hot, add their own taste and texture to the dinner.

An unlikely sounding dessert, Carrot Pudding is sweet, rich and really good. Lightly spiced with nutmeg and saffron, it is served warm, topped with pistachio nuts. Serves 8 to 10.

Wine Suggestion: Beer is the best choice for this menu.

Fish stuffed with Chutney and Chicken Curry are served with Lentil Soup. Spicy Rice, Green Beans with Coconut and fried bread.

PARTY PLAN FOR INDIAN DINNER MENU

1 Week Before:

Make Clarified Butter; cover and refrigerate.
Make Chutney; cover and refrigerate.
Make pastries; cool, wrap in aluminum foil. Freeze.

2 Days Before:

Make Lentil Soup; cover and refrigerate.
Make Chicken Curry; cover and refrigerate.

1 Day Before:

Prepare Carrot Pudding through step 2 in recipe; cover and refrigerate.
Fry bread; cover tightly.
Chill beer.

That Day: Afternoon

Cut green beans for Green Beans with Coconut and prepare through step 1 in recipe; cover and refrigerate.
Prepare garnishes and Side Dishes for menu; cover and refrigerate.

1 Hour 30 Minutes Before Serving:

Make Fish Stuffed with Chutney.
Make Spicy Rice.

30 Minutes Before Serving:

Complete Green Beans with Coconut.
Heat Lentil Soup.
Heat oven to 375°; heat pastries.
Heat Chicken Curry.

15 Minutes Before Dessert:

Heat Carrot Pudding; garnish.
Make tea.

SAMOSAS (Deep-fried Filled Pastries)

Makes about 40 appetizers

2 cups all-purpose flour
¾ teaspoon salt
¼ cup butter or margarine
¾ cup unflavored yogurt
   Lamb or Shrimp Filling
   (recipes follow)
1 quart vegetable oil
   *Ti leaf, lemon wedges and
   parsley, if desired

1. Mix flour and salt; cut in butter. Stir in yogurt. Shape dough into ball; cover with damp cloth. Refrigerate 2 hours.

2. Prepare either Lamb or Shrimp Filling.

3. Roll ¼ of the dough ¹⁄₁₆ inch thick on lightly floured cloth-covered board. Cut into 4-inch circles. Cut each circle in half. Moisten edges with water. (Cover remaining dough with damp cloth until needed.)

4. Place 1 teaspoonful filling on each half circle. Fold dough over filling forming triangle. Press edges together securely; place on baking sheet and cover. Refrigerate while preparing remaining pastries. (Pastries can be stored in refrigerator no longer than 24 hours before frying.)

5. Heat oven to 225°. Heat oil in deep fat fryer or kettle to 375°. Fry about 5 pastries at a time until light brown on both sides, about 4 minutes. Keep warm in oven while frying remaining pastries.** Arrange pastries on ti leaf on platter. Garnish with lemon wedges and parsley.

*TIPS: *Ti leaves can be purchased in florist shops.*

**Samosas can be stored wrapped tightly in aluminum foil in freezer no longer than 2 weeks. To serve, heat oven to 375°. Place pastries on ungreased baking sheet. Bake until hot, about 10 minutes.

LAMB FILLING   *Makes about 2 cups*

½ cup finely chopped onion
2 cloves garlic, finely chopped
2 tablespoons vegetable oil
¾ pound ground lamb
1 tablespoon curry powder
1 teaspoon salt
1 teaspoon crushed coriander seed
1 teaspoon crushed cumin seed
½ teaspoon freshly ground black pepper
3 tablespoons unflavored yogurt

Cook and stir onion and garlic in oil over medium heat 8 minutes. Mix in remaining ingredients except yogurt. Cook, stirring constantly, until meat loses red color. Mix in yogurt; reduce heat. Cook over low heat, stirring occasionally, 15 minutes. Cool slightly and cover. Refrigerate.

SHRIMP FILLING   *Makes about 2 cups*

½ cup finely chopped onion
1 clove garlic, finely chopped
2 tablespoons butter or margarine
¾ pound shrimp, shelled, deveined, chopped
¼ cup diced peeled tomatoes
1 teaspoon salt
1 teaspoon crushed coriander seed
1 teaspoon crushed cumin seed
⅛ teaspoon crushed red peppers
2 hard-cooked eggs, finely chopped

Cook and stir onion and garlic in butter over medium heat 8 minutes. Mix in remaining ingredients except eggs. Cook, stirring frequently, 5 minutes. Cool slightly; stir in eggs and cover. Refrigerate.

DAL SHORBA (Lentil Soup)   *Makes about 2 quarts*

5 cups chicken broth
4 cups water
2 cups lentils

½ cup chopped onion
1 clove garlic, finely chopped
2 teaspoons Indian curry powder
1 teaspoon crushed coriander seed
1 teaspoon salt
¼ teaspoon crushed red peppers
2 tablespoons butter or margarine

½ cup light cream
Lemon slices, if desired

1. Mix broth, water and lentils in large saucepan. Heat to boiling; reduce heat and cover. Simmer over low heat 1 hour.

2. Cook and stir onion, garlic, curry, coriander, salt and red peppers in butter over medium heat 7 minutes. Stir spice mixture into lentils; cover. Cook over low heat 20 minutes.

3. Puree about 3 cups of the lentil mixture in covered blender container. Repeat until all lentil mixture has been pureed. Stir in cream. Heat until hot. (If soup is too thick, stir in small amount cream.)* Garnish with lemon slices.

*TIP: *Dal Shorba can be prepared 48 hours in advance. Store covered in refrigerator. To serve, heat until hot.*

PATRANI MACHLI (Fish Stuffed with Chutney)

2 teaspoons salt
2 cloves garlic, finely
    chopped
1 teaspoon crushed coriander
    seed
1 teaspoon crushed cumin seed
½ teaspoon freshly ground
    black pepper
*2 whole red snappers (about 2
    pounds each), split, boned

1 cup Chatni (recipe follows)

3 eggs, beaten
½ cup cornstarch
1 teaspoon salt
½ teaspoon freshly ground
    black pepper

1 cup vegetable oil
   Ti leaves, if desired
   Lemon wedges

1 pound apples, chopped
    (about 5 cups)
½ pound dried apricots or
    peaches, chopped (about 2
    cups)
3 limes or lemons, cut into
    thin wedges, seeds removed
1½ cups packed brown sugar
1 cup cider vinegar
2 cloves garlic, finely chopped
2 teaspoons ground ginger
1½ teaspoons salt
1 teaspoon ground cinnamon
1 teaspoon chili powder
½ teaspoon ground coriander
½ teaspoon ground cloves
½ teaspoon freshly ground
    black pepper
¼ teaspoon crushed red peppers

1. Mix 2 teaspoons salt, the garlic, coriander, cumin and ½ teaspoon pepper. Rub cavity and outside of fish with spice mixture; cover. Let stand 30 minutes.

2. Spread ½ cup Chatni in cavity of each fish. Close opening with skewers; lace.

3. Mix eggs, cornstarch, 1 teaspoon salt and ½ teaspoon pepper. Dip fish into egg mixture.

4. Heat ½ cup of the vegetable oil in large skillet until hot. Place 1 fish in hot oil; reduce heat to medium. Fry fish 10 minutes on each side. Remove and keep warm. Repeat for second fish. Arrange fish on ti leaves on platter. Garnish with lemon wedges.

*TIP: *Four pounds fillet of sole can be substituted for red snappers. Reduce Chatni to ¾ cup and cooking time to about 4 minutes on each side.*

CHATNI (Chutney)   *Makes about 1 quart*

Mix all ingredients in large saucepan. Heat to boiling; reduce heat. Cook over low heat, stirring frequently, until soft and brown, about 1 hour. Cool slightly and cover. Serve at room temperature.

TIP: Chatni can be stored covered in the refrigerator 2 weeks.

MURGHI KARI (Chicken Curry)

2 tablespoons sesame seed
1 tablespoon salt
1 tablespoon finely chopped
   ginger root
2 teaspoons coriander seed
1 teaspoon cumin seed
1 teaspoon ground turmeric
½ teaspoon peppercorns
¼ teaspoon crushed red peppers
¼ teaspoon fennel seed

2 cups chopped onions
2 cloves garlic, finely chopped
⅓ cup Ghee (recipe follows)

2 broiler-fryer chickens (2½
   pounds each), cut up
¾ cup unflavored yogurt
½ cup chopped peeled tomatoes
2 tablespoons snipped
   coriander leaves or parsley
   Tomato wedges

1 pound unsalted butter

1. Place sesame seed, salt and spices in blender container; cover. Blend until powdered.

2. Cook and stir onions and garlic in Ghee in Dutch oven until onions are golden brown. Stir in spice mixture. Cook and stir 2 minutes.

3. Stir chicken into onion mixture. Cook over medium heat, stirring frequently, 5 minutes. Stir in yogurt and ½ cup tomatoes. Heat to boiling; reduce heat and cover. Cook over low heat, stirring occasionally, until thickest pieces are tender, about 45 minutes.* Sprinkle with coriander leaves. Garnish with tomato wedges.

*TIP: *Murghi Kari can be prepared 48 hours in advance. Cool slightly and cover; refrigerate. To serve, skim layer of fat from yogurt mixture. Heat until hot and garnish.*

GHEE (Clarified Butter)   *Makes about 1⅔ cups*

1. Cut 1 pound unsalted butter into 8 pieces; place in saucepan. Heat over medium heat, stirring frequently, until butter is melted. Heat over high heat to boiling, until butter foams; reduce heat. Cook over low heat 30 minutes.

2. Line strainer with several layers of damp cheesecloth. Pour butter slowly through cheesecloth into dry jar; cover. (If any solids go through, strain until Ghee is completely clear.) Refrigerate until needed. Let stand at room temperature just before using, about 30 minutes.

TIP: Ghee is traditionally preferred in many Indian recipes. Butter can be used but it has a much lower burning point, due to the milk solids. The milk solids are discarded when Ghee is prepared.

MASSALE DAR PILAU (Spicy Rice)

2	cups uncooked long grain rice
2	onions, thinly sliced
6	tablespoons Ghee (see above recipe)
1	cup unflavored yogurt
1½	teaspoons salt
2	cloves garlic, finely chopped
3	cardamom seeds, crushed
½	teaspoon ground turmeric
½	teaspoon ground ginger
¼	teaspoon crushed red peppers
3	cups hot chicken broth
	Green pepper rings and tomato wedges, if desired

1. Cover rice with water; let soak 30 minutes.

2. Cook and stir onions in Ghee in large saucepan until onions are brown. Drain rice. Cook and stir rice in onion mixture 5 minutes. Stir in remaining ingredients except broth, green peppers and tomatoes. Cook over high heat 5 minutes. Stir in broth; cover.

3. Heat rice mixture to boiling; reduce heat. Cook over low heat until rice is tender, about 25 minutes. Garnish with pepper rings and tomato wedges.

SAME KI BHAJI (Green Beans with Coconut)

1	cup flaked coconut
1	cup water
1	cup chopped onion
¼	teaspoon mustard seed
1	clove garlic, finely chopped
2	tablespoons vegetable oil
*2	pounds green beans, cut into 2-inch pieces
1	tablespoon crushed coriander seed
1½	teaspoons salt
1	teaspoon ground ginger
½	teaspoon ground turmeric

1. Measure coconut and water into blender container; cover. Blend on medium speed, scraping sides of container if necessary, 3 minutes; reserve.

2. Cook and stir onion, mustard seed and garlic in oil in 12-inch skillet or Dutch oven over medium heat, 5 minutes. Mix in remaining ingredients and reserved coconut mixture; cover.

3. Heat to boiling; reduce heat. Simmer, stirring occasionally, 15 minutes.

*TIP: *3 packages (9 ounces each) frozen cut green beans, thawed, can be substituted for 2 pounds fresh green beans.*

SIDE DISHES

Side dishes are often served with an Indian meal. They are passed and eaten with all the foods for texture and flavor contrast. Side dishes can include:

Hard-Cooked Egg—Chopped.
Nuts—Chopped.
Coconut—Toasted.
Onion—Chopped and mixed with yogurt.
Cucumber—Chopped and mixed with yogurt.
Chutney—See recipe on page 172.

PAPPADAMS (Bread)

Makes about 30

Vegetable oil
*1 package pappadams
(about 30)

Heat 2 inches oil to 375°. Fry bread in oil until brown, about 30 seconds on each side. Drain on paper toweling.**

*TIPS: *Pappadams can be purchased at specialty and gourmet shops.*

***Pappadams can be fried 48 hours in advance; cover tightly and store at room temperature.*

GAJAR HALVA (Carrot Pudding)

1 package (1 pound) carrots, pared, grated (about 5 cups)
1½ cups milk
½ cup whipping cream
1 cup ground blanched almonds
½ cup packed brown sugar
¼ cup butter or margarine
¼ teaspoon ground nutmeg
⅛ teaspoon ground saffron
¼ cup unsalted pistachio or pine nuts

1. Mix carrots, milk, and cream in saucepan. Heat to boiling, stirring constantly; reduce heat. Cook over medium heat, stirring frequently, until milk and cream are absorbed, about 45 minutes.

2. Stir in almonds, brown sugar, butter, nutmeg and saffron. Cook over low heat, stirring frequently, 20 minutes.*

3. Spoon Carrot Pudding on serving dish, mounding it in center. Garnish with pistachio nuts. Serve warm.

*TIP: *Gajar Halva can be prepared 24 hours in advance. Cool slightly and cover. Refrigerate. To serve, heat over low heat, stirring frequently, until warm. Proceed with step 3.*

Outdoor Edibles

Almost any kind of food tastes especially good when it is eaten out of doors. Fresh air has an amazing effect upon appetites, and an enjoyable feeling of relaxation is generated by open-air dining. Alfresco meals can be remarkably diverse, ranging from casual backyard barbecues to elegant luncheons or dinners on the patio, from wooden tables on the lawn loaded with food for a crowd to picnics anywhere.

Gather together cousins, uncles, aunts and grandparents from far and near this Fourth of July and treat them to the Family Reunion Spread, a truly splendid array of foods. It's an old-fashioned meal perfect for this traditional American custom—but this bountiful spread would be just as well received by any congenial group you choose to invite. The recipes are well-loved old standards, brightened with some innovative touches.

Our second outdoor menu is a picnic—an unusual one, in the Gallic style. The foods are specialties of Provence, a region in southeastern France which borders on Italy. Provençal cuisine is simple and well-cooked, with a strong Mediterranean flavor—olive oil, garlic, eggplant and zucchini are basic elements.

Entertain the carefree way with a buffet in your backyard. Set it out at midday or in the early evening: the Marinated Beef Menu is ideal for serving at midday or in the early evening, for it includes an interesting variety of party foods. Daytime outdoor meals are best served casually, but any of them can become elegantly formal at night. Special lighting and candles in hurricane lamps create a delightful atmosphere.

Three of our outdoor menus are based on grilled foods. Barbecue units have become immensely popular items; equipment can vary from an inexpensive portable grill purchased at the supermarket to a costly permanent unit. Charcoal briquets are most often used as fuel, and take about 30 to 45 minutes to reach the right stage for grilling. Coals should look gray in daytime and glow red at night—no flame should show. For best results, follow the manufacturer's directions included with your grill.

The Grilled Steak and Grilled Fish Menus both offer simple foods, perfectly cooked. Each meal includes fresh fruit, once as a dessert, the other time as an appetizer. The Grilled Turkey Menu provides an unexpected summertime meal; grilling on a spit gives the turkey an especially choice flavor. All three of these barbecue menus require very little preparation; the bulk of the entrée work is done by the grill and most of the other recipes may be made in advance.

A family spread includes crispy chicken, sloppy joes, baked beans and a trio of salads (see menu on page 178).

Family Reunion Spread

Raspberry preserves are layered between cake and frosting.

BAKED CHICKEN MENU

- GRANDMA'S BAKED CHICKEN
- CHILI JOES
- UNCLE HARRY'S BAKED BEANS
- COUSIN MARTHA'S POTATO SALAD
- HATTIE'S BEAN SALAD
- AUNT SUSAN'S CABBAGE SLAW
- HERBED BISCUITS

  WATERMELON SLICES
- AUNT CLARA'S PRESERVES CAKE

  ICED TEA OR COFFEE

• Recipes included

Pictured on page 177.

This traditional American summertime meal provides a wide variety of hot and cold dishes, perfect for a big holiday celebration. The menu can easily be adapted to serve fewer people by omitting some recipes and cutting the amounts in those you choose to use.

Baking chicken is an easy method of cooking it, and the meat stays moist and tender. Grandma's Baked Chicken has a crackly coating with a touch of garlic. Chili Joes, our updated version of sloppy joes, please kids and grownups alike. Everyone can make their own, ladling the chopped beef mixture onto hamburger buns.

Uncle Harry's Baked Beans are cooked slowly, the old-fashioned way, with molasses spiced with cloves. The three summer salads are old-time favorites, too. Avocado slices create a smooth texture contrast in Hattie's Bean Salad. Herbed Biscuits are fast and easy to make, since you use a packaged mix. Onion and parsley are added to the dough and caraway seeds sprinkled on top. Serve them hot from oven or grill.

Raspberry preserves blended with orange juice make the filling for Aunt Clara's Preserves Cake. Maple flavoring is a different idea for the white frosting. Substitute another kind of preserves or flavoring if you wish, but this combination is unusually good. Serves 16.

Wine Suggestion: Don't let yourself be fooled. Grandmother's recipes are rich and slightly on the heavy side. Take a big Italian wine like Barolo, or a BV Cabernet Sauvignon from Napa Valley.

PARTY PLAN FOR BAKED CHICKEN MENU

1 Day Before:

Prepare Chili Joes through step 2 in recipe; cover and refrigerate.
Prepare Uncle Harry's Baked Beans through step 5 in recipe; cover and refrigerate.
Make Cousin Martha's Potato Salad except do not garnish; cover and refrigerate.
Make Hattie's Bean Salad; cover and refrigerate.
Make Aunt Susan's Cabbage Slaw except do not garnish; cover and refrigerate.
Prepare Aunt Clara's Preserves Cake through step 1 in recipe; cover.

1 Hour 15 Minutes Before Serving:

Complete Aunt Clara's Preserves Cake.
Make Grandma's Baked Chicken.
Heat baked beans in oven until hot, about 30 minutes. (Add more water if necessary.)

30 Minutes Before Serving:

Make Herbed Biscuits.
Complete Chili Joes.

GRANDMA'S BAKED CHICKEN

4	large chicken breasts (3½ pounds), cut in half
5	large chicken legs (3 pounds), cut in half
½	cup shortening
½	cup butter or margarine
5	packages (.7 ounce each) cheese garlic salad dressing mix
3	cups finely crushed whole wheat flakes cereal

Heat oven to 400°

1. Wash chicken; pat dry. In oven, melt ¼ cup shortening and ¼ cup butter in each of two baking pans, 13 x 9 x 2 inches. Dip chicken into melted shortening mixture.

2. Mix salad dressing mix and cereal; coat chicken pieces thoroughly with mixture. Place skin sides down in pans.

3. Bake uncovered 30 minutes. Turn chicken; bake until thickest pieces are fork-tender, about 30 minutes.

CHILI JOES

3	pounds ground beef
¾	cup chopped onion
1	cup catsup
1	cup water
1	package (1 ounce) chili seasoning mix
1½	tablespoons packed brown sugar
1	tablespoon lemon juice
1	cup finely sliced celery
16	toasted hamburger buns

1. Cook and stir meat and onion in skillet until light brown; drain.

2. Mix catsup, water, chili seasoning, sugar and lemon juice. Stir catsup mixture and celery into meat.

3. Heat to boiling; reduce heat. Simmer uncovered 5 minutes. Serve on hamburger buns.

UNCLE HARRY'S BAKED BEANS

2   pounds dried navy or pea
    beans (4 cups)
4   quarts water
4   teaspoons salt
⅔   cup packed dark brown
    sugar
⅔   cup dark molasses
1   teaspoon dry mustard
½   teaspoon ground cloves

1   pound bacon, diced
2   medium onions, sliced

1. Cover beans with water in 6-quart Dutch oven. Heat to boiling; boil 2 minutes. Remove from heat; cover. Let stand at least 12 hours.

2. Stir in salt. Heat to boiling; reduce heat. Simmer uncovered until beans are just tender, 45 to 60 minutes. Drain, reserving liquid.

3. Mix sugar, molasses, mustard and cloves. Stir into beans.

4. Heat oven to 300°. Layer beans, bacon and onion in 4-quart casserole or two 2-quart casseroles or bean pots. Add enough reserved bean liquid and/or water to cover beans.

5. Bake covered until liquid is almost absorbed and beans are tender, about 3 hours.

6. Uncover casserole and bake, stirring occasionally, until liquid is absorbed, about 30 minutes.

COUSIN MARTHA'S POTATO SALAD

6   to 7 pounds red potatoes
¾   cup cider vinegar
6   tablespoons lemon juice
2¼ teaspoons salt
3   tablespoons sugar
3   onions, thinly sliced,
    separated into rings
1   cup thinly sliced radishes
1½ cups shredded unpared
    cucumber, drained (1 large)
6   hard-cooked eggs, chopped
1   tablespoon celery seed
1   cup mayonnaise or salad
    dressing
    Tomato slices
    Hard-cooked egg wedges

1. Cook unpared potatoes until done but still firm (do not overcook). Drain; cool and peel. Cut into cubes to measure 14 cups.

2. Mix vinegar, lemon juice, salt and sugar; pour over potatoes. Toss. Add remaining ingredients except tomatoes and egg wedges; toss. Refrigerate. Garnish with tomato slices and egg wedges.

HATTIE'S BEAN SALAD

3   cans (16 ounces each)
    kidney beans, drained
3   cans (8 ounces each) cut
    green beans, drained
1   large onion, thinly sliced,
    separated into rings
3   ripe avocados, peeled, sliced

¾   cup sugar
1   cup red wine vinegar
½   cup vegetable oil
1½ teaspoons salt
½   teaspoon pepper
¼   teaspoon dried basil leaves,
    crushed

1. Toss beans, onion and avocados.

2. Shake remaining ingredients in tightly covered jar. Pour dressing over salad; toss.

3. Refrigerate covered at least 3 hours. Just before serving, toss and drain.

AUNT SUSAN'S CABBAGE SLAW

8   cups shredded cabbage
       (about 1 medium head)
1   cup finely chopped celery
1   cup chopped red onion
½   cup shredded green pepper
1   cup mayonnaise or salad
       dressing
½   cup white vinegar
1½   teaspoons salt
¼   teaspoon pepper
       Paprika
       Green pepper rings

Toss cabbage, celery, onion and green pepper in large bowl. Mix remaining ingredients except paprika and green pepper rings; pour over cabbage mixture and toss. Refrigerate no longer than 24 hours. Attractive served in cabbage leaf-lined bowl. Sprinkle with paprika. Garnish with green pepper rings.

HERBED BISCUITS

3   cups biscuit baking mix
3   tablespoons instant minced
       onion
3   tablespoons parsley flakes
¾   cup cold water

     Caraway, poppy or sesame
       seeds

     Heat oven to 450°

1. Stir baking mix, onion, parsley flakes and water until a soft dough forms.

2. Drop by spoonfuls onto greased baking sheet. Sprinkle lightly with desired seeds.

3. Bake until light brown, 8 to 10 minutes. Serve hot.

TIP: To heat on a grill, wrap biscuits in a single layer in heavy-duty aluminum foil. Place foil packet on grill 3 to 4 inches from hot coals; heat 5 minutes on each side.

AUNT CLARA'S PRESERVES CAKE

1   package (18.5 ounces)
       yellow cake mix

1   cup raspberry preserves
2   tablespoons orange juice

1   package (7.2 ounces) fluffy
       white frosting mix
½   teaspoon maple flavoring

     Heat oven to 350°

1. Bake cake in baking pan, 13 x 9 x 2 inches, according to package directions. Cool 10 minutes. Remove from pan; cool cake on wire rack.

2. Split cake in half lengthwise to make 2 layers; return bottom layer to pan. Mix preserves and orange juice. Spread half of mixture over cut surface of bottom cake layer. Top with second cake layer. Spread remaining mixture over cake.

3. Prepare frosting according to package directions except stir in maple flavoring after beating. Frost top of cake (being careful not to form peaks which will burn).

4. Heat oven to 475°. Bake cake until frosting is light brown, 5 to 7 minutes. Serve at room temperature.

Picnic From Provence

Italian Olive Spread is subtly flavored.

Ratatouille can be served warm or cold.

Make colorful tarts with a variety of fruits.

RATATOUILLE MENU

•PATE DES OLIVES ITALIENNES
   (Italian Olive Spread)

ASSORTED SAUSAGES

CHEESE

FRENCH BREAD

•RATATOUILLE (Vegetable
   Casserole)

•TARTES AUX FRUITS (Fruit Tarts)

WINE

•Recipes included

Pâté des Olives Italiennes, a pungent spread for crackers or bread, is a special kind of appetizer to begin a special kind of picnic. Quickly made in a blender, this pâté combines Italian olives with anchovies, garlic and capers, plus an added fillip of rum in the flavoring.

A time-honored Provençal specialty, Ratatouille is a vegetable casserole that incorporates many of the elements of Mediterranean cookery. Eggplant, zucchini, tomatoes and green peppers are cooked in olive oil, then combined with an assortment of herbs and briefly baked. Ratatouille is an unusual yet ideal choice for a picnic, for it's equally good hot or cold. It may even be reheated with fine results, and makes an excellent casserole to serve with any meal. Serves 4.

Wine Suggestion: With this kind of picnic I would suggest a chilled rosé, such as Chateau de Selle from Provence or Cabernet Rosé from Simi wineries of California.

Picnic fare is completed with breads, cheeses, meats and wine.

PARTY PLAN FOR RATATOUILLE MENU

1 Day Before:	Make Italian Olive Spread; cover and refrigerate.
	Prepare Fruit Tarts through step 2 in recipe; cover.
That Morning:	Complete Fruit Tarts.
	Make Vegetable Casserole. (If serving warm, bake just before serving.)

PATE DES OLIVES ITALIENNES (Italian Olive Spread)

*2   jars (6½ ounces each)
      Italian olives, drained,
      pitted
1   tablespoon olive oil
2   small cloves garlic, crushed
1   tablespoon capers, drained
2   anchovy fillets, drained
1   small bay leaf
⅛   teaspoon ground thyme
1   tablespoon rum
      Crackers, toast rounds,
      bread or cherry tomatoes

Measure all ingredients except crackers into blender container; cover. Blend on medium-high speed, scraping down sides of blender frequently, until mixture is consistency of caviar, about 2 minutes. Refrigerate. Use as spread for crackers, toast rounds, bread or as a filling for cherry tomatoes.

TIP: *Greek olives can be substituted; omit anchovy fillets. Do not substitute ripe olives for Italian olives.

RATATOUILLE (Vegetable Casserole)

1   medium eggplant (about 1
      pound), cut into 3 x ⅜ x
      ⅜-inch strips
3   small zucchini (about ½
      pound), cut into ¼-inch slices
1   teaspoon salt

3   tablespoons olive oil
2   tablespoons olive oil
2   medium onions, sliced
½   large green pepper, cut into
      ¼-inch strips (about 1 cup)
4   medium cloves garlic,
      crushed
½   teaspoon salt
⅛   teaspoon pepper

2   medium ripe tomatoes, peeled
¼   teaspoon salt
      Dash pepper

3   tablespoons snipped parsley
1   teaspoon dried oregano
      leaves
1   teaspoon dried marjoram
      leaves
¼   teaspoon ground thyme
¼   teaspoon ground savory

1. Toss eggplant, zucchini and 1 teaspoon salt in bowl; let stand 30 minutes. Drain and pat dry.

2. Cook and stir eggplant and zucchini in 3 tablespoons olive oil in skillet until light brown;* transfer vegetables to bowl. Measure 2 tablespoons olive oil into skillet; return to heat. Cook onions, pepper and garlic in olive oil until onions are tender, about 8 minutes. Sprinkle with ½ teaspoon salt and ⅛ teaspoon pepper.

3. Cut tomatoes into eighths. Scoop out seeds by gently running finger through seeded areas; discard seeds. Arrange tomatoes on top of onions and peppers. Sprinkle with ¼ teaspoon salt and dash pepper; cover. Cook over low heat 5 minutes. Uncover; cook 5 minutes.

4. Heat oven to 400°. Mix parsley, oregano, marjoram, thyme and savory. Layer half the eggplant mixture in ungreased 1½-quart casserole; sprinkle with 1 tablespoon herb mixture. Layer half the tomato mixture over herbs; sprinkle with 1 tablespoon herb mixture. Repeat with remaining eggplant and tomato mixtures and herbs; cover.

5. Bake until hot, 12 to 15 minutes. Serve hot or cold.

TIP: *More olive oil can be added if necessary.

½　cup butter or margarine,
　　　softened
½　cup sugar
1　egg yolk
2　teaspoons water
1　teaspoon vanilla
1　tablespoon grated orange
　　　peel
1¾　cups all-purpose flour

　　Orange Glaze (recipe
　　　follows)
3　cups sliced bananas,
　　　peaches, pears or small
　　　whole berries

　　Heat oven to 350°

½　cup sugar
1　tablespoon plus 1½ teaspoons
　　　cornstarch
⅛　teaspoon salt
1　cup orange juice
2　teaspoons grated orange peel
1　tablespoon orange-flavored
　　　liqueur

1. Beat butter until fluffy. Mix in sugar gradually, beating until light and fluffy. Stir in egg yolk, water, vanilla and orange peel. Mix in flour gradually. Divide into 12 equal parts; press in 3-inch fluted tart pans (1¼ inches deep).*

2. Bake until light brown, 15 to 20 minutes; cool. Tap pans lightly to remove shells.

3. Prepare Orange Glaze. Arrange about ¼ cup fruit in each tart. Spoon Orange Glaze over fruit.

*TIP: *3½-inch tart pans can be substituted for 3-inch tart pans. Press dough 1¼ inches up sides.*

ORANGE GLAZE
Mix sugar, cornstarch and salt in small saucepan. Stir in orange juice gradually, mixing until smooth. Heat to boiling, stirring constantly. Boil and stir 2 minutes. Stir in orange peel; cover and cool. Stir in orange liqueur.

Backyard Buffet

Shown are marinated roast beef, antipasto, creamy dips and turkey chunks.

MARINATED BEEF MENU

- **APPLE-MINT JULEPS**
- **BERRY PATCH PUNCH**
- **CHUNKY ONION DIP**
- **DEVILED HAM DIP**
- **BUFFET ANTIPASTO WITH BREADSTICKS**
- **TURKEY SESAME CHUNKS**
- **MARINATED BEEF ROUND WITH PETITE BUNS**
- **FRESH FRUIT PLATTER**

• Recipes included

Apple-Mint Juleps and Berry Patch Punch give guests a cool choice of drinks. The juleps are made individually in separate glasses, but the non-alcoholic punch is concocted all at once. Any kind of vegetable from celery to zucchini is fine for dunking into two cold dips.

Thin slices of beef, marinated in wine and spices before roasting, go on or with simple-to-make buttered Petite Buns. The beef is delicious hot or cold. The buns are made from frozen bread dough, but any type of roll may be substituted. To make Turkey Sesame Chunks, spear pieces of cooked turkey on skewers and dip them in a hot lemon, soy sauce and butter mixture, then into toasted sesame seeds. Turkey is always popular and this is an unusual new way to serve it.

The Buffet Antipasto introduces *giardiniera,* spicy-hot bottled vegetables, along with artichoke hearts, mushrooms, ripe olives and tuna. Fruit—whole strawberries and wedges of cantaloupe and honeydew—make an easy, summery dessert. Serves 10.

Wine Suggestion: The variety and marination calls for a wine, and a red one, which can balance the taste—like Rioja, Marques de Riscal or a Pinot St. George, Christian Brothers.

Apple-Mint Juleps and Berry Patch Punch are party starters.

The buffet setting is as colorful as the food.

PARTY PLAN FOR MARINATED BEEF MENU

1 Day Before:	Make Chunky Onion Dip; cover and refrigerate.
	Make Deviled Ham Dip; cover and refrigerate. (To serve, bring to room temperature.)
	Make Buffet Antipasto; cover and refrigerate.
	Prepare Marinated Beef Round through step 1 in recipe; refrigerate.
That Morning:	Make Petite Buns; cool and wrap in aluminum foil.
	Prepare Berry Patch Punch through step 1 in recipe; refrigerate.
	Prepare vegetables for dips; cover and refrigerate.
2 Hours 30 Minutes Before Serving:	Make Turkey Sesame Chunks.
	Complete Marinated Beef Round.
	Make fruit platter; cover and refrigerate.
As Guests Arrive:	Complete Berry Patch Punch.
	Make Apple-Mint Juleps.

APPLE-MINT JULEPS

20   mint sprigs
10   teaspoons powdered sugar
5   cups crushed ice
10   ounces bourbon
2½ cups apple cider
      Mint sprigs

Crush 2 mint sprigs with 1 teaspoon sugar in each of 10 glasses. Stir in ½ cup ice, 1 ounce bourbon and ¼ cup apple cider. Add ice, if necessary, to fill glass. Decorate edge of glass with mint sprig.

BERRY PATCH PUNCH

Makes about 3 quarts

2   packages (10 ounces each)
      frozen raspberries, thawed
1   cup bottled lime juice
1   can (6 ounces) frozen
      orange juice concentrate,
      thawed
½ cup water

      Ice cubes
2   quarts ginger ale, chilled
      Mint sprigs

1. Mix raspberries, lime juice, orange juice and water; refrigerate.

2. Pour chilled mixture over ice cubes in punch bowl. Stir in ginger ale gently. Garnish with mint.

CHUNKY ONION DIP

Makes about 1½ cups

1   package (8 ounces) cream
      cheese, softened
⅓ cup chopped Bermuda onion
⅓ cup chili sauce
3   tablespoons mayonnaise or
      salad dressing
¼ teaspoon Worcestershire
      sauce
      Assorted fresh vegetables,
      chilled

Mix all ingredients except assorted vegetables with fork until slightly lumpy; cover. Refrigerate at least 1½ hours. Serve with chilled vegetables.

DEVILED HAM DIP

Makes about 1¼ cups

2   cans (4½ ounces each)
      deviled ham
¼ cup dairy sour cream or
      salad dressing
1   tablespoon horseradish
4   to 6 drops red pepper sauce
      Assorted fresh vegetables,
      chilled

Mix deviled ham, sour cream, horseradish and pepper sauce. Serve with chilled vegetables.

BUFFET ANTIPASTO

1 jar (14 to 16 ounces)
    giardiniera (hot-mix
    vegetables), well drained
1 can (6 ounces) marinated
    artichoke hearts (with
    liquid)
1 can (8 ounces) button
    mushrooms, drained
1 can (6 ounces) pitted ripe
    olives, drained
1 can (15 ounces) tomato sauce
1 can (6 to 7 ounces) water-
    packed tuna, well drained
2 teaspoons fresh grated
    lemon peel
¼ cup fresh lemon juice

Mix all ingredients; cover. Refrigerate at least 24 hours, mixing once or twice (flavors will blend). Garnish with lemon twists if desired. Serve with wooden picks.

TIP: This recipe is hot! Mild-mix giardiniera can be used if preferred.

TURKEY SESAME CHUNKS

1 frozen turkey roll
    (2 pounds)

1 cup butter or margarine
¼ cup vegetable oil
½ cup lemon juice
¼ cup soy sauce
*1 to 1½ cups toasted sesame
    seed

1. Cook turkey roll according to package directions. Cool. Cut into ¾-inch cubes.

2. Heat butter, vegetable oil, lemon juice and soy sauce in metal fondue pot until bubbly; transfer to source of heat at table. Arrange turkey cubes on platter around fondue pot.

3. Spear turkey cubes on wooden skewers; dip into melted butter mixture, then into sesame seed.

*TIP: *To toast sesame seed: Spread seed in shallow pan. Toast in 350° oven until golden brown, 10 to 15 minutes, stirring occasionally.*

MARINATED BEEF ROUND

⅓ cup vinegar
⅓ cup vegetable oil
1 cup Burgundy wine or grape
    juice
¼ cup finely chopped onion
2 teaspoons ground cinnamon
1 teaspoon salt
½ teaspoon ground nutmeg
5 whole cloves

1 beef round roast (about 4
    pounds)
    Petite Buns (recipe follows)

1. Shake all ingredients except beef and Petite Buns in tightly covered jar; pour over meat in shallow glass dish and cover. Refrigerate, turning occasionally, 12 to 24 hours.

2. Heat oven to 325°. Remove meat from marinade; reserve marinade. Place meat on rack in shallow roasting pan. Insert meat thermometer so tip is in center of thickest part of meat. Basting occasionally with marinade, roast uncovered to 160° (medium), about 2 hours. Serve hot or cold, sliced very thin, in buttered Petite Buns.

2 loaves (1 pound each)
    frozen bread dough

1 tablespoon milk
    Sesame seeds or poppy seeds
    or instant minced onion

PETITE BUNS   *Makes 30 buns*

1. Thaw and let bread dough rise according to package directions.

2. Divide each loaf into 15 pieces; shape each piece into ball. Place on greased baking sheet with sides just touching. Brush with milk; sprinkle with sesame seeds. Let rise in warm draft-free place until double, about 1 hour.

3. Heat oven to 375°. Bake until golden brown, 15 to 20 minutes.

A Summer Barbecue

Swagger Steak is cooked on the grill and served with macaroni salad.

Steaks are tops on the list of favorites for backyard barbecue meals. The Swagger Steak is a juicy sirloin, grilled and served with a tangy hot sauce. The sauce, excellent with any meat, is a blend of brown sugar, vinegar, honey, chili sauce and beer.

Macaroni Toss is quick and easy to make and an ideal dish for hot weather. Chilled macaroni is mixed with cooked green beans, raw carrots and celery, spiced and tossed with Italian dressing. As an alternative, a light green salad would also be fine with the steak.

The different layers of a parfait showing through the glass are always lovely. Melon Ambrosia Parfaits are tall, cool and simple to put together. Melon balls and coconut are layered and garnished with frozen ginger ale and mint sprigs. Use honeydew, cantaloupe or watermelon, or any fresh fruit cut into chunks or balls, or whole green grapes. This dessert could also be a summery offering for late-evening guests. Serves 6.

Wine Suggestion: One beautiful big Burgundy should make it a perfect meal— Pinot Noir from Sonoma Vineyards or Pommard, Clos de la Commaraine.

Melon balls and coconut are attractively layered in parfait glasses.

PARTY PLAN FOR GRILLED STEAK MENU

1 Day Before:	Make Marinated Vegetables; cover and refrigerate.
3 Hours Before Serving:	Make Macaroni Toss; cover and refrigerate. Prepare Melon Ambrosia Parfaits through step 2 in recipe; refrigerate.
30 Minutes Before Serving:	Make Swagger Steak.
5 Minutes Before Dessert:	Complete Melon Ambrosia Parfaits.

MARINATED VEGETABLES

Makes 4 cups

1   cup diagonally sliced
    carrots (about 2 medium)
½   cup diagonally sliced celery
    (about 1 stalk)
½   cup small cauliflowerets
½   cup green pepper cubes
    (about 1 medium)
½   cup diagonally sliced
    zucchini (about 1 medium)
½   cup sliced fresh mushrooms
    (about 2 medium)
½   jar (7-ounce size) Spanish
    olives, drained
¾   cup vegetable oil
⅓   cup white vinegar
2   tablespoons mixed pickling
    spice
1½ teaspoons salt
1   teaspoon celery seed
4   bay leaves
2   small onions, sliced
½   lemon, thinly sliced
    Lettuce leaves

1. Heat 1 inch salted water (½ teaspoon salt to 1 cup water) to boiling. Add carrots, celery, cauliflowerets, green pepper and zucchini; cover. Heat to boiling; reduce heat.

2. Cook until tender, 12 to 15 minutes; drain. Place vegetables in shallow glass baking dish. Stir in mushrooms and olives.

3. Mix remaining ingredients except lettuce leaves and breadsticks; pour over vegetables. Cover and refrigerate, stirring occasionally, at least 24 hours, no longer than 7 days. To serve, spoon vegetables into lettuce-lined shallow bowl. Spear vegetables with cocktail forks or wooden picks. Serve with breadsticks or melba toast if desired.

SWAGGER STEAK

1   beef loin sirloin steak,
    boneless (2 to 3 pounds),
    1½ to 2 inches thick
1   teaspoon salt
½   teaspoon pepper
⅔   cup chili sauce
½   cup beer
⅓   cup packed brown sugar
2   tablespoons vinegar
2   tablespoons honey
1   tablespoon Worcestershire
    sauce
1   tablespoon lemon juice
½   cup finely chopped onion

1. Grill steak 4 inches from medium-hot coals 15 minutes on each side. (Steak will be medium done.) Season steak with salt and pepper after turning and after removing from grill. Garnish meat platter with watercress and radishes if desired.

2. Mix remaining ingredients in saucepan. Heat to boiling; reduce heat. Simmer uncovered 15 minutes while steak is cooking. Serve with steak.

MACARONI TOSS

1	package (7 ounces) elbow macaroni
*2	cups fresh green beans, cooked, drained, cooled
1	cup shredded carrots
1	cup sliced celery
½	cup Italian salad dressing
¼	teaspoon dried oregano leaves, crushed
	Lettuce leaves
	Carrot curls, if desired

1. Cook macaroni according to package directions. Drain; rinse with cold water.

2. Mix macaroni, green beans, carrots and celery. Add dressing and oregano; toss lightly until all ingredients are evenly coated and cover. Refrigerate at least 1 hour. Serve in lettuce-lined bowl. Garnish with carrot curls.

*TIP: *One package (9 ounces) frozen green beans, cooked, drained and cooled, can be substituted for fresh green beans.*

MELON AMBROSIA PARFAITS

1	bottle (6 ounces) ginger ale
1	medium cantaloupe
1	honeydew melon
1	cup shredded coconut
	Mint sprigs

1. Pour ginger ale into ice cube tray; freeze until slushy, about 3 hours.

2. Cut melon into balls with melon ball cutter. Alternate cantaloupe, coconut and honeydew in parfait glasses; refrigerate at least 1 hour.

3. Top each parfait with a scoop of frozen ginger ale slush. Garnish with mint.

Great Fish Grill

Grilled fish topped with piccalilli has sensational flavor.

GRILLED FISH MENU

FRESH FRUIT CUP

•**FISH 'N' PICCALILLI**

•**CITRUS-ARTICHOKE SALAD**
ROLLS AND BUTTER

•**ALMOND CRUNCH CREAM PIE**
COFFEE

•Recipes included

In summertime, when fresh fruit is abundant, there is no reason to offer guests anything less in a fruit cup. Choose your favorite fruits and add a dollop of sherbet or sprig of mint.

Whitefish, grilled to perfection, is a welcome change from meat or fowl for an outdoor meal. It's flaky and tender, with a delicate taste. Serve the fish with a zesty piccalilli mixture of green tomatoes, onion, sweet red pepper, spices and vinegar. Piccalilli is an excellent relish for hamburgers, too.

Citrus-Artichoke Salad is a refreshing choice to serve alongside the fish. The unusual but flavorful combination of ingredients are lightly tossed with a French-style dressing. To round out the menu, offer your favorite rolls, heated or cold.

Almond Crunch Cream Pie has a macaroon-flavored crust with a crunchy texture. The vanilla-pudding filling is laced with almond extract, and chopped almonds are sprinkled on top. This attractive dessert would be ideal year-round. Serves 6.

Wine Suggestion: Grilled fish is the lightest, most elegant preparation. It calls for a similarly delicate, delightful wine. Here is one lightly pastimey—Pouilly-Fumé Ladoucette from Loire or Fumé Beringer from California.

Onion rings are a pleasing flavor contrast with fruit salad.

PARTY PLAN FOR GRILLED FISH MENU

1 Day Before:	Make Piccalilli Sauce; cover and refrigerate.
3 Hours 30 Minutes Before Serving:	Make Almond Crunch Cream Pie; cool and refrigerate. Make Citrus-Artichoke Salad; cover and refrigerate.
1 Hour Before Serving:	Make Fish 'n' Piccalilli.

FISH 'N' PICCALILLI

1	whole whitefish (2½ to 3 pounds), cleaned, head removed
½	teaspoon salt
¼	teaspoon pepper
½	cup butter or margarine, melted
	Piccalilli Sauce (recipe follows)

1. Wash fish in cold water and pat dry with paper toweling. Rub cavity with salt and pepper. Close opening with skewers; lace.

2. Place fish in lightly greased hinged grill. Grill 5 inches from medium coals 25 minutes; turn. Grill, basting frequently with melted butter, until done, about 25 minutes. Serve with Piccalilli Sauce.

PICCALILLI SAUCE

1½ pounds green tomatoes,
    sliced ⅛ inch thick
1   medium onion, sliced ⅛
    inch thick
1   tablespoon salt

1   cup cider vinegar
½ cup sugar
1   sweet red pepper, cut into
    thin strips
2   teaspoons mustard seed
1½ teaspoons celery seed
    Dash ground cloves
    Dash cinnamon
    Dash pepper

1. Layer tomatoes, onion and salt in glass dish, 9 x 9 x 2 inches; cover. Refrigerate at least 12 hours; drain.

2. Mix remaining ingredients in medium saucepan. Add tomato mixture. Heat to boiling; reduce heat. Simmer 30 minutes. Refrigerate covered.

CITRUS-ARTICHOKE SALAD

*1 package (9 ounces) frozen
    artichoke hearts

2   oranges, pared, sectioned
1   grapefruit, pared, sectioned
1   small red onion, thinly sliced,
    separated into rings
**8 cups salad greens, broken into
    bite-size pieces
1   bottle (8 ounces) French-style
    oil-and-vinegar dressing

1. Cook artichoke hearts according to package directions; drain and refrigerate.

2. Place artichokes and remaining ingredients except dressing in salad bowl. Toss with dressing.

TIPS: *One can (8 ounces) whole artichoke hearts can be substituted for frozen artichoke hearts. Drain; cut artichoke hearts in half.

**Use combination of romaine and fresh spinach or curly endive.

ALMOND CRUNCH CREAM PIE

    Almond Crust (recipe follows)
1   package (3¼ ounces) vanilla
    regular pudding and pie
    filling
1½ cups milk
1   teaspoon almond extract

1   cup chilled whipping cream
1   tablespoon sugar

2   tablespoons chopped almonds,
    toasted

1. Make Almond Crust.

2. Mix pudding mix and milk in small saucepan. Heat to boiling, stirring constantly. Remove from heat; stir in almond extract. Transfer to bowl; cover with plastic wrap. Refrigerate until cool, about 1½ hours.

3. Beat whipping cream in chilled bowl until stiff. Fold half of the whipped cream into pudding. Stir sugar into remaining whipped cream.

4. Pour pudding into pie shell. Top with dollops of sweetened whipped cream. Refrigerate no longer than 2 hours before serving. Sprinkle with almonds just before serving.

ALMOND CRUST

1½ cups natural almonds

1   egg white
¼ cup sugar
½ teaspoon almond extract

    Heat oven to 375°

1. Place ½ cup of the almonds in blender container; cover. Blend until almonds are finely chopped. Repeat with remaining almonds.

2. Beat egg white until foamy. Gradually beat in sugar and almond extract; beat until stiff. Fold in chopped nuts.

3. Spread nut mixture carefully in generously buttered and floured 9-inch pie plate; press with back of spoon.

4. Bake until light brown, about 15 minutes. While warm, gently loosen side of crust with small spatula; carefully twist to free from plate. Cool in plate on rack.

A smooth cream pie is almond-crusted and topped.

A Patio Dinner

Frozen Lime Dessert is tart and refreshing.

GRILLED TURKEY MENU

- **TURKEY WITH SPICY CRANBERRY GLAZE**

- **VINEYARD POTATO SALAD**
  CRISP RELISH TRAY
  FRESH CORN ON THE COB
  BREAD AND BUTTER

- **FROZEN LIME DESSERT**
  ICED TEA

- Recipes included

Grilled turkey is an easy main course to serve for a summer dinner. It cooks slowly on a spit for several hours, giving you plenty of time to prepare the rest of the meal. A pungent cranberry sauce and Italian salad dressing mixture is brushed on the turkey as it turns, creating an attractive glaze.

Potato salad is always a hot weather favorite, and our version is extra special—white wine makes the difference. Fresh corn on the cob, steaming hot and dripping with butter, is a traditional midsummer treat that goes perfectly with any open-air meal. A pinch of basil or tarragon in the melted butter adds a nice, different flavor to the corn.

Refreshingly cool, the Frozen Lime Dessert is fun to make. The tart lime filling, an attractive pale green, is spooned into a refrigerator tray over a crushed chocolate creme cookie base. More cookie crumbs are sprinkled on top before freezing. This dessert will keep for one week in the freezer; it is a good choice to have on hand for unexpected guests.

For a beverage, serve iced tea with lots of lemon slices. To vary it, try serving the tea in sugar-rimmed glasses. Rub the rim of the glass with a lemon quarter, then roll in a saucer of coarse sugar. Serves 6 to 8.

Wine Suggestion: A good rosé wine only—Rosé d'Anjou from France or Grignolino Rosé, Heitz, from California.

Grilled turkey with cranberry glaze is a great summer entrée.

PARTY PLAN FOR GRILLED TURKEY MENU

1 Day Before: Make Frozen Lime Dessert; store in freezer.

4 Hours 15 Minutes Before Serving: Make Turkey with Spicy Cranberry Glaze.
Make Vineyard Potato Salad; cover and refrigerate.

30 Minutes Before Serving: Make relishes and cook corn on the cob.

TURKEY WITH SPICY CRANBERRY GLAZE

1   **turkey (8 to 10 pounds)**
    Salt

    Butter, melted, or vegetable oil

1   **can (16 ounces) jellied cranberry sauce**
¾   **cup bottled Italian salad dressing**
½   **teaspoon dried rosemary leaves, crushed**

1. Sprinkle turkey cavity with salt. Fasten neck skin to back with skewer. Flatten wings over breast; tie string around breast to hold wings securely. Tie drumsticks securely to tail. Insert spit rod through center of bird from breast end toward tail. Secure turkey on spit with holding forks. Check balance by rotating spit in palms of hands.

2. Arrange medium-hot coals at back of firebox;* place foil drip pan under spit area. Insert meat thermometer so tip is in thickest part of thigh and does not touch bone. Place spit in rotisserie. Brush turkey with butter. Cook turkey 3 hours.

3. Mix cranberry sauce, Italian dressing and rosemary in saucepan. Heat, stirring constantly, until mixture bubbles. Cook turkey, brushing several times with cranberry mixture, until thermometer registers 175° and drumsticks feel very soft, about 1 hour longer. Garnish with cherry tomatoes and parsley if desired.

*TIP: *Add coals at intervals to maintain heat if necessary.*

VINEYARD POTATO SALAD

4½   **cups diced peeled cooked new potatoes (about 2 pounds)**
⅓   **cup Chablis or other dry white wine, if desired**

3   **tablespoons vegetable oil**
¼   **cup dairy sour cream**
1   **teaspoon salt**
½   **teaspoon sugar**
¼   **teaspoon pepper**
1   **teaspoon lemon juice**
¼   **cup thinly sliced radishes**
2   **tablespoons snipped parsley**
2   **green onions (with tops), thinly sliced**

    Lettuce leaves
    Watercress, if desired

1. Toss potatoes and wine in bowl; let stand 15 minutes.

2. Add remaining ingredients except lettuce and watercress; toss until potatoes are coated. Cover. Refrigerate at least 1 hour (to blend flavors).

3. Serve in lettuce-lined bowl; garnish with watercress.

FROZEN LIME DESSERT

1	can (5⅓ ounces) evaporated milk
2	egg yolks
¼	cup sugar
½	teaspoon grated lime peel
¼	cup fresh lime juice Few drops green food color
2	egg whites
¼	cup sugar
8	creme-filled chocolate sandwich cookies (1½ inches in diameter), crushed

1. Pour evaporated milk into refrigerator tray; freeze until icy, about 20 minutes.

2. Mix egg yolks, ¼ cup sugar, the lime peel, lime juice and food color in top of double boiler. Cook over boiling water until thickened, stirring constantly, about 3 minutes. Remove lime mixture from boiling water; place in bowl of cold water to cool.

3. Beat egg whites until foamy. Beat in ¼ cup sugar, 1 tablespoon at a time; beat until stiff and glossy. Fold into lime mixture.

4. Wash bowl and beaters. Rinse with cold water; dry. Beat icy evaporated milk until stiff. Fold into lime mixture.

5. Spread cookie crumbs in bottom of buttered refrigerator tray, reserving 1 tablespoon crumbs for top. Spread lime mixture over crumbs in tray; sprinkle with reserved crumbs. Freeze until firm, about 1½ hours, no longer than 1 week. Cut into wedges to serve.

TIP: Place tray bottom in hot water for a few seconds before slicing for easier removal of crumb crust.

8 Buffet Spectaculars

Entertaining buffet-style can be as simple or as grand as you want it to be. The menus in this chapter are designed for those times when you want something out of the ordinary. Most of the recipes are made from scratch and are well worth the time and effort. You'll have four memorable buffet spectaculars equal to the most outstanding occasions.

Buffets take up little space and are the simplest meals of all to serve. Guests help themselves from an attractive array of dishes set out anywhere that is convenient—in the dining room, living room, or outdoors on a terrace. Setting up a buffet table should be done in an organized fashion, preferably in a progressive arrangement. Put plates, napkins and cutlery at one end. Salads, soups and entrées follow, with vegetable dishes, condiments and other extras interspersed. Electric hot trays, chafing dishes and fondue pots are helpful in keeping hot dishes hot. Desserts come last, with their own plates. Dessert can also be arranged on a separate table or tea cart, along with coffee, cream and sugar, cups and saucers, and the necessary cutlery.

Our Southern-style buffet recreates the famed hospitality of the Old South with a well-balanced selection of characteristic regional dishes. Savannah, Georgia, was the inspiration for this ceremonial menu which begins with one of the South's most treasured symbols—the Mint Julep. Traditionally, a julep is served in frosted silver cups and garnished with a sprig of fresh mint.

The Duck Buffet Menu is ideal all year but would be especially good for a Christmas celebration. The foods are hearty—roast ducklings, a thick soup and a rich fudge pie dessert. It is a menu with a holiday air, combining delicious flavors and aromas with great visual appeal.

Hot spiced cider is a warm way to welcome guests to a cold-weather Beef and Ribs Buffet. Serve the cider in a glass pitcher or a punch bowl, so that the clove-studded orange may be admired. Two meat entrées, beef and spareribs, share the autumn table with three nicely contrasting salads, plus a Pineapple Cheesecake topped with sour cream.

From a pomegranate-studded cheese ball appetizer to an unusual after-dinner drink of crème de menthe and lemonade, the final buffet offering in this chapter is truly elegant. Every dish is not only eye-catching, but has a special touch that takes it far from the ordinary.

Every Southern cook has a favorite recipe for pilau. Shrimp Pilau is seasoned with tomatoes, salt pork, onion and green pepper (see menu on page 204).

Dining Southern Style

Mint Juleps are served in frosted silver cups with assorted appetizers.

BAKED HAM AND PILAU MENU

- MINT JULEPS
- TOASTED SAVORIES
- CRINOLINE CHEESE SQUARES
- CHUT-NUT BALLS
- PICKLED BLACK-EYED PEAS
    WITH PASTRY CUPS
- HERITAGE BAKED HAM
- SHRIMP PILAU
    Pictured on page 203.
- SQUASH CASSEROLE
    TOSSED GREEN SALAD
    ASSORTED PICKLES (Watermelon,
      Cantaloupe, Beet, Okra)
    HOT BISCUITS AND BUTTER
- STRAWBERRIES SAVANNAH
    COFFEE OR ICED TEA

• Recipes included

Served with four unique appetizers, Mint Juleps are a fitting introduction to this menu reminiscent of the Old South. You can make the appetizers as much as a week ahead and freeze them. Pecans are called for in the crunchy Toasted Savories, but any favorite nut could be used. Chut-Nut Balls, a unique combination of fruit-spicy chutney and peanut butter, are super rich and sweet.

A word about hams: this recipe uses a Georgia or Virginia variety. Both types of Southern hams are hickory-smoked and aged in a pepper coating. Before baking, a ham of this type should be soaked in water for at least 12 hours to remove much of the salty taste. Southern hams are a real delicacy; sliced very thin, they are often served as appetizers. Your local specialty or gourmet shop may carry them, or they can be ordered by mail. If you must substitute, a smoked bone-in ham could be used—but it will lack the distinctive flavor of the Southern ham.

Mace is a popular spice in Southern cooking. The recipe for Strawberries Savannah uses just a touch of this warm and potent spice. Mace is almost the same as nutmeg, but more pungent. Both are part of the same tropical plant—nutmeg is the seed; mace is the seed's outer coating. Serves 8.

Wine Suggestion: A mellow, warm Rhône wine, a Côte-Rotie Gerin from France, is a good choice, or a Pinot Noir such as Paul Masson from California.

Georgia ham is slowly baked with molasses, then topped with bread crumbs and spices.

PARTY PLAN FOR BAKED HAM AND PILAU MENU

1 Week Before:
Make Toasted Savories, Crinoline Cheese Squares and Chut-Nut balls; wrap and freeze.
Prepare Pickled Black-Eyed Peas with Pastry Cups through step 4 in recipe; freeze.

1 Day Before:
Prepare Heritage Baked Ham through step 1 in recipe.

5 to 7 Hours Before Serving:
Complete Heritage Baked Ham.
Prepare Strawberries Savannah through step 1 in recipe; refrigerate.

2 Hours Before Serving:
Defrost Toasted Savories, Crinoline Cheese Squares, Chut-Nut Balls and Pastry Cups.
Make tossed salad; cover and refrigerate.

50 Minutes Before Serving:
Make Shrimp Pilau.
Make Squash Casserole.
Make biscuits.

10 Minutes Before Guests Arrive:
Complete Pickled Black-Eyed Peas with Pastry Cups.

As Guests Arrive:
Make Mint Juleps.

15 Minutes Before Dessert:
Complete Strawberries Savannah.

MINT JULEPS

16   teaspoons sugar
24   mint leaves

16   cups crushed ice
      Bourbon
8   mint sprigs

1. Place 2 teaspoons sugar and 3 mint leaves in each 10-ounce silver julep cup or glass. Crush sugar and mint leaves together with muddler until blended.

2. Fill cups with crushed ice and stir mint mixture through ice with long-handled silver spoon until frosty. Pour bourbon on ice and serve with a sprig of mint.

TOASTED SAVORIES

Makes 2 cups

2   egg whites
*2   cups unsalted pecans

1   teaspoon salt
1   teaspoon dry mustard
1   teaspoon garlic powder

     Heat oven to 300°

1. Cover baking sheet with aluminum foil; grease and set aside.

2. Beat egg whites just until foamy. Drop pecans into egg whites and stir to coat. Lift with fork or slotted spoon to drain; place on foil.

3. Mix salt, dry mustard and garlic powder; pour into empty salt-shaker. Sprinkle salt mixture on nuts.

4. Bake 25 minutes or until coating is set. Lift foil to loosen nuts and break them apart; cool. Store in airtight container no longer than 1 week. Store in freezer no longer than 3 weeks.

*TIP: *If pecans are salted, put in strainer, run hot water over them to remove salt. Dry between paper toweling.*

CRINOLINE CHEESE SQUARES

Makes about 3 dozen

*1   **stick pie crust mix**
½   **cup shredded sharp Cheddar cheese**
⅛   **to ¼ teaspoon cayenne or red pepper**

Heat oven to 400°

1. Crumble pie crust stick into bowl; stir in cheese and pepper. Mix dough for one-crust pie according to package directions. On floured board, roll dough ⅛ inch thick. Cut into 1½-inch squares.

2. Bake until light brown, 8 to 10 minutes. Store in airtight container no longer than 3 days. Store in freezer no longer than 1 month.

TIP: *½ packet free-flowing pie crust mix can be substituted for pie crust stick. Or a double recipe can be made, using 2 sticks or 1 packet mix. Divide dough in half and roll out separately.

CHUT-NUT BALLS

Makes about 3 dozen

½   **cup chutney, drained, chopped**
⅓   **to ½ cup chunky peanut butter**
½   **cup peanuts, finely chopped**

Mix chutney with enough peanut butter to make a stiff mixture. Spoon mixture by level teaspoonfuls onto buttered waxed paper; refrigerate 1 hour. Shape into balls; roll in chopped peanuts. Store covered in refrigerator no longer than 5 days. Store in freezer no longer than 2 weeks.

PICKLED BLACK-EYED PEAS WITH PASTRY CUPS

Makes about 3 dozen

½   **cup Pickled Black-Eyed Peas (recipe follows)**
*1   **stick pie crust mix**

Heat oven to 450°

1. Make Pickled Black-Eyed Peas.

2. Mix dough for one-crust pie according to package directions; shape into smooth ball.

3. Pinch off small pieces of dough and roll into ½-inch balls. Place balls on baking sheet and press center of each ball carefully with finger or small melon ball cutter to make deep impression. Smooth edges; prick well with fork.

4. Bake until edges are light brown, 8 to 10 minutes; cool. Store in airtight container no longer than 1 week. Store in freezer no longer than 3 weeks.

5. Heat Pickled Black-Eyed Peas before serving. Serve hot in pastry cups.

TIP: *½ packet free-flowing pie crust mix can be substituted for pie crust stick.

PICKLED BLACK-EYED PEAS

Makes 1½ cups

Mix all ingredients; cover. Refrigerate at least 12 hours. Remove garlic clove. Store covered in refrigerator no longer than 2 weeks.

1   **can (16 ounces) black-eyed peas or ⅔ cup dried black-eyed peas, cooked, drained**
¼   **cup vegetable oil**
2   **tablespoons wine vinegar**
1   **clove garlic, lightly scored**
2   **tablespoons finely chopped onion**
¼   **teaspoon salt**
⅛   **teaspoon pepper**

HERITAGE BAKED HAM

1   Georgia or Virginia ham
    (12 to 16 pounds)

1   quart ginger ale
⅔   cup molasses

2   cups dry bread crumbs
½   cup packed brown sugar
½   teaspoon ground cloves
¼   teaspoon ground allspice

1. Scrub ham with brush. Place ham in large container and completely cover with water. Refrigerate 12 to 24 hours; rinse.

2. Place ham in large kettle and cover with water. Heat to boiling; reduce heat. Simmer uncovered 1 hour. Place ham on rack in large roasting pan with cover. Pour ginger ale and molasses over ham; cover.

3. Heat oven to 350°. Bake 4 to 6 hours (about 20 minutes per pound). Baste ham once every hour during baking with mixture in pan.

4. Remove ham from roasting pan. Heat oven to 425°. Trim off excess fat and skin. Return ham to roasting pan; sprinkle with mixture of bread crumbs, brown sugar, cloves and allspice.

5. Bake until crumb mixture browns, about 10 minutes.

SHRIMP PILAU

1   cup diced salt pork or bacon
    (about 6 ounces)

1   medium onion, chopped
1   medium green pepper,
    chopped
1   can (28 ounces) tomatoes,
    undrained
1   teaspoon salt
½   cup water
1½ cups uncooked regular rice

*1½ pounds raw shrimp, peeled,
    deveined

1. Cook salt pork in large kettle or Dutch oven until crisp and brown. Remove pork and set aside, reserving fat.

2. Cook and stir onion and green pepper in fat until tender. Stir in tomatoes, salt and water. Stir in rice and reserved salt pork. Heat to boiling; reduce heat. Simmer uncovered 10 minutes.

3. Place shrimp on top of rice; cover. Cook 15 minutes. Mix in shrimp; cover and let stand 5 minutes before serving.

*TIP: *One package (16 ounces) frozen uncooked peeled and deveined shrimp can be substituted for fresh shrimp. Rinse off ice crystals before using.*

SQUASH CASSEROLE

4   medium yellow summer squash
    (straightneck or crookneck)
1   teaspoon salt
1   teaspoon sugar

1   tablespoon butter or
    margarine
½   teaspoon salt
2   tablespoons flour
1   cup milk

¼   teaspoon pepper
½   cup chopped onion
1   cup shredded Cheddar cheese
    (about 4 ounces)
1   cup soda cracker crumbs

1. Cut squash into ½-inch slices. Cook in 1 inch (about 1 quart) boiling water with 1 teaspoon each salt and sugar until tender, about 15 minutes.

2. Melt butter in small saucepan; stir in ½ teaspoon salt and the flour. Stir in milk gradually; cook over medium heat, stirring constantly, until sauce thickens.

3. Heat oven to 350°. Place half of the squash slices in ungreased 1½-quart casserole; sprinkle with half of the pepper. Arrange half of the onion and cheese over squash slices; pour on half of the sauce. Sprinkle with half of the cracker crumbs; repeat.

4. Bake until top is brown and edge is bubbly, about 30 minutes.

Ground mace, a Southern favorite, flavors Strawberries Savannah.

STRAWBERRIES SAVANNAH

3   pints strawberries, washed,
    hulled, cut in half
⅓   to ½ cup powdered sugar
⅓   cup orange juice or orange
    liqueur
½   cup whipping cream
½   cup dairy sour cream
2   tablespoons powdered sugar
½   teaspoon ground mace

1. Mix strawberries, ⅓ to ½ cup powdered sugar and the orange juice. Refrigerate at least 2 hours.

2. Measure whipping cream, sour cream, 2 tablespoons powdered sugar and the mace into chilled mixer bowl. Beat with electric mixer until fluffy. Refrigerate no longer than 30 minutes. To serve, top strawberries with cream mixture.

Autumn Buffet

An autumn buffet includes roast duckling halves served on rice.

DUCK BUFFET MENU

- **POTATO SOUP**

- **RHUBARB CONSERVE**
  BREAD AND BUTTER

- **ROAST LONG ISLAND DUCKLINGS**
  WITH CRANBERRY SAUCE,
  STEWED APPLE SLICES AND
  RICE
  BUTTERED BROCCOLI

- **SPINACH-ARTICHOKE SALAD**

- **FUDGE NUT PIE**
  COFFEE OR TEA

- Recipes included

This handsome buffet centers on three roast Long Island ducklings served in an unusual way. Hot cooked rice sprinkled with slivered almonds is used as a base atop a bed of lettuce leaves. Then the halved ducklings are arranged on the rice, with a special cranberry sauce spooned on. Apple slices stewed in wine are placed around the ducklings as garnish.

Begin the meal with a thick Potato Soup, which can be made a day ahead, refrigerated and reheated. The potatoes are broken up but not mashed, imparting an unusual texture to the soup. The salad includes a crisp assortment of fresh greens, plus artichoke hearts and shallots (mild onions). If shallots are not available, substitute green onions. Rhubarb Conserve is made with frozen rhubarb cooked with raspberry gelatin and tapioca. Place it on the table in small individual bowls; it is eaten like jam, with bread. Buttered broccoli is suggested as a vegetable, but any green vegetable would be fine.

The Fudge Nut Pie is very easy and quick to make. It's a cross between a brownie and fudge, and is delicious hot or cold with ice cream. Serves 6.

Wine Suggestion: Those crisply cooked Long Island ducks have to be served with strong, masculine wines—Fixin, from Clos Du Perrière, or a well-aged Zinfandel Cresta Blanca, from California.

PARTY PLAN DUCK BUFFET MENU

1 Day Before:
Make Potato Soup except do not garnish. Store covered in refrigerator.
Prepare Rhubarb Conserve through step 2 in recipe; refrigerate.
Make Dressing for Spinach-Artichoke Salad; refrigerate.

3 Hours Before Serving:
Make Roast Long Island Ducklings and Cranberry Sauce.
Prepare salad ingredients; cover and refrigerate.

30 Minutes Before Serving:
Make Fudge Nut Pie.
Heat Potato Soup until hot; garnish.
Complete Spinach-Artichoke Salad.
Cook broccoli and rice.
Make Stewed Apple Slices.

POTATO SOUP
Makes 1 quart

2   large potatoes, pared, cut
      in julienne strips
1   small onion, finely chopped
1½ cups water
2   cups milk
½   teaspoon garlic salt
½   teaspoon celery salt
⅛   teaspoon dried thyme leaves,
      finely crushed
¼   teaspoon salt
2   tablespoons butter or
      margarine
    Croutons
    Snipped parsley

1. Heat potatoes, onion and water to boiling in medium saucepan; cover. Cook until potatoes are tender, about 12 minutes. Break potatoes into small pieces with a fork but do not mash.

2. Stir in milk, garlic salt, celery salt, thyme leaves, salt and butter. Heat *just* to boiling but do not boil. Garnish with croutons and parsley.

RHUBARB CONSERVE
Makes about 1½ cups

2   packages (16 ounces each)
      frozen rhubarb
½   package (3-ounce size)
      raspberry-flavored gelatin
      (3 tablespoons)
1½ tablespoons instant tapioca

    Bread

1. Thaw rhubarb according to package directions. Mix all ingredients except bread in medium saucepan. Heat, stirring occasionally, to a full boil; remove from heat.

2. Let stand 20 minutes; stir. Cover and refrigerate.

3. Serve in small bowls with bread.

TIP: Use remaining package of gelatin for salad or dessert at some other time. Pour ½ cup boiling water over remaining gelatin, stirring until gelatin is dissolved. Stir in ½ cup cold water. Refrigerate until firm.

ROAST LONG ISLAND DUCKLINGS

3   ducklings (3 to 4 pounds each), cut lengthwise in half or quartered
2   teaspoons monosodium glutamate

6   large lettuce leaves
6   cups hot cooked rice
¾   cup butter or margarine, melted
¾   cup slivered almonds
    Cranberry Sauce (recipe follows)
    Stewed Apple Slices (recipe follows)
6   parsley sprigs

Heat oven to 325°

2   tablespoons sugar
1   tablespoon cornstarch
1   cup cranberry juice
2   to 3 tablespoons vinegar
½   teaspoon instant chicken bouillon
2   tablespoons butter or margarine

3   Winesap apples, cored
¼   cup butter or margarine
1   lemon
2   tablespoons sugar
½   cup white wine

1. Slash skin around bottom edge of duckling halves (this keeps ducklings from curving while roasting); remove large pieces of fat. Tuck neck skin under wing. Sprinkle monosodium glutamate over ducklings.

2. Place 3 halves cut sides down on rack in each of 2 baking pans, 13 x 9 x 2 inches. Roast uncovered until golden brown and meat is done, about 2½ hours. (Ducklings are done when juices are no longer pink when cut between leg and body and drumstick meat feels very soft.)

3. Arrange lettuce leaves on large serving platter; fluff 1 cup rice on each lettuce leaf. Drizzle each with 2 tablespoons butter and sprinkle with 2 tablespoons almonds. Place duckling halves on rice; spoon Cranberry Sauce over each duckling. Garnish with Stewed Apple Slices and parsley sprigs.

CRANBERRY SAUCE

1. Mix sugar and cornstarch in saucepan. Stir in cranberry juice gradually. Add remaining ingredients.

2. Cook, stirring constantly, until mixture thickens and boils. Boil and stir 1 minute.

STEWED APPLE SLICES

1. Cut each unpared apple crosswise into 6 slices. In large skillet, cook in butter until light brown, about 2 minutes on each side. Squeeze lemon juice over apple slices and sprinkle with sugar.

2. Pour in wine; heat to boiling. Reduce heat and cover. Simmer just until tender, about 5 minutes. Serve warm.

TIP: The following apples can be substituted for Winesap: Rome Beauty, Baldwin, Jonathan and Stayman.

SPINACH-ARTICHOKE SALAD

1	small bunch romaine, torn into bite-size pieces (about 5 cups)
5	ounces spinach, torn into bite-size pieces (about 5 cups)
1	cup radish slices
½	cup chopped celery
2	tablespoons chopped shallots
	Dressing (recipe follows)
2	hard-cooked eggs, sliced
*1	can (14 ounces) artichoke hearts, drained, halved
	Freshly ground pepper

Toss romaine, spinach, radish slices, celery and shallots with dressing. Garnish with egg slices and artichoke hearts. Sprinkle with freshly ground pepper.

TIP: *Marinated artichoke hearts can be substituted.

¼	cup vegetable oil
2	tablespoons apple cider vinegar
2	cloves garlic, crushed
1	teaspoon seasoned salt
¼	teaspoon salt

DRESSING
Shake all ingredients in tightly covered jar; refrigerate.

FUDGE NUT PIE

1	square (1 ounce) unsweetened chocolate, melted, cooled
½	cup butter or margarine, melted
½	cup all-purpose flour
1	cup sugar
1	teaspoon vanilla
2	eggs
¼	cup chopped walnuts or pecans
	Vanilla ice cream
	Heat oven to 350°

1. Mix all ingredients except nuts and ice cream until smooth.

2. Pour into greased 9-inch pie pan. Sprinkle with nuts.

3. Bake pie until sides begin to pull away from pan and top springs back when lightly touched with finger, about 25 minutes. Serve warm or cold with ice cream.

TIP: The center of the pie will rise during baking and fall when removed from the oven.

Potluck Party

Cider is spiced and served hot.

Cheesecake is flavored with pineapple, topped with sour cream.

BEEF AND RIBS MENU

- **HOT SPICED CIDER**
  PARTY NIBBLES
  FRESH FRUIT

- **MARINATED BEEF ROAST**
- **SPICY BARBECUED SPARERIBS**
- **JULIENNE CARROTS WITH**
    WALNUTS
- **HOT GERMAN POTATO SALAD**
- **MINTED LIME MOLD**
- **POTLUCK BEAN SALAD**
  ROLLS AND BUTTER

- **PINEAPPLE CHEESECAKE**
  COFFEE OR TEA

• Recipes included

Give your guests the chance to dine on ribs and a roast together this autumn. Marinated Beef Roast has a subtle tang yet is not too hotly spiced. The marinade's distinctive flavor comes from beer, although apple cider provides a suitable substitute. The meaty spareribs come out of the oven beautifully glazed with their own barbecue sauce, and are attractive with onion and lemon slices.

German potato salad is typically served hot so that its spicy bacon, vinegar and sugar dressing will be at its best. Potluck Bean Salad goes one better than the prevalent three-bean version—it has four beans. One kind, garbanzo (also called chick-pea), may be purchased dried or in cans.

The lime gelatin mold has an unexpected flavor of peppermint. Included in this recipe are pears, honeydew and cantaloupe balls, though any fruit could be used. If you use fresh pineapple, remember that it contains an enzyme which will prevent gelatin from setting unless the fruit is heated to boiling first.

Crushed pineapple is folded into the Pineapple Cheesecake, with a topping of sour cream. You may make this excellent cake a day ahead, and—another bonus—it will keep up to ten days in the refrigerator if any is left over. Serves 12.

Wine Suggestion: Spicy marination might trick us into difficult choices—but a simple wine will be just right. Beaujolais, Village of Jadot, will be perfect. Or a good winemaker in California, like Heitz, will do a fine Burgundy to match this.

PARTY PLAN FOR BEEF AND RIBS MENU

1 Day Before:
Make Pineapple Cheesecake; cool and refrigerate.
Prepare Potluck Bean Salad through step 1 in recipe; cover and refrigerate.
Prepare Minted Lime Mold through step 3 in recipe; refrigerate.
Prepare Marinated Beef Roast through step 2 in recipe; refrigerate.

2 Hours 30 Minutes Before Serving:
Complete Marinated Beef Roast.
Make Spicy Barbecued Spareribs.

1 Hour 30 Minutes Before Serving:
Make Hot German Potato Salad.
Unmold Minted Lime Mold and garnish; refrigerate.

45 Minutes Before Serving:
Make Julienne Carrots with Walnuts.
Make Hot Spiced Cider; keep warm on low heat.
Remove Marinated Beef Roast from oven; cover with aluminum foil.
Make gravy.
Bake Hot German Potato Salad.
Complete Potluck Bean Salad.

HOT SPICED CIDER
Makes 1 quart

1	teaspoon whole cloves
1	stick cinnamon (3 inches)
1	teaspoon whole allspice
2	quarts apple cider
½	cup packed brown sugar
¼	teaspoon salt
1	orange, if desired
	Whole cloves, if desired

1. Tie 1 teaspoon whole cloves, the cinnamon and allspice in small cloth bag. Mix cider, sugar and salt in large saucepan; add spice bag.

2. Heat to boiling; reduce heat and cover. Simmer 20 minutes. Remove spice bag to serve. Stud orange with whole cloves; place in cider.

MARINATED BEEF ROAST

1	beef round rump roast, boneless or beef sirloin tip roast (about 4 pounds)
1	bottle (12 ounces) beer or 1½ cups apple cider
½	cup vegetable oil
2	tablespoons lemon juice
1	medium onion, sliced
1	clove garlic, crushed
1	bay leaf
1	teaspoon salt
¾	teaspoon dried thyme leaves
½	teaspoon dry mustard
¼	teaspoon pepper
½	cup water
2½	tablespoons flour

1. Pierce meat with fork about 20 times. Place meat in plastic bag in 2½-quart glass bowl.

2. Mix 1 cup of the beer, the oil, lemon juice, onion, garlic, bay leaf, salt, thyme, mustard and pepper. (Reserve remaining beer.) Pour marinade over meat. Refrigerate, turning occasionally, at least 6 hours, no longer than 24 hours.

3. Heat oven to 350°. Remove roast from marinade; reserve marinade. Place meat in roasting pan. Insert meat thermometer so tip is in center of thickest part of meat and does not rest in fat. Roast until thermometer registers 160°, about 2 hours.

4. Remove meat to warm platter; keep warm while preparing gravy. Add reserved ½ cup beer to reserved marinade. Add enough water to measure 2 cups. Skim fat from pan drippings; stir marinade into drippings and heat. Shake water and flour; stir slowly into hot liquid. Heat to boiling, stirring constantly. Boil and stir 1 minute. Season to taste.

On next pages, Marinated Beef Roast, Spicy Barbecued Spareribs, Hot German Potato Salad, Minted Lime Mold, Julienne Carrots with Walnuts and Potluck Bean Salad will rate compliments.

SPICY BARBECUED SPARERIBS

6   pounds pork spareribs, cut
      into serving-size portions
1   teaspoon salt
½   teaspoon pepper
1   lemon, thinly sliced
1   medium onion, thinly sliced

1   bottle (14 ounces) catsup
1   cup water
⅓   cup vinegar
¼   cup Worcestershire sauce
3   tablespoons lemon juice
2   to 3 teaspoons chili powder
2   teaspoons paprika
1½ teaspoons salt
1   tablespoon ground coriander
½   teaspoon garlic powder
⅛   teaspoon red pepper sauce

1. Sprinkle spareribs with 1 teaspoon salt and the pepper. Place spareribs meaty sides up in roasting pan. Arrange lemon and onion slices on top of ribs.

2. Bake uncovered at 350° for 1 hour. Drain off fat. Mix remaining ingredients; pour over meat and cover.

3. Bake, basting several times, until done, about 1½ hours longer. Uncover during last 15 minutes to brown.

JULIENNE CARROTS WITH WALNUTS

3   pounds carrots (about 12)

2   tablespoons sliced green
      onions and tops

½   cup butter or margarine,
      softened
2   packages (3¼ ounces each)
      English walnuts, broken

1. Scrape carrots and remove ends. Cut carrots into julienne strips.

2. Heat 1 inch salted water (½ teaspoon salt to 1 cup water) to boiling. Add carrots and onions; cover. Heat to boiling; reduce heat. Simmer until tender, about 25 minutes.

3. Drain carrots; toss with butter and walnuts. Season to taste.

HOT GERMAN POTATO SALAD

4½ pounds potatoes (about 12
      medium)

9   slices bacon, diced
1½ cups chopped onion
¾   cup chopped celery

3   tablespoons flour
1   tablespoon plus 1 teaspoon salt
1½ cups water
1   cup cider vinegar
1   cup sugar
⅓   cup snipped parsley

1½ cups sliced radishes
      Whole radishes, if desired

1. Pare potatoes. Heat 1 inch salted water (½ teaspoon salt to 1 cup water) to boiling. Add potatoes; cover tightly. Heat to boiling; reduce heat. Simmer until tender, 30 to 35 minutes; drain and set aside.

2. Fry bacon until crisp in large skillet; remove and drain on paper toweling. Cook and stir onion and celery in bacon fat until tender.

3. Stir in flour and salt. Cook over low heat, stirring constantly, until bubbly. Remove from heat; stir in water, vinegar and sugar. Heat to boiling, stirring constantly. Boil and stir 1 minute. Stir in bacon and parsley.

4. Heat oven to 350°. Cut potatoes into thin slices. Toss potatoes and bacon mixture in ungreased 3½-quart casserole; cover. Bake 30 minutes. Stir in sliced radishes. Garnish with whole radishes.

MINTED LIME MOLD

1   cup water
1   can (6 ounces) frozen
      limeade concentrate
2   packages (3 ounces each)
      lime-flavored gelatin

1. Heat 1 cup water and the limeade concentrate to boiling. Pour over gelatin in large bowl; stir until gelatin is dissolved.

2. Stir in ½ cup cold water, the ginger ale and peppermint extract. Refrigerate until partially set.

½ cup cold water
1¼ cups ginger ale
⅛ teaspoon peppermint extract

2 cups diced pears
1 cup honeydew melon balls
1 cup cantaloupe melon balls

Greens

3. Stir in pears, 1 cup honeydew melon balls and 1 cup cantaloupe melon balls. Turn into 7-cup mold. Refrigerate until firm.

4. Unmold onto greens. Garnish with cantaloupe melon balls and mint if desired.

POTLUCK BEAN SALAD

1 can (16 ounces) butter beans, drained
1 can (16 ounces) kidney beans, drained
1 can (15½ ounces) cut green beans, drained
1 can (15½ ounces) garbanzo beans, drained
3 hard-cooked eggs, chopped
½ cup chopped onion
½ cup chopped celery
½ cup sweet pickle relish
½ cup mayonnaise or salad dressing
1 tablespoon prepared mustard
½ teaspoon salt
¼ teaspoon pepper

1. Mix all ingredients except greens in large bowl; cover. Refrigerate at least 4 hours, no longer than 24 hours.

2. Serve in bowl lined with greens; garnish with slices of hard-cooked egg if desired.

PINEAPPLE CHEESECAKE

1½ cups graham cracker crumbs
3 tablespoons sugar
¼ cup butter or margarine, melted
¼ teaspoon ground cinnamon

1 carton (16 ounces) creamed cottage cheese (small curd)
4 eggs
3 packages (8 ounces each) cream cheese, softened
2 tablespoons flour
1 cup sugar
1¼ teaspoons vanilla
¼ teaspoon salt
2 cans (8¼ ounces each) crushed pineapple, well drained

Sour Cream Topping (recipe follows)

Heat oven to 300°

1. Mix graham cracker crumbs and 3 tablespoons sugar. Stir in butter and cinnamon. Press mixture evenly in bottom and 1½ inches up side of 10-inch springform pan. Bake 10 minutes; cool.

2. Mix cottage cheese and eggs in blender on high speed until smooth.

3. Beat cream cheese, flour, 1 cup sugar, the vanilla, salt and cottage cheese mixture in large mixer bowl until smooth. Gently fold in drained pineapple. Pour into baked graham cracker crust.

4. Bake 1½ hours. Turn off oven. With oven door ajar, let cake cool in oven 1 hour. Remove cake and spread with Sour Cream Topping.

5. Heat oven to 350°. Bake 10 minutes. Cool slightly and refrigerate.* To serve, loosen crust with thin-blade knife, then remove side of springform pan.

*TIP: *Cheesecake can be refrigerated no longer than 10 days.*

SOUR CREAM TOPPING
Mix all ingredients.

1 pint dairy sour cream
3 tablespoons sugar
1 teaspoon vanilla

An Elegant Buffet

Whole mushrooms and cherry tomatoes accent Green Pepper Steak.

Salad flavors include soy and ginger.

Zucchini is baked with two toppings.

SOLE AND PEPPER STEAK MENU

- HOT TOMATO COCKTAILS
- JEWEL CHEESE BALL
  ASSORTED CRACKERS
- SOLE AU GRATIN WITH SHRIMP
  SAUCE
- GREEN PEPPER STEAK
- SPINACH RICE
- BAKED ZUCCHINI
- FAR EAST SALAD
- FROZEN LEMON CREME DE
  MENTHE
- ALMOND-CRUSTED CHOCOLATE
  TORTE

COFFEE

• Recipes included

According to ancient Greek mythology, because Persephone ate part of a pomegranate, she was forced to remain with Hades, ruler of the nether world, for part of each year. Pomegranate seeds add an exotic look to the Jewel Cheese Ball appetizer—the juicy seeds resemble red corn kernels and taste like berries.

Sherry brings out the delicate flavor of the fish in the Sole au Gratin recipe. Freshly cooked shrimp are added along with Swiss cheese to the creamy sauce. The second buffet entrée contrasts nicely—Green Pepper Steak, sirloin strips simmered with green peppers and whole mushrooms.

Two vegetable dishes also grace this buffet. Spinach and cooked rice flavored with curry go into a good casserole that may be put together in advance, ready for baking. The other vegetable offering is zucchini, cut lengthwise and topped with salad dressing and a basil-herbed mixture of bread crumbs. The salad has an Oriental air—bean sprouts, soy sauce, ginger and refreshing mandarin oranges blend with slices of Bermuda onion.

With coffee, our Frozen Lemon Crème de Menthe provides a delicious after-dinner drink, served in stemmed glasses with straws. It is easily made with lemonade concentrate. Serves 12.

Wine Suggestion: The richness and mellowness of the Pinot Chardonnay grapes is a marvelous accompaniment for this delectable menu—a California Chardonnay (for example, Sonoma Vineyards), or from France, a good white Burgundy, a Meursault.

Shrimp and sole are richly sauced and flavored with sherry.

PARTY PLAN FOR SOLE AND PEPPER STEAK MENU

3 Days Before:

Prepare Jewel Cheese Ball through step 1 in recipe; cover and refrigerate.

Make Almond-Crusted Chocolate Torte; store in freezer.

1 Day Before:

Prepare Green Pepper Steak through step 1 in recipe; cover and refrigerate.

Prepare Spinach Rice through step 1 in recipe; cover and refrigerate.

Prepare Baked Zucchini through step 2 in recipe; cover and refrigerate.

Prepare salad and dressing ingredients; cover and refrigerate.

Prepare Frozen Lemon Crème de Menthe through step 1 in recipe.

That Day:

Measure and assemble ingredients for final preparation of recipes; refrigerate perishables.

20 Minutes Before Guests Arrive:

Complete cheese ball.

Heat Hot Tomato Cocktails.

45 Minutes Before Serving:

Make Sole au Gratin with Shrimp Sauce.

Bake Spinach Rice.

Place Baked Zucchini in oven with the rice.

15 Minutes Before Serving:

Complete Green Pepper Steak.

Complete salad.

Remove crème de menthe mixture from freezer to thaw.

HOT TOMATO COCKTAILS

Makes 1½ quarts

8　cans (6 ounces each) spicy tomato cocktail

1　or 2 avocados

1. Heat tomato cocktail to simmering, stirring occasionally.

2. Peel avocado. Cut in half crosswise; remove pit and slice.

3. Fill mugs or cups with ½ cup hot spicy tomato cocktail. Garnish with avocado slice. Serve immediately.

JEWEL CHEESE BALL

1　package (8 ounces) cream cheese, softened

1　package (4 ounces) blue cheese, softened

2　cups (8 ounces) shredded Cheddar cheese

2　tablespoons dry sherry or apple juice

½　teaspoon Worcestershire sauce

　Seeds from 1 pomegranate or ¾ cup quartered cranberries
　Parsley
　Assorted crackers and melba toast rounds

1. Mix all ingredients except pomegranate seeds, parsley and crackers; refrigerate at least 4 hours. Shape into ball; wrap in plastic wrap and refrigerate at least 2 hours, no longer than 1 week.

2. Press pomegranate seeds into cheese ball. Garnish with parsley. Serve with assorted crackers and melba toast rounds.

SOLE AU GRATIN WITH SHRIMP SAUCE

2	pounds sole fillets, cut in half
¼	cup dry sherry or apple juice
2	tablespoons lemon juice
½	teaspoon salt
2	tablespoons butter or margarine
2	tablespoons flour
¼	teaspoon pepper
½	teaspoon prepared mustard
1	teaspoon instant chicken bouillon
½	cup whipping cream
½	cup (2 ounces) shredded Swiss cheese
1	pound frozen cleaned raw shrimp, cooked, or 12 ounces cooked whole shrimp
1	tablespoon snipped parsley
3	lemon slices, cut in half

Heat oven to 350°

1. Arrange fillets in large shallow baking dish or pan. Mix sherry and lemon juice; pour over fish. Sprinkle with salt.

2. Bake uncovered 15 minutes; drain broth and reserve. Bake until fish flakes, about 10 minutes. While fish bakes, add enough water to reserved broth to measure 1 cup.

3. Melt butter in medium saucepan over low heat. Stir in flour, pepper, mustard and chicken bouillon. Cook over low heat, stirring until mixture is smooth and bubbly. Remove from heat; stir in reserved broth and the whipping cream. Heat to boiling, stirring constantly. Boil and stir 1 minute. Add cheese and shrimp, reserving several shrimp for garnish if desired. Heat over low heat, stirring constantly, until cheese is melted.

4. Alternate layers of fish and sauce in large chafing dish, ending with sauce. Sprinkle with parsley. Garnish with lemon and reserved shrimp. Serve in chafing dish over low flame.

GREEN PEPPER STEAK

	Beef sirloin tip steak (about 3 pounds)
⅓	cup vegetable oil
1¼	teaspoons salt
¼	teaspoon pepper
½	cup chopped onion
1	clove garlic, finely chopped
1	can (10½ ounces) condensed beef broth
2	medium green peppers, cut into strips
1	pound fresh mushrooms
⅓	cup cornstarch
¼	cup water
1	tablespoon soy sauce
2	cups cherry tomatoes, halved

1. Slice beef into thin strips, 2 inches long. Brown meat in oil in Dutch oven. Stir in salt, pepper, onion, garlic and broth. Heat to boiling; reduce heat and cover. Simmer until meat is tender, 20 to 30 minutes.*

2. Stir in green peppers and whole mushrooms; cover. Simmer until vegetables are crisp-tender, 3 to 4 minutes. Mix cornstarch, water and soy sauce. Pour into meat mixture, stirring constantly, until mixture boils and thickens, about 1 minute. Add tomatoes; cook uncovered 2 to 3 minutes.

*TIP: *At this point, meat can be covered and refrigerated no longer than 24 hours. At serving time, heat to boiling and proceed with step 2.*

SPINACH RICE

1	package (10 ounces) frozen chopped spinach, thawed, drained
6	cups cooked rice
¼	cup chopped onion
1	teaspoon salt
1	teaspoon curry powder
1	cup milk
2	eggs, beaten

1. Mix all ingredients. Spoon into buttered 2½- or 3-quart casserole.*

2. Bake uncovered at 350° until set, 30 to 40 minutes.

*TIP: *At this point, rice can be covered and refrigerated no longer than 24 hours. Bake until set, 40 to 50 minutes.*

BAKED ZUCCHINI

6   medium zucchini

¼   cup creamy French salad
      dressing

2   tablespoons prepared
      mustard

¼   cup butter or margarine,
      melted

1   cup dry bread crumbs

1   teaspoon dried basil leaves

1   teaspoon salt

1. Cut off ends of zucchini. Heat 1 inch salted water (½ teaspoon salt to 1 cup water) to boiling. Add whole unpared zucchini; cover and heat to boiling. Reduce heat; simmer until tender, 12 to 15 minutes. Drain; cool slightly.

2. Heat oven to 350°. Cut each zucchini lengthwise in half. Place cut sides up in buttered baking dish, 13½ x 9 x 2 inches. Stir together salad dressing and mustard; spread on zucchini. Mix remaining ingredients; sprinkle on top.*

3. Bake zucchini uncovered until hot, about 20 minutes.

TIP: *At this point, zucchini can be covered and refrigerated no longer than 24 hours. Bake until hot, about 30 minutes.

FAR EAST SALAD

4   large heads bibb lettuce

1   head lettuce

1   medium Bermuda onion, sliced

2   cans (11 ounces each)
      mandarin orange segments,
      drained

1   can (16 ounces) bean
      sprouts, drained

⅓   cup vegetable oil

2   tablespoons wine vinegar

1   tablespoon soy sauce

1   teaspoon salt

½   teaspoon ground ginger

¼   teaspoon freshly ground
      pepper

1. Tear bibb and head lettuce into bite-size pieces. Toss onion, orange segments and bean sprouts. Shake remaining ingredients in a tightly covered jar.*

2. Toss with greens and orange-bean sprouts mixture.

TIP: *At this point, ingredients can be covered and refrigerated in separate containers no longer than 24 hours. Toss just before serving.

FROZEN LEMON CREME DE MENTHE

Makes about 2 quarts

1   can (12 ounces) frozen
      lemonade concentrate, thawed

5   cups water

1½   cups green crème de menthe

1. Mix all ingredients. Pour into two 9 x 5 x 3-inch metal loaf pans. Cover with aluminum foil and freeze until slushy, about 3½ hours.*

2. Spoon into stemmed glasses; break up slightly and serve with straws.

TIP: *At this point, mixture can be stored in freezer. Let thaw at room temperature until slushy, about 1¼ hours. Serve as directed.

Make the chocolate torte ahead and freeze for an easy-to-serve dessert.

ALMOND-CRUSTED CHOCOLATE TORTE

½   cup butter or margarine
1   cup all-purpose flour
½   cup sugar
½   cup chopped slivered
      almonds, toasted

1   cup chilled whipping cream
1   quart chocolate ice cream
¼   cup golden rum or
      1 tablespoon rum flavoring

1. Melt butter in large skillet; stir in flour, sugar and almonds. Cook over medium heat, stirring constantly, until mixture is golden and crumbly, 6 to 8 minutes. Reserve ¾ cup crumb mixture; pat remaining crumb mixture in buttered 9-inch springform pan. Freeze at least 3 hours.*

2. Beat cream in chilled small mixer bowl until soft peaks form. Soften ice cream slightly in chilled large bowl; gently but quickly fold rum and whipped cream into ice cream. Spoon into crumb-lined pan. Freeze until partially set, about 1 hour; sprinkle with reserved crumb mixture. Return to freezer and freeze until firm, at least 2 hours, no longer than 2 weeks.

TIP: *You will want to be sure that your freezer maintains 0° F. or below for this dessert.

Dinners to Remember

The dinners in this chapter have been designed for occasions when you want to gather your guests at the table and serve them unusually splendid menus, course by course. Each menu is unique, and all provide in full "the pleasures of the table."

These dinners are meant to be presented with pride to an appreciative group. They should be leisurely savored, accompanied by good wines and your most attractive table settings. Yet they're not as complicated as might be expected. Many of the recipes offer time-saving shortcuts or can be prepared, at least in part, ahead of time. The menus are planned for three or four couples—just the right number for sumptuous entertaining.

The Heritage Dinner offers a time-honored Southern recipe— Spiced Beef. Once called Hunters Round, this spicy marinated dish had its Dixie origins in 18th-century tidewater Virginia. Thomas Jefferson's daughter, Martha, served it at Monticello; and back home in Tennessee, President James Polk and his wife, Sarah, considered it essential to their traditional Christmas dinners.

The Gourmet Dinner revolves around a handsome stuffed crown roast of pork, served with artichoke bottoms filled with Hollandaise sauce. This creamy blend of egg yolks, butter and lemon has been called the queen of sauces. Even the best of cooks have been known to shudder at the thought of Hollandaise sauce curdling, but careful handling easily insures against such a disaster. Butter should be melted very slowly to allow the egg yolks to cook and thicken the sauce smoothly.

A dinner with a harvesttime touch is the Roast Pork Loin Menu. Squash Soup and roast pork with stuffed onions are hearty offerings when the air has a nippy tang, and the dessert provides a seasonal flourish with a fluffy-topped cranberry pie.

Traditional British favorites are on display in our final menu. Instead of beef, however, we have chosen a lamb loin roast from which you create a Lamb Wellington. Impressive to see and delicious to eat, the combination of perfectly cooked meat and light pastry makes a memorable dinner entrée.

Spark Orange Consommé with a touch of red wine (see menu on page 228).

Heritage Dinner

Spiced Beef and Sprouts Salad are unique flavors in this menu.

SPICED BEEF MENU

•ORANGE CONSOMME
Pictured on page 227.

• SPICED BEEF

• DUCHESS NESTS WITH GARDEN
    PEAS

• SPROUTS SALAD

    DINNER ROLLS AND BUTTER

•EGGNOG PIE

    COFFEE OR TEA

• Recipes included

Start off the meal in a special way—with Orange Consommé. It is very light and has a pleasantly tart flavor. Orange slices, halved, make an attractive garnish.

The Spiced Beef offers alternatives. When the beef roast is marinated a full 24 hours, it will be quite spicy. If you prefer a milder dish, just cut down on the marinating time. It is an excellent entrée served either hot or cold. Duchess Nests made with whipped sweet potatoes are an attractive change.

Brussels sprouts for the salad are only partially cooked so that they will retain a somewhat crisp and crunchy texture. They, too, are marinated, and colorfully garnished with tomato slices.

Eggnog Pie is a delicious dessert the year around. Melted currant jelly swirled over the top adds a tangy extra flavor to the creamy pie. Serves 8.

Wine Suggestion: One of those Burgundies that makes you remember the best days of your life will make this menu a perfect dinner. Try Corton, Clos du Roi, or an alternate choice from California: Pinot Noir, Freemark Abbey.

Garnish Eggnog Pie with currant jelly and whipped cream.

PARTY PLAN FOR SPICED BEEF MENU

1 Day Before:	Prepare Eggnog Pie through step 4 in recipe; refrigerate. Prepare Sprouts Salad through step 2 in recipe; cover and refrigerate.
5 to 7 Hours Before Serving:	Prepare Spiced Beef through step 2 in recipe. (If more pungent flavor is desired, prepare the day before.)
2 Hours 30 Minutes Before Serving:	Complete Spiced Beef. (For medium beef begin 3½ hours before serving.)
1 Hour 15 Minutes Before Serving:	Make Duchess Nests with Garden Peas.
15 Minutes Before Serving:	Make Orange Consommé. Complete Sprouts Salad.
10 Minutes Before Dessert:	Complete Eggnog Pie.

ORANGE CONSOMME

Makes 1½ quarts

6	beef bouillon cubes
6	cups boiling water
2	tablespoons tomato paste
2	tablespoons orange juice
1	tablespoon dry red wine
4	orange slices, cut in half

Dissolve bouillon cubes in boiling water; mix in tomato paste and orange juice. Heat, stirring constantly, until hot; stir in wine. Garnish with half orange slices. Serve with breadsticks if desired.

SPICED BEEF

1 beef sirloin tip roast
  (about 5 pounds)

2 cups white vinegar
1 cup dry red wine
1 cup packed brown sugar
1 tablespoon salt
2 teaspoons ground ginger
1 teaspoon ground allspice
1 teaspoon ground nutmeg
1 teaspoon ground cinnamon
1 teaspoon pepper
¼ to ½ teaspoon cayenne red
  pepper, if desired
1 bay leaf
2 medium onions, sliced

2 packages (11 ounces each)
  mixed dried fruits

1. Pierce meat with fork about 12 times. Place meat in 3-quart glass bowl.

2. Mix remaining ingredients except dried fruits in large saucepan. Heat to boiling, stirring constantly, until sugar is dissolved; pour over meat. Refrigerate until marinade is cool. Turn meat; cover with plastic wrap. Refrigerate, turning occasionally, 3 hours. (For a pungent flavor, refrigerate 24 hours.)

3. Heat oven to 350°. Place meat in Dutch oven or deep roasting pan; pour marinade over meat. Insert meat thermometer so tip is in center of thickest part of meat and does not rest in fat; cover.

4. Roast until thermometer registers 140°, about 2 hours. (For medium beef, roast until thermometer registers 160°, about 3 hours.) Stir dried fruits into marinade during last 45 minutes of roasting. Remove roast from oven; let stand 15 minutes for easier carving. Serve fruits and marinade with the beef.

TIP: Spiced beef is traditionally served cold or at room temperature in the South but can be served hot.

DUCHESS NESTS WITH GARDEN PEAS

*6 medium sweet potatoes
  (about 2¼ pounds)

3 eggs
¼ cup butter or margarine,
  melted
1 teaspoon salt
⅛ teaspoon pepper

2 tablespoons butter or
  margarine, melted

Garden Peas (recipe follows)

Heat oven to 500°

1. Cover potatoes with water. Heat to boiling; reduce heat and cover. Simmer until tender, 30 to 35 minutes. Drain. Slip off skins.

2. Beat potatoes in large mixer bowl until smooth. Beat in eggs, ¼ cup butter, the salt and pepper.

3. Fill decorators' tube with potato mixture; form 8 nests with large star tip on buttered baking sheet. Drizzle nests with 2 tablespoons butter.

4. Bake until light brown, about 10 minutes. Make Garden Peas while nests are baking. Remove nests from oven. Let stand 5 minutes before removing from baking sheet. Place nests on platter; fill each with Garden Peas.

*TIP: *2 cans (18 ounces each) vacuum-pack sweet potatoes can be substituted. Complete recipe starting with step 2.*

GARDEN PEAS
Cook and stir onion in butter until tender. Add water, sugar, salt and peas. Heat to boiling, separating peas with fork. Top peas with lettuce leaf and cover; reduce heat. Simmer until peas are tender, about 5 minutes; discard lettuce and drain peas.

⅓ cup finely chopped onion
3 tablespoons butter or
  margarine
1 cup water
1 tablespoon sugar
1 teaspoon salt
2 packages (10 ounces each)
  frozen peas
1 large lettuce leaf

230

SPROUTS SALAD

1	pint Brussels sprouts
2	medium unpared zucchini, sliced (about 2 cups)
¼	cup sliced green onions
1	cup vegetable oil
¼	cup fresh lemon juice
¼	cup vinegar
2	cloves garlic, crushed
2	teaspoons seasoned salt
1	teaspoon sugar
½	teaspoon dry mustard
½	teaspoon salt
¼	teaspoon crushed red peppers
	Salad greens
8	to 10 tomato slices

1. Heat 1 inch salted water (½ teaspoon salt to 1 cup water) to boiling. Add Brussels sprouts; cover. Heat to boiling; reduce heat. Cook just until crisp-tender, 4 to 5 minutes; plunge into cold water. Cut Brussels sprouts into thin wedges; toss with sliced zucchini and green onions.

2. Shake oil, lemon juice, vinegar, garlic, seasoned salt, sugar, dry mustard, salt and peppers in tightly covered jar; pour over sprouts mixture and cover. Refrigerate, stirring occasionally, at least 4 hours, no longer than 24 hours.

3. Serve salad on greens-lined plates; garnish with tomato slices.

EGGNOG PIE

15	almond windmill cookies, crushed (about 1½ cups crumbs)
¼	cup butter or margarine, melted
½	cup sugar
1	envelope unflavored gelatin
½	teaspoon salt
3	egg yolks
1¼	cups milk
3	tablespoons light rum
3	egg whites
¼	teaspoon cream of tartar
½	cup sugar
½	cup chilled whipping cream
½	cup currant jelly
	Whipped cream, if desired

Heat oven to 350°

1. Mix cookie crumbs and butter. Press mixture firmly and evenly against bottom and side of 9-inch pie pan. Bake 10 minutes; cool.

2. Mix ½ cup sugar, the gelatin and salt in saucepan. Mix egg yolks and milk; stir into sugar mixture. Heat over medium heat, stirring constantly, just to boiling; cover. Refrigerate until mixture mounds when dropped from a spoon. Stir in rum.

3. Beat egg whites and cream of tartar until foamy. Beat in ½ cup sugar, 1 tablespoon at a time; beat until stiff and glossy. (Do not underbeat.) Fold egg yolk mixture into meringue.

4. Beat cream in chilled bowl until stiff. Fold whipped cream into egg mixture. Pile filling into pie shell. Refrigerate until set, at least 3 hours.

5. Melt currant jelly over low heat; cool slightly. Drizzle jelly over pie. Garnish individual servings of pie with dollops of whipped cream.

A Gourmet Dinner

Tomato and Mushroom Salad is served before the main course.

CROWN ROAST OF PORK MENU

- **SHRIMP BOIL**

- **EGGS IN ASPIC**

- **TOMATO AND MUSHROOM SALAD**

- **STUFFED CROWN ROAST OF PORK FLAMBE**

- **ROAST POTATOES WITH FINES HERBES**

- **ARTICHOKE BOTTOMS WITH HOLLANDAISE SAUCE**
  BREAD AND BUTTER

- **LEMON SQUARES**

- **SPICED COFFEE AND/OR BRANDY**

- Recipes included

The elegant appetizer for this menu is an artistic delight called Eggs in Aspic. An easy-to-follow Step-By-Step Recipe illustrates the method of preparation. The result looks almost too lovely to eat—each cold poached egg is glazed with a clear gelatin aspic and decorated with flowers made from pieces of leek, olives and pimientos.

Crown roasts are impressive cuts of meat. They really look like crowns; the ribs are formed into a circle and tied together to form a coronet. This recipe fills the center of the crown with a mixture of onions, mushrooms, diced apples and bread stuffing. The meat is glazed with apricot preserves and apple brandy during roasting. At serving time, each bone tip is garnished with a kumquat, and the roast is flambéed with additional brandy.

The tender bottom of the artichoke provides a delicately flavored base for an easily made Hollandaise sauce. Artichokes, native to the Mediterranean, were popular in Italy as early as the 16th century. You can purchase the bottoms in cans. Cashew-crusted Lemon Squares are a light dessert. Serve them as an accompaniment to coffee spiced with cardamom and sweetened with coffee liqueur. Serves 8.

Wine Suggestion: This is a big, wintery dinner menu and matched only by a big, fiery wine. Try to put your hands on a few bottles (one will not do) of Hungarian Bull's Blood or Egri Bikaver with which to fight this dinner. Anything else will be only a substitute.

Elegant crown roast of pork is generously stuffed, glazed, garnished and flamed.

PARTY PLAN FOR CROWN ROAST OF PORK MENU

1 Day Before:	Prepare Shrimp Boil through step 3 in recipe; cover and refrigerate. Prepare Eggs in Aspic through step 6 in recipe; cover and refrigerate. Prepare Tomato and Mushroom Salad through step 1 in recipe; cover and refrigerate. Prepare Lemon Squares through step 3 in recipe; cover and refrigerate.
That Afternoon:	Prepare salad greens and garnishes for menu; refrigerate. Slice tomatoes for Tomato and Mushroom Salad; cover and refrigerate.
3 Hours 45 Minutes Before Serving:	Prepare Stuffed Crown Roast of Pork Flambé through step 3 in recipe.
2 Hours Before Serving:	Complete Eggs in Aspic; refrigerate.
1 Hour 15 Minutes Before Serving:	Make Roast Potatoes with Fines Herbes. Prepare Artichoke Bottoms with Hollandaise Sauce through step 2 in recipe. Complete Shrimp Boil; arrange in serving dish. Cover and refrigerate. Complete Tomato and Mushroom Salad. Complete Artichoke Bottoms with Hollandaise Sauce.
15 Minutes Before Serving:	Remove roast from oven and garnish bone tips with kumquats; arrange potatoes on platter with roast. Flame roast with preserves mixture and brandy.
10 Minutes Before Dessert:	Prepare Spiced Coffee. Complete Lemon Squares and serve with Spiced Coffee or brandy.

SHRIMP BOIL

Sauce (recipe follows)

1. Prepare Sauce; refrigerate.

3   **quarts light beer**
1   **bottle (1¾ ounces) pickling spice**
3   **pounds frozen shelled shrimp**

2. Heat beer and pickling spice to boiling in large kettle over high heat; reduce heat. Simmer uncovered 10 to 15 minutes. Heat to rolling boil; add frozen shrimp. Simmer uncovered 2 to 3 minutes.

3. Remove shrimp from broth; refrigerate shrimp and broth separately until cold. Pour cold broth over shrimp and return to refrigerator.*

4. Remove shrimp from broth with slotted spoon; rinse shrimp with cold water to remove any spices. Serve with wooden picks for dipping in Sauce.

*TIP: *Shrimp Boil can be prepared to this point 24 hours in advance.*

SAUCE
Mix all ingredients.

2   **cups catsup**
1   **tablespoon horseradish**
     Juice of 1 lime

EGGS IN ASPIC

See STEP-BY-STEP RECIPE on page 237.

TOMATO AND MUSHROOM SALAD

½	cup olive oil
¼	cup dry white wine
1	tablespoon capers
1½	teaspoons salt
½	teaspoon cracked pepper
5	ounces large mushrooms (about 10), sliced
4	to 6 tomatoes, sliced Salad greens

1. Mix oil, wine, capers, salt and pepper; pour over mushrooms in glass bowl. Cover with plastic wrap. Refrigerate, stirring occasionally, at least 2 hours, no longer than 24 hours.

2. Remove mushrooms with slotted spoon from bowl. Arrange tomato slices on salad greens on individual salad plates; sprinkle with salt if desired. Top with mushrooms. Pour about 1 tablespoon marinade over each salad.

STUFFED CROWN ROAST OF PORK FLAMBE

*1	pork rib crown roast (about 5 pounds) Vegetable oil Salt Pepper
¼	cup butter or margarine
3	green onions and tops, sliced
4	large fresh mushrooms, sliced
2	tart apples, diced
3	cups packaged stuffing mix
½	cup applesauce
3	tablespoons apple brandy
1	jar (10 ounces) apricot preserves
½	cup apple brandy
	Preserved kumquats
	Heat oven to 325°

1. Brush meat with vegetable oil; rub salt and pepper into meat. Place meat on triple thickness of aluminum foil the same diameter as roast. Place in roasting pan. Cover bone tips with small pieces of foil. Insert meat thermometer in thickest part of meat so tip does not touch bone or rest in fat.

2. Heat butter in large skillet until it bubbles. Cook and stir onions in butter until tender. Add mushrooms; cook and stir until mushrooms are just tender. Add apples; cook and stir 1 minute. Stir in stuffing mix, applesauce and 3 tablespoons brandy (add more applesauce if stuffing seems dry). Pack in prepared roast, mounding high. Cover stuffing with foil cap.

3. Roast 2½ hours. Remove foil from stuffing. Heat apricot preserves and ¼ cup of the brandy in small saucepan (reserve ¼ cup preserves mixture for flambé). Brush remaining preserves mixture on meat every 10 minutes. Roast until meat thermometer registers 170°, about ½ hour.

4. Remove roast from oven. Let stand 15 minutes. Cut ends off kumquats; scoop out centers with melon baller. Garnish bone tips with kumquats. Heat reserved ¼ cup preserves mixture; float remaining ¼ cup brandy on top. Ignite and pour over roast.

TIP: *2 racks pork spareribs (about 3 pounds each) can be substituted. Tie each rack spareribs in circle; place bone tips up on rack in open shallow roasting pan. Pack stuffing in center of each; cover stuffing with foil cap. Follow steps 3 and 4 above.

ROAST POTATOES WITH FINES HERBES

8	small baking potatoes
¼	cup butter or margarine, melted
2	teaspoons paprika
1	teaspoon fines herbes
	Heat oven to 325°

1. Cut unpared potatoes lengthwise in half. Brush cut surfaces with melted butter; sprinkle with paprika and herbes. Place on baking sheet.

2. Bake until tender, about 1 hour. Serve on platter with roast if desired.

ARTICHOKE BOTTOMS WITH HOLLANDAISE SAUCE

3 egg yolks
¼ cup lemon juice
½ cup firm butter

2 cans (14 ounces each)
    artichoke bottoms, chilled
    Paprika

1. Stir egg yolks and lemon juice briskly with wooden spoon in small saucepan. Add half the butter; stir over very low heat until butter is melted.

2. Add remaining butter; stir briskly until butter is melted and sauce thickens.* Cool slightly; cover. Refrigerate 1 hour.

3. Drain artichoke bottoms on paper toweling. Arrange on serving platter; spoon about 1 tablespoon sauce into each artichoke bottom. Sprinkle with paprika. Garnish with watercress if desired.

TIP: *Melt butter very slowly to allow eggs to cook and thicken sauce without curdling.

LEMON SQUARES

½ cup butter or margarine,
    softened
1 cup all-purpose flour
½ cup salted cashews, finely
    ground

1 cup powdered sugar
1 package (8 ounces) cream
    cheese, softened
½ cup chilled whipping cream

2 packages (3¾ ounces each)
    lemon instant pudding and
    pie filling
3 cups milk
1 tablespoon grated lemon peel

¼ cup chilled whipping cream
    Grated lemon peel

    Heat oven to 375°

1. Mix butter, flour and cashews. Press in bottom of baking pan, 13 x 9 x 2 inches. Bake until light brown, about 15 minutes; cool on wire rack.

2. Beat powdered sugar and cream cheese until fluffy. Beat ½ cup whipping cream in chilled small mixer bowl until soft peaks form; stir in cream cheese mixture. Spread on cooled nut mixture; refrigerate.

3. Mix pudding, milk and 1 tablespoon lemon peel. Pour over cream cheese mixture; refrigerate no longer than 24 hours.

4. Beat ¼ cup whipping cream in chilled small mixer bowl until soft peaks form. Spoon on dessert; sprinkle with grated lemon peel.

SPICED COFFEE

    Coffee for 8 cups strong
    coffee
2 or 3 cardamom pods, crushed

8 ounces coffee liqueur

1. Prepare strong coffee, adding crushed cardamom pods to coffee grounds.

2. Pour 1 ounce liqueur into each footed demitasse or small mug. Pour hot coffee to within ¾ inch of cup rim. Spoon whipped cream on coffee if desired.

1.

2.

3.

4.

5.

6.

8	**eggs**
1	**can (10½ ounces) chicken broth**
¼	**teaspoon celery salt**
	Dash garlic powder
1	**envelope unflavored gelatin**
	Leek or scallion tops
	Large pitted ripe olives or truffles
	Pimiento
	Parsley sprigs

1. Heat water (1½ to 2 inches) to boiling in large skillet or saucepan; reduce to simmer. Break each egg into measuring cup or saucer; slip eggs, one at a time, into water, holding cup or saucer close to water's surface. Slip 3 eggs into water (photo 1). Cook eggs until whites are set and yolks still feel soft when touched gently, 3 to 4 minutes; repeat with remaining eggs. Lift poached eggs with slotted spoon; place eggs in enough ice water to cover (photo 2). Refrigerate until cold.

2. Mix chicken broth, celery salt and garlic powder in saucepan. Heat until fat floats to the top (do not boil). Skim fat from surface with paper toweling; refrigerate broth until cold.

3. Sprinkle gelatin on cool chicken broth to soften. Stir over low heat until gelatin is dissolved. Remove from heat and place saucepan in ice water; stir until mixture coats back of metal spoon.

4. Lift eggs with slotted spoon from ice water. Trim any ragged edges with kitchen shears or sharp pointed knife (photo 3). Place eggs on rack over baking sheet. Spoon gelatin mixture (aspic) over each egg (photo 4). Refrigerate eggs on rack to set aspic, about 15 minutes (reserve but do not refrigerate remaining aspic).

5. Drop leek or scallion tops into boiling water. Boil 1 to 2 minutes; drain and rinse with cold water. Spread on paper toweling; pat dry.

6. Cut olives and pimiento into flower shapes, leek tops into stems and leaves. Dip each piece of decoration into aspic and arrange on eggs in desired design (photo 5). Refrigerate to set design, about 15 minutes. Remove from refrigerator and coat again with aspic (photo 6). Repeat coating-setting process until eggs have been coated 4 or 5 times.*

7. Gently loosen eggs from rack just before serving; trim any ragged edges of aspic. Place eggs on serving dishes; garnish with parsley.

TIP: *If aspic thickens, return to heat to soften.*

A Bountiful Dinner

Start the dinner with a delicious soup made with squash.

ROAST PORK LOIN MENU

- SQUASH SOUP

- ROAST LOIN OF PORK WITH
  ALMOND-STUFFED ONIONS
- ASPARAGUS VINAIGRETTE
  ROLLS AND BUTTER

- RED BOTTOM PIE
  COFFEE OR TEA

• Recipes included

The nutty flavor of butternut squash comes through in our recipe for Squash Soup. This satisfying dinner opener is made with cubes of squash and whole canned tomatoes simmered in a beef-vegetable stock. Sherry adds a nice touch, and accentuates the uniqueness of the soup.

Roast pork is an old favorite. Simple and good, it goes well with onions stuffed with croutons and almonds, then baked in apple juice. The roast, served on a platter surrounded by the stuffed onions, provides an especially handsome entrée for this menu.

The day before, prepare Asparagus Vinaigrette, a cool contrast to the pork. Cooked asparagus spears and Bermuda onion are marinated in a clear French dressing and are served cold.

Red Bottom Pie puts together two complementary flavors. Cranberry relish mixed with orange juice forms the red base. The top is a creamy layer of white, touched with rum, and frosted cranberries add a sugarplum garnish. The pie may be made a day ahead and refrigerated. Serves 6.

Wine Suggestion: Pork should be served with a fairly strong, big wine. The best of Italian wines, Barolo, is excellent with it. Sonoma Vineyard Pinot Noir is also a fine choice.

PARTY PLAN FOR ROAST PORK LOIN MENU

1 Day Before:	Make Red Bottom Pie except do not garnish; refrigerate. Make Asparagus Vinaigrette; cover and refrigerate.
3 to 3 Hours 30 Minutes Before Serving:	Make Roast Loin of Pork.
1 Hour 30 Minutes Before Serving:	Make Almond-Stuffed Onions and place around roast. Make Squash Soup.
10 Minutes Before Dessert:	Garnish Red Bottom Pie.

SQUASH SOUP

Makes about 1¼ quarts

1   **small butternut squash**
4   **slices bacon, diced**
¼   **cup chopped onion**
1   **medium clove garlic, crushed**
1   **can (16 ounces) whole tomatoes, undrained**
2½   **cups water**
¼   **cup snipped parsley**
2½   **tablespoons beef-vegetable flavor liquid**
1   **bay leaf**
¼   **teaspoon dried basil leaves**
⅛   **teaspoon ground thyme**
3   **tablespoons dry sherry, if desired**

1. Pare squash and remove seeds. Cut squash into ½-inch cubes (about 3 cups); set aside.

2. Cook bacon until almost crisp in 2½-quart saucepan. Drain off fat; return 1 tablespoon to saucepan.

3. Cook and stir onion and garlic in 1 tablespoon fat until onion is tender. Stir in tomatoes, water, squash, parsley, beef-vegetable flavor liquid, bay leaf, basil leaves and thyme. Heat to boiling; reduce heat and cover. Simmer until squash is tender, 20 to 25 minutes. Remove bay leaf; stir in sherry.

ROAST LOIN OF PORK WITH ALMOND-STUFFED ONIONS

1   **pork center loin roast, (about 5 pounds)**
½   **clove garlic**
1   **teaspoon dill weed**
1   **teaspoon salt**

    Almond-Stuffed Onions (recipe follows)

    Heat oven to 325°

1. Rub meat with garlic and dill weed; sprinkle with salt.

2. Place meat fat side up in shallow roasting pan. Insert meat thermometer in center of thickest part of meat, away from fat or bone.

3. Roast uncovered 2½ to 3 hours, to internal temperature of 170°. Allow to stand at room temperature 15 to 20 minutes before carving. Serve Almond-Stuffed Onions around roast.

On next pages, Roast Loin of Pork with Almond-Stuffed Onions.

ALMOND-STUFFED ONIONS

6 medium onions, about 3 inches in diameter

¾ cup coarsely chopped almonds

1½ cups croutons

¾ teaspoon salt

¼ teaspoon pepper

¼ teaspoon sage

⅛ teaspoon thyme

¼ cup butter or margarine, melted

1 cup apple juice

1. Cut a thin slice off root end of each onion; cut a ¼-inch slice off opposite end. Carefully remove center of each onion with vegetable parer or melon ball cutter, leaving a ⅜-inch shell (at least 2 rings). Arrange onion shells in ungreased 2-quart casserole.

2. Toss almonds, croutons, salt, pepper, sage, thyme and butter. Fill each onion shell with stuffing. Spoon any remaining stuffing on top of onions. Pour apple juice around onions. Put casserole in oven about 40 minutes before roasting time for pork is complete.

3. Bake covered 40 minutes. Uncover (when pork roast is removed from oven) and bake until tender, about 20 minutes.

ASPARAGUS VINAIGRETTE

Clear French Dressing (recipe follows)

2 packages (10 ounces each) frozen asparagus spears, cooked, drained

1 medium Bermuda onion, finely chopped

Salt

Pepper

½ cup snipped parsley

1 cup vegetable oil

½ cup vinegar

2 tablespoons sugar

2 teaspoons salt

½ teaspoon celery seed

½ teaspoon dry mustard

¼ teaspoon grated onion

1 small clove garlic, peeled, finely chopped

1. Make Clear French Dressing.

2. Arrange a single layer of asparagus spears in glass dish. Spread chopped onion on top; season with salt and pepper. Sprinkle with snipped parsley and drizzle with dressing. Refrigerate at least 12 hours.

CLEAR FRENCH DRESSING

Mix all ingredients.

A cranberry layer is topped with rum-chiffon filling.

RED BOTTOM PIE

1	package (10 ounces) frozen cranberry relish, thawed
¼	cup orange juice
1	tablespoon cornstarch
2	egg yolks
⅓	cup sugar
1	envelope unflavored gelatin
¼	teaspoon salt
1	cup milk
2	tablespoons light rum
2	egg whites
¼	teaspoon cream of tartar
⅓	cup sugar
½	cup chilled whipping cream
	10-inch baked pie shell
	Nutmeg, if desired
	Frosted Cranberries (recipe follows)
	Huckleberry leaves
½	cup fresh or thawed cranberries
	Water
⅓	cup sugar

1. Mix cranberry relish, orange juice and cornstarch in saucepan. Cook and stir over medium heat until mixture thickens. Boil and stir 1 minute. Cool.

2. Mix egg yolks, ⅓ cup sugar, the gelatin, salt and milk in saucepan. Cook over medium heat, stirring constantly, just until mixture boils. Place pan in bowl of ice and water or in refrigerator; stir occasionally until mixture mounds when dropped from spoon. Stir in rum.

3. Beat egg whites and cream of tartar until foamy. Beat in ⅓ cup sugar, 1 tablespoon at a time; beat until stiff and glossy. (Do not underbeat.) In chilled bowl, beat cream until stiff; fold gelatin mixture into cream. Carefully fold mixture into meringue.

4. Spread cranberry mixture in bottom of baked pie shell. Spoon gelatin mixture on top; sprinkle lightly with nutmeg. Refrigerate until set, at least 3 hours. Garnish with Frosted Cranberries and huckleberry leaves if desired.

FROSTED CRANBERRIES
Dip cranberries individually in water, then in sugar. Dry on paper toweling.

Fare Extraordinaire

Trifle is lavished with whipped cream and almonds.

LAMB WELLINGTON MENU

• **MUSHROOM SOUP**

• **LAMB WELLINGTON**
  BUTTERED CARROT RINGS
  FRESH SPINACH SALAD
  HOT ROLLS AND BUTTER

• **RUM TRIFLE**
  COFFEE

• Recipes included

For this hearty dinner, a fairly light soup starter is just right. This Mushroom Soup simmers fresh mushrooms in a beef bouillon liquid, flavored with thyme and either Madeira or sherry wine. Try a simple raw spinach salad, which may be drizzled with your favorite dressing, and buttered carrots.

A Step-By-Step Recipe provides complete instructions on how to prepare the impressive Lamb Wellington. The meat is marinated in a wine, spice and mushroom mixture, then rolled up and roasted. Not only is the lamb wrapped in pastry, but pastry cups filled with cooked peas add their own appeal to the Wellington.

Trifle is an English dessert. The English traditionally make theirs with ladyfingers and macaroons surrounding a brandy-flavored boiled custard. That's much more time-consuming than this version, which uses a purchased angel food cake, a packaged mix or your favorite recipe. Chopped almonds and raisins soaked in rum add both extra flavor and contrasting texture to this creamy dish. Serves 6.

Wine Suggestion: A classically difficult dish which reminds me of Bordeaux estates, so I like to select for it as elegant a Bordeaux as I can find: Château Pichon-Longueville-Baron of a good vintage! A Cabernet Sauvignon from Heitz is a good California alternative.

Flaky pastry is a decorative and flavorful addition to lamb.

1 Day Before:	Prepare Rum Trifle through step 3 in recipe; cover and refrigerate. Prepare Mushroom Soup through step 1 in recipe; cool slightly. Refrigerate. Prepare Lamb Wellington through step 1 in recipe; refrigerate.
3 Hours Before Serving:	Complete Lamb Wellington. Make salad; cover and refrigerate.
15 Minutes Before Serving:	Cook carrots. Complete Mushroom Soup.
10 Minutes Before Dessert:	Complete Rum Trifle.

MUSHROOM SOUP

Makes about 2 quarts

1   **pound fresh mushrooms, sliced**
½   **cup chopped onion**
3   **tablespoons butter or margarine**
8   **cups water**
2   **tablespoons instant beef bouillon**
2   **carrots, sliced (about 2 cups)**
¼   **teaspoon ground thyme**
1   **teaspoon salt**
⅛   **teaspoon pepper**
½   **cup dry Madeira or sherry wine**

1. Cook and stir mushrooms and onion in butter in Dutch oven until tender; reduce heat. Simmer 10 minutes. Stir in water, bouillon, carrots and thyme. Heat to boiling; reduce heat and cover. Simmer 1 hour.

2. Stir in salt, pepper and wine. Heat to boiling. Garnish with snipped parsley if desired.

LAMB WELLINGTON

See STEP-BY-STEP RECIPE on page 247.

RUM TRIFLE

½   **cup rum**
¾   **cup chopped almonds**
¾   **cup golden raisins**

1   **package (3 ounces) vanilla regular pudding and pie filling**
½   **cup chilled whipping cream**

1   **angel food cake**

½   **cup chilled whipping cream**
     Sliced almonds
8   **maraschino cherries, cut into flower shapes**

1. Pour rum over chopped almonds and raisins in small bowl. Let stand 1 hour.

2. Prepare vanilla pudding and pie filling according to package directions for pudding except use 2½ cups milk; cool. Beat ½ cup whipping cream in chilled bowl; fold into pudding.

3. Cut cake into ½-inch cubes (about 8 cups). Layer ⅓ of the cake cubes, almond mixture and pudding in glass bowl; repeat twice, ending with pudding. Cover. Refrigerate at least 3 hours, no longer than 24 hours.

4. Beat ½ cup whipping cream in chilled bowl just before serving. Spread over pudding. Garnish with sliced almonds and cherry flowers.

1.

2.

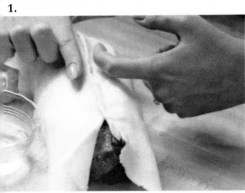

3.

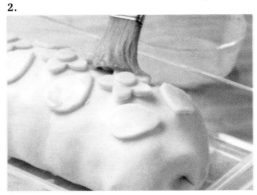

4.

*1   lamb loin roast (about 3½ pounds), boned
2   cups rosé wine
¼   cup chopped mushrooms
¼   cup snipped parsley
1   teaspoon dried tarragon leaves, crushed
1   teaspoon salt
½   teaspoon pepper
1   clove garlic, crushed

     Pastry for two-crust pie
1   egg
1   tablespoon water

     Fresh tarragon or parsley
     Pastry Cups (recipe follows)
     Herbed Wine Sauce (recipe follows)

1. Remove excess fat from lamb. Mix wine, mushrooms, parsley, 1 teaspoon tarragon, the salt, pepper and garlic. Pour over lamb in large glass or ceramic bowl and cover. Refrigerate at least 8 hours.

2. Heat oven to 325°. Remove lamb from marinade. Strain marinade, reserving both wine and mushroom mixtures. Spread mushroom mixture over meat. Roll up evenly as for jelly roll (photo 1). Tie with heavy string at several points around lamb. Place lamb on rack in shallow baking pan. Insert meat thermometer so tip is in center of thickest part of meat (photo 2).

3. Bake until meat thermometer registers 160°, about 1½ hours. Remove meat from oven; let stand 30 minutes. Remove string; pat lamb dry with paper toweling.

4. Increase oven temperature to 425°. Roll pastry into 12-inch square. Cut off a 2-inch strip from one side for design. Place lamb in center of pastry. Bring up sides; seal seam and ends securely (photo 3). Moisten with water if necessary. Place pastry-wrapped lamb seam side down in jelly roll pan or shallow baking dish. Roll out 2-inch strip of pastry; cut out small designs. Garnish top of pastry with cutouts. Mix egg and water; brush over top and sides of pastry (photo 4).

5. Bake until pastry is golden brown, about 35 minutes. Place on platter; garnish with fresh tarragon and Pastry Cups, if desired. Serve Herbed Wine Sauce over lamb.

*TIP: *A 4- to 5-pound leg of lamb, partially boned, can be substituted for the loin. Remove excess fat from fleshy part of leg. Proceed as directed above. You will need to use care in shaping this roll since it is less symmetrical than the loin.*

2 tablespoons flour
¾ teaspoon bottled brown
  gravy sauce

Pastry for one-crust pie
1 package (10 ounces) frozen
  peas

HERBED WINE SAUCE
Stir reserved wine slowly into 2 tablespoons flour in saucepan. Heat, stirring constantly, until mixture thickens. If desired, stir in ¾ teaspoon bottled brown gravy sauce.

PASTRY CUPS   *Makes*
1. Roll pastry on lightly floured cloth-covered board to ¼-inch thickness. Cut into thirty-two 2-inch circles (half with holes in the center). Reroll pastry as necessary.

2. Brush circles with remaining egg and water mixture; stack 4 together (top 2 with holes). Place pastry cups on ungreased baking sheet Bake with lamb, until golden brown, about 15 minutes.

3. Cook peas according to package directions while pastry cups bake. Fill pastry cups with peas.

Index

251

Mail Order Sources

SPECIALTY FOOD ITEMS

Marshall Field and Co.
Gourmet Foods Section
Mail Order Department
111 N. State Street
Chicago, Illinois 60602
(312) 781-1000
No minimum order

Stop & Shop
Specialty Gourmet Shop
16 W. Washington
Chicago, Illinois 60602
(312) 726-8500
$2.50 minimum order

Calloway Gardens Country Store
(Georgia Hams)
U.S. Highway 27
Pine Mountain, Georgia 31822
(404) 663-2281

INDIAN FOODS

Sahadi Importing Co.
187 Atlantic Avenue
Brooklyn, New York 11201
(212) 624-4550
$15.00 minimum order

Bezjian Grocery
4725 Santa Monica Blvd.
Hollywood, California 90029
(213) 663-1503
$10.00 minimum order

India Grocers
5002 N. Sheridan Road
Chicago, Illinois 60640
(312) 334-3351
No minimum order

CHINESE FOODS

Wing Chong Lung Co.
922 S. San Pedro St.
Los Angeles, California 90015
(213) 627-5935
No minimum order

Shing Chong and Co.
800 Grant Avenue
San Francisco, California 94108
(415) 982-0949
No minimum order

Star Market
3349 N. Clark Street
Chicago, Illinois 60657
(312) 472-0599
No minimum order

Oriental Import-Export Comapny
2009 Polk Street
Houston, Texas 77002
(713) 223-5621
$10.00 minimum order

Legal Sea Foods Market
234 Hamshire Street
Cambridge, Massachusetts 02139
(617) 354-8473
No minimum order

MIDDLE EASTERN FOODS

Kasso Brothers
570 9th Avenue
New York, New York 10036
(212) 736-7473
$20.00 minimum order

American Oriental Grocery
20736 Lahser Road
Southfield, Michigan 48075
(313) 352-5733
No minimum order

Photography Credits

Cover Photo: Robert Keeling

Mark Barinholtz: pages 45–46, 198–199. Tom Benda: page
94. Norman Bilisko: page 26. Fred Brodersen: pages 48,
90–91, 98–99, 108–109, 111, 128–129, 195, 220–221, 225,
238, 240–241, 245. Taber Chadwick: pages 68–69, 71,
142–143. George de Gennaro: page 190. Michael Ditlove:
page 28. Larry Gordon: pages 76, 160–161, 165. Kazu:

page 197. Robert Keeling: pages 16, 64, 67, 203–205, 209.
Dick Krueger: pages 12–13, 244. Gene Perraud: pages
182–183. Dan Randolph: pages 121–123, 127. Bill Sla-
dick: pages 25, 42, 59–60, 62, 243. Richard Tomlinson:
pages 11, 22, 33–34, 38, 40, 50, 54, 56, 72–73, 79–81,
86–87, 94–95, 102–103, 114, 136–137, 148–149, 153–154,
168–169, 177–178, 186–187, 191, 210, 214–215, 227–229,
234–235.